The European Debt Crisis

The European Debt Crisis: Causes, Consequences, Measures and Remedies

Edited by

Ali Ari

CAMBRIDGE
SCHOLARS
PUBLISHING

The European Debt Crisis:
Causes, Consequences, Measures and Remedies,
Edited by Ali Ari

This book first published 2014

Cambridge Scholars Publishing

12 Back Chapman Street, Newcastle upon Tyne, NE6 2XX, UK

British Library Cataloguing in Publication Data
A catalogue record for this book is available from the British Library

ISBN (10): 1-4438-5616-9, ISBN (13): 978-1-4438-5616-4

TABLE OF CONTENTS

Part III: Measures

Part IV: Remedies

LIST OF TABLES

LIST OF FIGURES

INTRODUCTION

EUROPEAN DEBT CRISIS: CAUSES, CONSEQUENCES, MEASURES AND REMEDIES

ALI ARI
KIRKLARELI UNIVERSITY

This collection brings together most interesting papers presented at the CES International Conference on the European Debt Crisis, held in Kirklareli in Turkey on May 17-18, 2012. The idea of organising this Conference developed in late 2011 when the advanced economies, in particular the US, the Eurozone member states and the UK were struggling to find a way out of the on-going global financial crisis which has been affecting the world economy since late 2007. Today, the US authorities seem to have resolved the crisis, although growth and employment rates are not yet encouraging: however, Europe remains in crisis. This book intends to provide answers, from both theoretical and empirical perspectives, to the following questions, which have been posed many times since 2007 but remain unanswered: What caused the global crisis? What are the consequences of this crisis? Why, despite the implementation of several measures, is the crisis still affecting the world economy? How can the situation of on-going crisis be brought to an end, particularly in the European Union (EU)? Will the Eurozone be dismantled? Finally, how can future crisis episodes in the world economy be prevented?

In this introduction, I shall begin by presenting a brief account of the global financial crisis and the European debt crisis; then, I shall provide a brief overview of the papers included in the volume.

A brief account of the global financial crisis

The crisis that started in the US mortgage credit market in 2007—the now world-famous subprime market (Bénassy-Quéré et al., 2009)—is a typical banking crisis. This crisis occurred as a result of banks increasing non-performing loans, which in turn prevented them from honouring their obligations to other banks or financial institutions. Here, the important question is: why did banks' non-performing loans increase to such an extent in 2007?

The answer to this question lies in a number of global economic and financial developments of the 1990s and early 2000s: firstly, the increasing financial instability and crisis episodes in emerging markets during the 1990s resulted in capital flows to advanced economies, particularly to the US (the "flight to quality"); secondly, increases in savings in some emerging economies like China (due to distortions in the Chinese economy which artificially keeps savings high) and Middle Eastern countries (due to a sharp rise in oil prices between the end of 1998 and August 2007) increased the demand for US financial assets; in parallel, US equity prices rose and the dollar appreciated. The rise in equity prices increased the level of perceived wealth in the US, thus reducing domestic savings (Siebert, 2010).

This excessive money supply, accompanied by a lax FED monetary policy after 2001 (Obstfeld and Rogoff, 2009), reduced real interest rates and eased credit conditions in the US financial sector. This led to extensive leverage, i.e., debt-financed financial investment, which tended to cause consumption to rise and savings to fall. As a result, US house prices rose steadily, by 7-8% per year in the period 1998-1999, by 9-11% per year from 2000-2003 and by 15-17% in 2004-2005 (Bernanke, 2010). This "bubble" was also fed by the self-fulfilling expectations of market participants: households, investors and financial institutions. This euphoric atmosphere led banks to take riskier investment decisions (i.e., investment in subprime mortgages) in a lax regulatory environment. Subprime mortgage credits are financial products that aim to give access to home ownership to poorer and therefore less credit-worthy households. These high-yield mortgages are riskier, and contracts are designed to mitigate these risks by collateralizing them, on the assumption of rising house prices. This strategy was effective while house prices were rising, which was the case until late 2006 (Bénassy-Quéré et al., 2009).

On the other hand, increasing consumption in the US economy, due to eased credit conditions in the presence of low interest rates and the overvalued US dollar reducing the country's trade competitiveness, led to huge trade deficits. Those deficits were generally financed by the high saving surpluses of the emerging economies, particularly China and the Middle Eastern countries. Thus, at the time of the the outbreak of the financial crisis, the world economy was characterised by significant global imbalances.

The outbreak of the crisis

In the second half of 2006, when some regulatory agencies in the US criticized excessive risk-taking and leveraging of the financial institutions and put forward the existence of a housing bubble, the FED increased nominal interest rates. This led to a decline in house prices, and thus to an increase in default rates. On the other hand, increasing interest rates reduced the already-low level of investment in the US real sector, causing an increase in unemployment rates. Increasing unemployment also led to rising default rates on mortgages. Increases in default rates substantially increased banks' non-performing loans. Although mortgaged homes were taken back by banks through foreclosure, banks recorded huge losses because of declining home prices (collateral). This resulted in a liquidity squeeze in the financial markets.

However, as stated by Bénassy-Quéré et al. (2009), this liquidity problem could have been tolerated if these subprime loans had not been securitised. Securitisation is the technique through which bank loans are transformed into marketable securities. Furthermore, securitised subprime loans were also pooled with other types of mortgage-based securities to form structured assets (which are riskier, but with a higher return in comparison to standard fixed-income instruments). This is why defaults on subprime securities affected the whole range of asset-backed securities. In this sense, the more complex a product was, the more difficult it became to value it (Bénassy-Quéré et al., 2009). The financial innovation process, initially considered favourable to long-term growth, led to the emergence of what are now termed "toxic products". All this financial innovation is indeed related to the excessive deregulation of the financial system, a process which has been on-going since the 1980s.

Once liquidity dried up, and risk was re-priced in August 2007, interbank rates sharply rose. This led to the failure of two large hedge funds, and a run on Northern Rock. Central banks provided direct and instant liquidity to financial institutions, in order to help them face debt repayments. However, this lender of last resort action did not calm the existing tensions in the financial markets, as market participants were unwilling to lend to potentially bankrupt counterparties. This uncertainty and loss of confidence forced banks to sell their assets. This resulting fall in asset prices in turn led to a further deterioration in the banks' balance sheets. Furthermore, as the value of many complex assets became unclear, the banks' published accounts did not provide accurate information concerning the true extent of the damage, which exacerbated the lack of confidence in the financial markets even further. As a result, many banks, illiquid or insolvent, were condemned to a bail-out by the national authorities.

The panic spread worldwide in September 2008, when the investment bank Lehman Brothers went bankrupt. This caused a massive loss of confidence, and illiquidity became the most important problem in the financial system. Central banks cut interest rates to zero and engaged in a near-total substitution of the interbank market (Bénassy-Quéré et al., 2009). The global crisis seriously affected the real economy, as credit conditions became completely restrictive, while the fall in equity prices reduced the ability of large companies to finance their investments. As a result, advanced economies recorded large contractions, unemployment rates increased substantially and world trade decreased considerably. Emerging countries were also heavily affected by the global financial crisis, as they also recorded a decrease in economic growth and employment. One may affirm that trade and finance were the two main channels in crisis contagion, from advanced to developing economies.

Governments and central banks in the US and the EU responded to the crisis with a more aggressive interest rate policy, and substantial liquidity provisions to the financial markets (Blanchard, 2009). They also used expansionist fiscal policies in an effort to increase consumption, production and employment. Moreover, to prevent further collapses in the financial system, bank rescue and guarantee plans were implemented: bail-outs, recapitalisation and nationalisation of illiquid and insolvent banks, and a provision for credit and debt guarantees to all banks (Aït-Sahalia et al., 2010). The IMF, the World Bank and regional development banks were also mobilised to counter the effect of the global crisis. These measures could not prevent a world recession in 2009, but in 2010 and its aftermath the world economy recorded positive growth, thanks to the rapid recovery of the emerging markets. However, these expansionary policies, accompanied by nationalisation of the private sector debt stock, resulted in a dramatic rise in public debt, and created serious roll-over concerns. As a result, some Eurozone countries, namely the so-called PIIGS countries, have suffered the on-going sovereign debt crisis.

A brief overview of the Eurozone debt crisis

As stated by Wolf (2012), in its origin the Eurozone crisis is not a fiscal crisis, although fiscal deficits and massive debt stocks caused the sovereign debt crisis in the Eurozone. Prior to the outbreak of the global financial crisis, the debt stocks of the crisis countries were actually quite low, with the exception of Greece and Italy. Liquidity provisions and the nationalisation of private banks during the period 2007-2009 resulted in an increasing debt burden in these countries. Of course, the crisis was not caused only by increasing fiscal deficits and rising public debt. There are other macroeconomic and structural factors that have led to the outbreak of the sovereign debt crisis in Eurozone.

First, as affirmed by many economists, the Economic and Monetary Union (EMU) is a monetary union without a fiscal union. Nonetheless, this design, permitting the free riding of fiscal policies within a framework of common monetary policy, led to differences in inflation rates within the Eurozone member countries. Inflation differences in turn led to a decrease in the trade competitiveness of high-inflation countries, i.e., Greece, Spain. As the option of improving the competiveness of the economy through exchange rate depreciation was not available, because of the common currency, trade deficits rose steadily in the Southern peripheral countries. One may also affirm that while the Maastricht criteria and the Stability and Growth Pact (SGP) had put in place some strict fiscal rules to be respected, these rules were violated several times, even by "good students" such as France and Germany.

Moreover, the continuing structural differences between member countries impacted on the effectiveness of the common monetary policy implemented by the European Central Bank (ECB), which, over time, created macroeconomic imbalances within the Union. The main structural differences between member states were reflected in aggregate productivity and price and wage competitiveness, which in turn directly affected external balances (Darvas, 2012).

Furthermore, with the transition to monetary union, capital inflows increased towards peripheral countries. The resulting low interest rates led to a decrease in household savings and increased consumption, causing external deficits and an increase in private debt stock. As in the pre-crisis period, the focus on fiscal issues within the SGP or Maastricht criteria targeted the public sector, neglecting private-sector behaviour, which resulted in unsustainable credit and housing booms in countries such as Ireland and Spain. This observation explains quite clearly why countries with very low public debt stock at the beginning of the global crisis in 2008 suffered a sovereign debt crisis in its aftermath.

Last but not least, the governance problems and decision-making issues within the Union were also important factors in the deepening of the crisis. In several cases, the response of European policymakers was partial, inadequate and late, which undermined their credibility in terms of resolving the crisis (Darvas, 2012).

What, then, is to be done, if the on-going crisis is to be resolved? For us there is only one option: beyond putting together a large enough financial bail-out to restore market confidence, a complementary economic union with well-defined and re-written rules, to be respected by all members and supported by the key institutions, must be adopted. This will strengthen the real economy and restore sustainable growth within the Union.

The Book

This book is divided into four interlinked sections: Causes, Consequences, Measures, and Remedies.

Part One is composed of two papers that, taken together, provide a systematic theoretical and empirical overview of the global financial crisis and the European debt crisis.

In their paper "Greece in the Great Depression and the European Debt Crisis: Transmission and Process", Ayfer Gedikli and Abdullatif Ceviker compare the situation of the Greek economy during the Great Depression of 1929 and the global crisis of 2008. The authors first show that the effects of both crises on the world economy (and on the Greek economy in particular) lead to similar consequences in terms of economic recession and rising unemployment rates. However, they state that during the recent global crisis, central banks were quite active, as they injected substantial amounts of liquidity to ease borrowing conditions. This is contrary to the situation during the Great Depression, where central banks did not take enough measures. Moreover, again contrary to the Great Depression, governments acted together through international cooperation instead of launching protectionist policies, which contributed to the international economy recovering more quickly. On the other hand, the authors show that although the economic situations were different, both crises affected the Greek economy deeply. Greece's entry to the EU, and then the EMU, boosted its economy by providing the country with large funding opportunities at low interest rates. Nevertheless, the acceptance of the euro as the common currency put the Greek monetary policy in the hands of the EMU authorities, resulting in a lack of adjustment mechanisms to deal with the crisis at a supranational level. In this sense, Greece heavily depends on the actions and implemented measures of the European authorities, if it is to successfully overcome the present debt crisis.

In his paper "Public Debt Crises in the Eurozone and Possible Effects on Sovereign Credit Rankings", Ata Ozkaya provides an econometric analysis of whether selected European countries and Turkey have followed sustainable debt policies over the last 12 years. He shows that Ireland, Portugal, Greece and Spain pursued unsustainable debt policies over the reviewed period, contrary to France, Italy, Poland and Turkey. On the other hand, he observes that during the same period, the primary balances of Poland, Portugal, Ireland, Greece, and the UK economies deteriorated and exhibited a negative trend, while the debt stock to GDP ratio of each country increased. Moreover, the author finds that even if the UK's debt stock is sustainable in the long-run, the disrupted structure of the UK primary surplus may lead to instability. Finally, Ozkaya reconstructs the credit ratings of the 25 selected countries, according to a set of macroeconomic fundamentals during three non-overlapping periods: 2005-2010, 2011, and 2012-2013. He illustrates the mismatch between actual credit rankings and the current situation of countries: the US and Italy do not merit their actual ratings; Turkey should have a better rating; and it is also probable to expect a further downgrade in the credit ratings of the UK, France and Spain.

Part Two is composed of three papers that analyse the consequences of the global and European crises on the financial system and the real economy. It also examines, from a theoretical and an empirical perspective, how the crisis was transmitted to other economies

In his paper "The Effects of the Global Crisis on Emerging Economies", Jean-Pierre Allegret first analyses the transmission of the global financial crisis to emerging economies and, second, he examines the responses of policymakers in emerging markets to this crisis. He shows that financial and trade linkages were the main transmission channels of the crisis, as the sudden capital outflows and the collapse in export demand severely affected emerging economies. The author emphasizes that the impact of the global crisis on emerging markets was relatively short-lived, in contrast with past crises, as the majority of developing markets (except the emerging European countries) were better equipped—in terms of macroeconomic fundamentals—to respond to the current crisis with more counter-cyclical policy easing. Moreover, Allegret claims that the dramatic rebound of net capital inflows to emerging economies is now the main challenge for policymakers, as these capital flows raise many concerns for monetary policy and exchange rates. He thus suggests a more extensive use of capital controls to contain massive capital inflows, as implemented in Brazil and South Korea.

Ali Ari and Raif Cergibozan's paper "The Transmission of Financial Crises from Advanced to Emerging Economies: The Turkish Case" analyses, via logit models, the transmission channels of external shocks to the Turkish economy. The authors show that US interest rates representing global shocks and variables representing financial linkages had a significant impact on the occurrence of crises in Turkey. Therefore, they affirm that even if the Turkish economy seems more stable in the post-2001 period, it still remains vulnerable to external shocks as the May 2004, May 2006 and October 2008 events confirmed. According to the authors, the economic growth strategy, which is heavily dependent on export earnings and short-term capital inflows, is the main reason behind the problems of external vulnerability for the Turkish economy.

In their paper "European Automotive Industry: Before and After the Global Financial Crisis", Adem Baltaci and Huseyin Burgazoglu focus on the impact of the global financial crisis on the real sector, particularly on the European automotive industry. Through a descriptive analysis, they show that like other manufacturing sectors, the automotive sector in the EU—the biggest motor vehicle manufacturer in the world—was severely affected by the global crisis, in terms of production, export revenues, employment and new car sales. They show that the competitiveness of the sector was nevertheless affected positively by both the global financial crisis and the European debt crisis.

Part Three, composed of three papers, assesses the effectiveness of policy measures taken to fight the global and the European crises.

Cemil Erarslan and Yuksel Bayraktar's paper, entitled "Efficiency of the FED's Monetary Policy during the Global Financial Crisis", assesses the effectiveness of monetary policies pursued by the FED in fighting the global financial crisis. Firstly, the authors show that the occurrence of the 2007-2008 financial crisis in the US economy was caused by inconsistencies in the FED's monetary policy. On the other hand, they show that the traditional and unconventional monetary policy implemented by the FED during the crisis was quite successful in preventing a further deepening of the crisis within the US financial system. Here, the authors emphasize the importance of buying troubled assets on financial markets in order to resolve the current crisis, even if this policy places the burden of the crisis on the taxpayer. Finally, the authors underline the fact that international coordination with other central banks would increase the effectiveness of monetary policy in fighting the global financial crisis.

In his paper "A Note on the New Monetary Policy of the Central Bank of Turkey", Fatih Ozatay discusses the new objective imposed on central banks, in the aftermath of the global financial turmoil: monetary policy should focus on financial stability in addition to price stability. Through the example of the Central Bank of Turkey (CBT), Ozatay analyses a new monetary policy framework designed with two ultimate aims, the development of appropriate policy tools and new institutional setups. He shows, through an analysis of the Turkish case, that inflation targeting and macroprudential policy can undermine each other's effectiveness if appropriate monetary policy tools are not selected. He also states that to develop an effective monetary policy, which aims at both price and financial stability, appropriate institutional arrangements should be implemented, with the responsibilities and powers of the institutions clearly identified.

In their paper "Central Banking since the Eighties", Philippe Gilles and Cecile Bastidon assess—from a historical perspective—the evolution of central banking and monetary policies and the emergence of several financial crises over the last three decades. They show that until the global crisis, the role of central banking was limited to conventional lending of last resort, with only minor variants. In contrast, in the current crisis, central banks have been forced to adopt so-called "unconventional monetary policies" which are threefold: large official interest rate cuts, new credit facilities and large asset purchases. However, a worsening of central banks' credibility may occur as a result of the implementation of unconventional monetary policies, as central banks purchase part of the government bonds issuances, required to finance the banking sector rescue programmes and recovery policies, in order to maintain the desired level of liquidity. The authors conclude that crisis management monetary policies should be strictly limited in time and that central banks should conduct a particularly careful monitoring of market liquidity indicators, which are for the most part, correlated to the interbank market.

Part Four, composed of three papers, evaluates the policy options available to exit the European debt crisis. It also proposes economic policy actions and structural measures to counteract global or common shocks in the future.

The paper "The European Crisis and its Reflections on Turkey" prepared by Ali Ari, Mehmet Hondur, Muhsin Kar, Kivilcim Metin Ozcan, Guray Vural and Dilek Yigit, aims firstly to identify the causes of the European debt crisis. The authors show that the Eurozone structural problems and expansionary fiscal measures taken to offset the negative impacts of the global crisis were the main causes of the European debt crisis. The paper also examines the policy measures taken to fight the crisis, and their effects on the financial market and the real economy. The authors show that emergency expansionary policies could not offset the effects of the crisis on the real economy, but that structural reforms have been relatively successful in re-establishing confidence in the financial markets and in overseeing a slight recovery in the real sector. Finally, the paper evaluates the following four probable exit scenarios from this on-going crisis: monetary expansion, fiscal austerity, exit from the EMU, and fiscal transfers from Northern European countries to Southern ones. The authors conclude that Europeans need to make a quick decision, and that the solution is closely related to the following questions: which option will result in the least cost, who will shoulder the burden of the crisis, and what future do Europeans imagine for themselves?

Eleftherios Thalassinos' paper, entitled "Country Risk and Financial Crisis", analyses the concept of country risk and its evolution since the 1980s. The author shows that credit ratings assigned to a particular country by rating agencies actually plays an important role in the opinion-making of investors about a country. Bearing this in mind, such ratings may lead to a crisis in a country by influencing capital flows. As stated by Thalassinos, even if a country's risk is affected by many "objective" determinants including domestic and external political, economic and financial factors, the rating is not free of "subjective" elements, and the scoring systems of different agencies do not necessarily converge, as can be observed in the current global crisis. The author adds that the ratings have a pro-cyclical effect, which can encourage speculation. Therefore, some necessary reforms should be implemented.

In her paper "De-coupling in Global Economic Activity: Trends and Some Predictions for the Future", Sumru Altug discusses the phenomenon of "de-coupling" in the recent global financial crisis and its aftermath. Through a series of graphs, she shows that a form of de-coupling exists in global economic activity, as developing and developed economies performed quite differently during the global crisis. She states that cyclical fluctuations are driven by a complex set of factors. While the nature of trade and financial links and the role of alternative policy regimes have often been considered, country-specific and idiosyncratic differences also imply a role for institutions in the transmission of global or common shocks, especially informal institutions such as norms, codes of conduct or other behavioural factors. Lastly, the author affirms that with increased globalisation, the future of both emerging and developed economies will depend on their mutual reactions and institutional changes. In this sense, Altug suggests a policy for sustainable development which focuses on both macroeconomic indicators and the institutional and cultural environment.

References

Bernanke B.S. 2010, "Monetary Policy and the Housing Bubble," *Speech at the Annual Meeting of the American Economic Association,* Atlanta, GA, 3 January.

Aït-Sahalia Y., J. Andritzky, A. Jobst, S. Nowak and N. Tamirisa 2010, "Market Response to Policy Initiatives during the Global Financial Crisis", *NBER Working Paper,* 15809.

Bénassy-Quéré A., B. Coeuré, P. Jacquet and J. Pisani-Ferry 2009, "The Crisis: Policy Lessons and Policy Challenges", *CEPII Working Paper,* 2009-28.

Blanchard O. 2009, "The Crisis: Basic Mechanisms, and Appropriate Policies", *IMF Working Paper,* 09-80.

European Commission 2009, "Economic Crisis in Europe: Causes, Consequences and Responses", *The European Economy Series,* 7.

Darvas Z. 2012, "The Euro Crisis: Ten Roots, but Fewer Solutions", *Bruegel Institute Policy Contribution,* 2012-17.

Obstfeld M. and K. Rogoff 2009, "Global Imbalances and the Financial Crisis: Products of Common Causes", *CEPR Discussion Papers,* 7606.

Siebert A. 2010, "Global Imbalances and the Financial Crisis", *European Parliament Policy Note,* IP/A/ECON/FWC/2009_040/C7.

Wolf M. 2012, "Why the Eurozone Crisis is not Over", *Speech at the Peterson Institute for International Economics,* Washington, DC, 3 May.

PART I:

CAUSES

CHAPTER ONE

GREECE IN THE GREAT DEPRESSION AND THE EUROPEAN DEBT CRISIS: TRANSMISSION AND PROCESS

AYFER GEDIKLI
ISTANBUL MEDENIYET UNIVERSITY
AND ABDULLATIF CEVIKER
ISTANBUL MEDENIYET UNIVERSITY

1. Introduction

It is the "Holy Grail" for economists to analyse the macroeconomic effects of the Great Depression. The effects of the 1930s were so deep that economic science broke with the traditional "classical school" and launched Keynesian economics to overcome the effects of the Depression (Bernanke, 1994). In particular, monetary shocks and budget deficits played an important role in the Great Depression. Although those shocks had a destructive effect upon all economies, these effects were much deeper in developing countries such as Greece. Nowadays, according to some economists, the world is experiencing a second depression. When we compare the Great Depression with the current global crisis and European debt crisis, it is obvious that we understand the challenges of the world's economic system very poorly, and that we may indeed be prisoners of our own traditional beliefs. Thus, in this paper, we aim to understand the transmission channels and the influence of the Great Depression and the global financial crisis on developing countries, particularly on the Greek economy, via an analysis of the impact of fiscal and governmental policies.

Before explaining the transmission channels of the two crises to Greece, it is necessary to give a theoretical explanation of the nature of contagion. In the recent literature, contagion is defined as the transmission of economic shocks and fluctuations from one country to another. A broad definition of contagion for the World Bank is "the cross-country transmission of shocks or the general cross-country spillover effects".

Moser (2003) defines financial contagion as a result of adverse shocks that have the potential to trigger financial crises. Further, Fratzscher (2003) defines contagion as the "transmission of a crisis to a particular country due to its real and financial interdependency with countries that are already experiencing a crisis". More specifically, contagion is a process observed through co-movements in exchange rates, stock prices, sovereign spreads, and capital flows.

In the last 30 years, open economy activities and globalisation have led to closer relations between countries. Some crisis transmission problems and volatility have arisen, due to these close relations, such as common creditors and the actions of investors operating in international financial centres. Furthermore, trade links, regional patternships, and deep connections between economies and macroeconomic similarities make countries vulnerable to volatility. Microeconomic conditions, institutional factors, and the actions of specific financial agents are also effective in spreading shocks (Dornbusch et al., 2000).

The IMF categorises crisis transmission channels into two groups: country-specific factors and common factors. Country-specific factors include a country's vulnerability, its economic characteristics, and its trade and financial links. Financial stress can increase as a reaction to capital outflows following a financial strike. In addition, financial stress can increase as a result of asset losses in a country that has invested in the country which is in crisis (IMF, 2009).

Common factors comprise commodity prices, global output and interest rates. These can also be called global factors, and may be manifested in herd market behaviour, cross-country contagion, and common lender effects (the blanket withdrawal of funds by highly exposed financial institutions). The process of contagion by spreading market disturbances from one country to another can be explained by investors' irrational behaviour, or the "herding" effect. In many ways, a crisis results in large capital losses for international institutional investors. These losses may induce investors to sell off securities in other markets to raise cash in anticipation of the higher frequency of redemptions. Commercial banks may also face liquidity problems when there is a great outflow in the financial sector. If there is such a panic, investors exert pressure in order to pull their funds urgently. This situation may lead banks to experience difficulty satisfying the demands of their clients. Liquidity and incentive problems can also be considered as financial links in contagion (Dornbusch et al., 2000).

Like the IMF, the World Bank classifies the transmission of a crisis in terms of fundamental links and herding behaviour. Fundamental transmission links cover both real and financial links. Fratzscher (2000), Camarazza et al. (2000) and Kaminsky and Reinhart (2003) highlight the financial channel.[1] The greater the degree of financial integration, the more extensive the contagious effects of a common shock or a real shock to another country. Under these circumstances, local and global shocks can be transmitted across countries because of their financial linkages. For example, if the collateral value of leveraged institutions falls, because of a negative shock in one country, leveraged companies need to increase their reserves. To fulfill this transaction, they need to sell their valuable holdings in countries which are as yet unaffected by the crisis. This transaction transmits the shock to the target countries.[2] Balakrishnan et al. (2009) show that the current crisis affected all segments of the financial system, and spread to all major regions in both advanced and emerging economies. Nearly 70% of the stress experienced in advanced economies was transmitted to emerging economies, and transmission was fast. Differences among emerging countries in the degree of transmission were associated with the extent of these financial linkages, and were generally measured according to the stock of foreign liabilities to advanced economies. Bank lending, portfolio flows, and direct investments were important channels in the transmission of the current crisis. In fact, the most virulent responses to the crisis were initially experienced in Emerging Europe, which has strong banking linkages to Western European banks (Balakrishnan et al., 2009).

On the other hand, transmission of a crisis can occur through real/trade links. Glick and Rose (1999), Eichengreen and Rose (1999), Forbes (2001) emphasize trade links as the mode of crisis transmission. Real links represent the basic economic relationships among economies, and these are mostly associated with international trade. Real links of contagion can be explained as affecting the economic fundamentals of a related country through trade links and currency devaluations in an economy where local shocks occur. Strikes of banks, firms or industries, the spread of business fluctuations across economies, and the diffusion of technology and growth convergence across countries are all are categorised as fundamental links. Because of the financial crisis in the source country, the major trading

---

[1] For further information, see Eichengreen et al. (1996), Dornbusch et al. (1999), Khan et al. (2005), Kaluza (2010).

[2] World Bank, http://go.worldbank.org/JIBDRK3YC0

partner of that country encounters a sharp currency depreciation that may result in declining asset prices and large capital outflows, initiated by investors in advanced economies following a crisis (IMF, 2009).

In parallel with these problems, the partner country could become the target of speculative attacks as investors anticipate a decline in exports to the crisis country, and these attacks may lead to a deterioration in the trade balance. The herding effect is due to international investors. Speculative trading by the behaviour of agents determine, for the most part, the change in prices which can lead to the spreading of shocks. After a shock strikes a country (or a group of countries), a significant change in asset prices in the local economy is to be expected (Kaluza, 2010). According to Corsetti et al. (1999), a game of competitive devaluation can result in deep and harmful currency depreciation. If market participants expect that a currency crisis will lead to a game of competitive devaluation, their intention is to sell their security holdings in other countries, curtail their lending, or refuse to roll over short-term loans to borrowers in those countries (Dornbusch et al., 2000). To overcome the harmful effects of the contagion of a crisis, countries may launch economic policies to immunise themselves, such as high trade barriers, tariffs or certain acts or agreements.

This paper is organised as follows: Section 2 analyses the Greek economy in the great depression years. Section 3 proposes a review of the Greek economy over the last decade. Finally, Section 4 concludes with a comparison of the impact of these two crises on the Greek economy.

2. The Greek economy in the Great Depression years

2.1 The Great Depression: Facts and process

The Great Depression lasted from 1929 through to 1939. Most economists agree that shocks to the domestic US economy were a primary cause of both the US and the world depressions. Friedman and Schwartz (1971) note that during the period of August 1929 to August 1931, the US transmitted the depression to the rest of the world. They refer to US gold stocks, the flow of gold, whether the US adhered to gold standard rules, and to the balance of payments. On the other hand, according to data from the Federal Reserve Bulletin of June 1933, between August 1929-August 1931, US reserves increased from 3.995 billion to 4.632 billion US$, and total reserves for the world (fifty countries) increased from 10.250 billion to 11.297 billion US$. Hence, gold reserves outside the US increased from 6.255 billion to 6.665 billion US$. From this data, one can conclude that although the Great Depression originated in the US, it was transmitted internationally to many other countries (Gertrud, 1985).

The Great Depression could be considered a structural crisis, with its slow accumulation, investment instability, and financial fluctuations. Friedman and Swartz (1963) emphasized that one of the main reasons for the Great Depression was the banking crisis. Bernanke (1995) claimed that banking panics, bankers' and speculators' attitudes and monetary contraction under the gold standard were the most important causes of the Great Depression. Bernanke (1995) also pointed out "the evidence that monetary shocks played a major role in the Great Depression, and these shocks were transmitted around the world primarily through the workings of the gold standard".

Following the monetary factor and international deflationary transmission, which has a clear correlation with the fluctuation of the monetary system, monetary hegemony can be considered as one of the reasons for the infection of the economies. In fact, the current economic situation of Europe confirms this approach to the transmission of crises (Bregianni, 2012). A series of bank panics in the US converted the recession into a serious crisis until 1930. Unlike the US, where banking was highly localised, continental European economies were dominated by financial systems in which a small number of very large banks were dominant (Bordo and James, 2009). Most countries experiencing monetary concentration had a common dependence on the international Gold Exchange Standard (GES) (Bernanke, 2000). The situation worsened after the collapse and rescue of the Creditanstalt bank, which spread financial contagion to the UK, France and to the rest of Europe. The lending flow abroad fell in 1928 and 1929 as a result of high interest rates and the booming stock market in the US. This decline in foreign lending might have been the reason for credit contraction and the reduction in output in borrower countries (Rothermond, 1996). In addition, banks in many debtor countries in South America and Central Europe accumulated mismatches between assets (in local currency) and liabilities (in US dollar or other key currencies), and this gave rise to an environment of vulnerability to currency turmoil. Moreover, global banks suffered large losses on their shareholdings because of a decline in their capitalisation. Therefore, they had to decrease their lending. In Germany, the government reorganised the Danat and Dresdener Bank by merging them. This policy was accepted as the origin of the banking collapse, since the government had to inject liquidity (Bordo and James, 2009). These events were the key factors in forcing the UK to abandon the gold standard. Consequently, falling prices affected credit flow and the real activity of economies. In the eastern part of the Europe, the situation was even more dramatic, as these countries were heavily dependent on these "great actors".

As regards the Great Depression, many authors claim that GES was one of the reasons for the transmission of the crisis (Bernanke and James, 1991). According to this approach, the fundamental cause of the Great Depression in the US was the decline in aggregate demand which led to a decline in production and an increase in stocks. There was a more than fourfold rise in the value of stock prices between 1921 and the peak in 1929. In 1928 and 1929, the Federal Reserve raised interest rates to slow the rapid rise in stock prices. Higher interest rates depressed interest-sensitive spending in sectors such as the construction and automobile industries. With this protection, US stock prices declined by 33% in 1929. These price declines forced some investors to liquidate their holdings, thus aggravating the fall in prices (Bernanke and James, 1991). The decrease in aggregate demand and the decrease in total supply affected the global economy via the gold standard.

During the 1930s, in most countries changes in output, a dramatic decrease in price levels, an increase in unemployment, and deep deflation pioneered the demand shocks. In 1933, the GDP was almost one third of that in 1929, and until the 1940s, the dollar value of the physical level of production was unable to recover and remained below the 1929 level. The wholesale price index declined by 33%, and the unemployment rate exceeded 20%. In 1933, about 13 million employees lost their jobs, which amounted to one person in every four among the labour force (Bernanke and James, 1991). The prices of primary commodities traded in the world markets declined even more dramatically during this period. The price of coffee, cotton, silk, and rubber fell by roughly half between September 1929 and December 1930. During the period 1929-1933, industrial production declined by 47%, and the real GDP of the US economy fell by 30%. World industrial production also decreased by almost 37%, world trade declined by 68%, and world agricultural prices decreased by 75% from the level they had reached between 1923-1925. By 1933, there was almost no foreign investment anywhere in Europe (Boyce, 2009). Despite all of these global effects, the timing, the spread from one country to another, the integration of the global economy and industrialisation levels were all significant factors in determining the severity of the crisis. Not only industrialised but also underdeveloped agricultural countries producing crops for export were experiencing the depression, because of the network of fixed exchange rates. As a result, as the price of crops used as raw material for industrial production decreased drastically, the income levels of producers dropped substantially whilst food prices increased.

Furthermore, the 1930 Smoot-Hawley tariff enactment, which aimed to boost farm incomes by protecting farms from foreign competition in agricultural products, led to a great rise in protectionist trade policies in the US and Europe (Bordo et al., 1997). Scholars believe that those policies may have reduced trade in the global economy, and may have contributed to the dramatic decline in the world trade price of raw materials, causing a severe balance of payments problem, especially in developing countries.

2.2 General economic conditions of Greece towards the Great Depression

After the war, the Greek economy was based on autarchy. The stronger European countries adopted a series of economic measures, such as protectionist legislation and tariff barriers, to maximise their natural resources and to became economicaly independent. These measures spread all over the Continent in a short time. Under the circumstances, the Greek government had to launch a programme which covered public investments and industrial development in order to decrease the Greek economy's dependence on imported products. With these precautions in place, the Greek economy grew rapidly (Lazaretou, 2005).

The country had to overcome tensions in the internal political situation, due to the exchange of Greek Muslims with Anatolian Greeks (Lazarevic, 2008). After the war in 1922, Greece was impoverished, and its population increased by a net inflow of one million Orthodox refugees from Anatolia. Despite the Muslim population leaving the country in large numbers, the total population increased by 25%, because of the arrival of Anatolian Greek refugees. At the same time, emigrant remittances began to fall after the implementation of restrictions on immigration in the US (Kostis and Petmezas, 1998).

In the 1920s, the immigrants from Anatolia had a tremendous effect on the country's social and economic life. These immigrants were more educated and affluent than the indigenous Greek people. These refugees played a triple role as consumers, labourers and entrepreneurs, and thus had a significant impact on the national economy (Pentzopoulos, 1962). The percentage of refugees was 27.6% and 13% in the agricultural and industrial sectors respectively. In the commercial sector, the percentage was 4.4%. The immigrant farmers not only increased the productivity of the agricultural sector, but also introduced and spread new varieties, adaptable to Macedonia and Trace. Most of them preferred to grow tobacco, which was in heavy demand on the global market. The heavy tariff protection and the sharp fall in real wages (due to the existence of an abundant labour force following the massive influx of refugees in 1922, plus the high inflation rate) were the forces driving this developing process (Lazaretou, 2005). However, immigrants contributed little as consumers: income is important to consumption, and because of the disadvantageous conditions for urban settlers, the refugees had to work as cheap manual labour. During this period, most of the factories were built near urban areas where labour was abundant and wages were low. As there was an unemployment problem, the refugee workers were eager to work for low wages, hoping to keep their job permanently.

Greece tried to develop its agriculture, to increase commercialisation in order to achieve the necessary financial assets needed to import consumer goods. In addition, Greece had to import certain raw materials and technology for planned industrialisation from abroad. To grow faster, Greece had to transfer certain technological improvements. Relatively poor economies are expected to grow faster than more advanced economies, because of their advantage of backwardness (Bernanke, 2000). This situation applied to Greece, and the country grew quickly towards the end of the decade. However, exports could not cover import expenditure. As a foreseeable consequence, there was a problem with the balance of payments and chronic budget deficits.

In the second half of the 1920s, there was a clear implication of the cyclical downturn which started in 1929. Towards the end of the decade, Greece was able to perform better than its western counterparts. Until 1929, a relatively stable period was recorded both in the agricultural and industrial sectors, at least partly as a consequence of following nationalistic economy policies. The textile industry in particular showed a remarkable improvement in this period. The main factors in this recovery were tax and financial benefits and protective customs policies, which hindered access to the domestic market and encouraged domestic investment, and foreign investments in cooperation with domestic investors.

Despite this success, it should be noted that Greece remained behind the industrialised western countries, as economic and financial disorder deprived the government of new investments. Since the economy was heavily based on agriculture, the products subject to export were agricultural crops which did not provide sufficient inflow of foreign assets for the stimulation of the domestic non-agrarian sector. As the export sector was non-competitive, the consequence was a deficiency between the capital supply and its demand, which brings non-proportionally high interest rates to national financial markets. Furthermore, in the first half of the 1920s, agriculture failed to recover, and did not provide enough support to satisfy capital demand.

Table 1-1 Greek international trade (1925-1938)

In 1914 FF	Imports x000	Exports x000	Mean Annual Growth Rate Imp.	Exp	Trade Deficit	Imports P.C	Exports P.C	Mean Annual Growth Rate Imp	Exp
1925-1929	676.610	338.365	9,68%	9,06%	99.96%	110.57	55.29	5.80%	5,30%
1930-1934	500.142	284.956	-5.22%	-3,16%	75.52%	76.18	43.41	-6.22%	-4,30%
1935-1938	627.572	407.688	5.66%	9,57%	53.93%	89.74	58.30	3,95%	7,62%

Source: Kostis and Petmezas (1998)

In the financial sector, the situation was similar to the other developing countries in Europe. As Greece had a shortage in national savings in the 1920s, the two basic motivating powers for economic development were the state and foreign capital. The state acted as a substitute for the insufficiently developed entrepreneurial environment and the insufficient accumulation of capital. For this reason, the role of the state in banking was crucial. The state provided long-term funds for agriculture, the most important sector, and encouraged industrialisation, and specialized mortgage banks with long-term loans were commonplace. In the meantime, there were no assets other than agricultural products available to finance the import of know-how and technology. This deficiency caused an excessive financial flow from creditors to debtors, and the only choice remaining was to attract foreign investment. This situation resulted in a dependence on foreign accumulation—foreign capital— in the area of industrial investments as well as the banking sector. In this context, it was inevitable for the Greek banking sector to apply for foreign capital from Western European capital centres like Vienna, Berlin, Paris, London and Rome. Such capital was substantial for Greece, since the domestic financial sector was shallow and underdeveloped. However, Greece did not have a good reputation in this area, because of its low creditworthiness and its political and social instability.

Until 1925, the growth rate in Greece was very high, but macroeconomic indicators were very unstable. There was an unbalanced economic structure and an unsolvable inflation problem, along with wide fluctuations in the drachma exchange rates, since the supply of consumer goods was not able to meet demand. The inflation rate was 22.5% in 1915, and climbed to 37.3% in 1918, reaching a peak of 66.4% in 1922. Inflation fell to moderate levels between 1924 and 1926 (Lazarevic, 2008). In the period 1924-1928, the inflation rate was 9.8%. It decreased to 3.1% in 1929, and fell dramatically in 1930 to -13%. After 1930, it started to rise again, reaching 5.7% and 7.6% in 1932 and 1933 respectively. It fell to 2.7% from 1934 to 1938, as shown in Figure 1-1.

From the mid-1920s towards the Great Depression, Greece tried to follow international monetary developments. From 1927, the government implemented a two-year stabilisation programme followed by fiscal consolidation, monetary stringency and a devaluation of the drachma. Foreign creditors demanded the restoration of convertibility as a pre-condition for lending. They also asked for the establishment of an independent central bank, the Bank of Greece. Greece changed the anchoring to the GES on 14 May 1928 to ensure financial credibility and implement reforms to increase economic growth rate (Lazaretou, 2005). Moreover, the amount of broad money reflects the size of the country's banking system. As the economy gradually relies more heavily on the banking activity than in the past, the amount of deposits will exhibit a strong upward trend over time. Furthermore, the underdeveloped nature of the economy and the low degree of financial integration were mirrored in the weak impact of both the banking and the public sectors, in favour of a larger contribution from the monetary base (Lazaretou, 2010).

Figure 1-1 Inflation development in Greece (1924-1938)

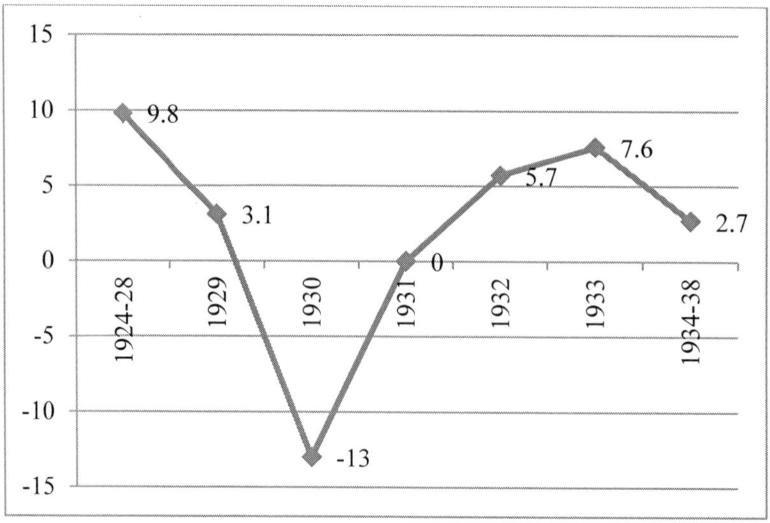

Source: Kavonius (2009)

Figure 1-2 Monetary aggregates for Greece (1922-1939)

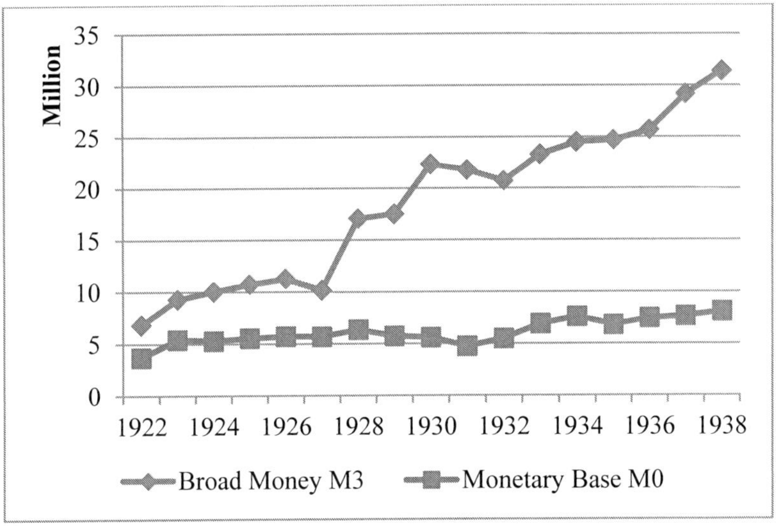

Source: Lazaretou (2010)

2.3 Real links of transmission of the crisis to Greece in the Great Depression

Greece always had a chronic deficit problem. Fixing the drachma to the pre-war exchange rate with UK sterling was not enough to cure the existing imbalances. In the second half of the 1920s, Greek exports to the UK accounted for only 12.2% of total volumes, while imports from the UK accounted for just 13.4%. Trade volumes with the US, Italy, and Germany were higher, in relative terms, and the exchange rate should have been pegged to an average of the major trading currencies (Lazarevic, 2008). In 1928-29, the trade balance showed an import surplus. Thus, the equilibrium point of supply and demand was unbalanced in favour of supply. At this point, the government decreased imports to bring the economy back to equilibrium. Their target was to equate increasing supply with decreasing demand, and the result was a smooth decline in the industrial sector. Although there is not enough reliable data on industrial production prior to the depression years, we can say that the harmful effects of the depression decreased after 1933, as shown in Figure 1-3. Just as Soldatos (1993) expresses, the general production index dropped to 88.8% in 1933 from 100% in 1928. Also, equipment imports, which were necessary for industrial investment, declined to 58.8% in the same year. After 1933, general and industrial production levels increased constantly. It should be highlighted that during the crisis years, the industrial sector was less affected by the crisis than other sectors in most of the developing countries, since a smaller proportion of this sector was linked to total economic activity.

As can be seen in Figure 1-4, the agricultural sector lost some of its market share in the crisis years, due to the lack of demand for Greek agricultural products like tobacco and currants. During the 1928-1932 period, demand for wine decreased by 68.6%, for tobacco by 43.2%, and for hides and skins by 53.1% (Triantis, 1951). Although production was reduced and relatively insignificant in this sector, overproduction was not a problem, since consumption was generally balanced by import restrictions (Aldcroft, 2002). Although agricultural and industrial production were increasing and the GDP was improving, as the population increased with the influx of refugees, income per capita did not improve as expected. Furthermore, both the GDP and income per capita hit a downturn after 1929, the year the Great Depression struck.

Figure 1-3 Industrial activity (1932-1939, 1928=100)

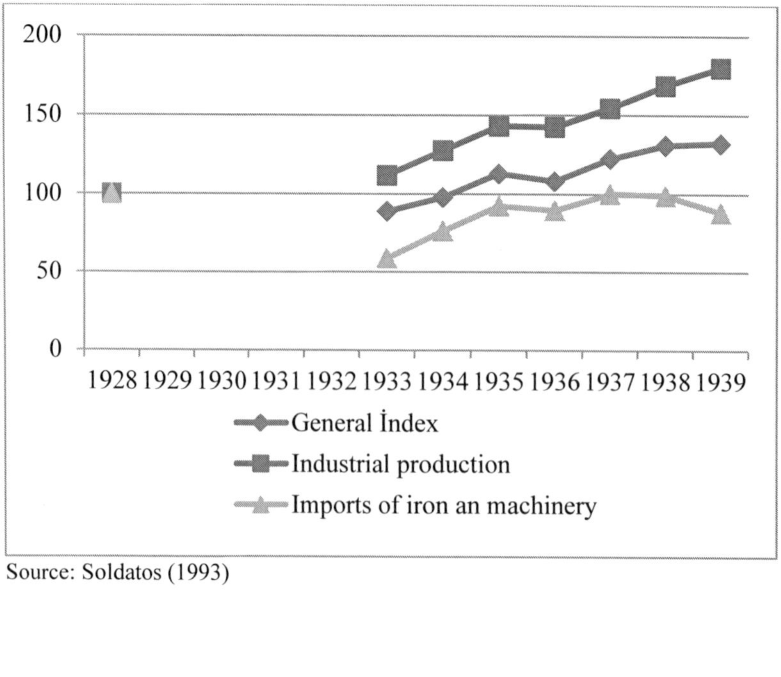

Source: Soldatos (1993)

Figure 1-4 Sector combinations (1928-1939)

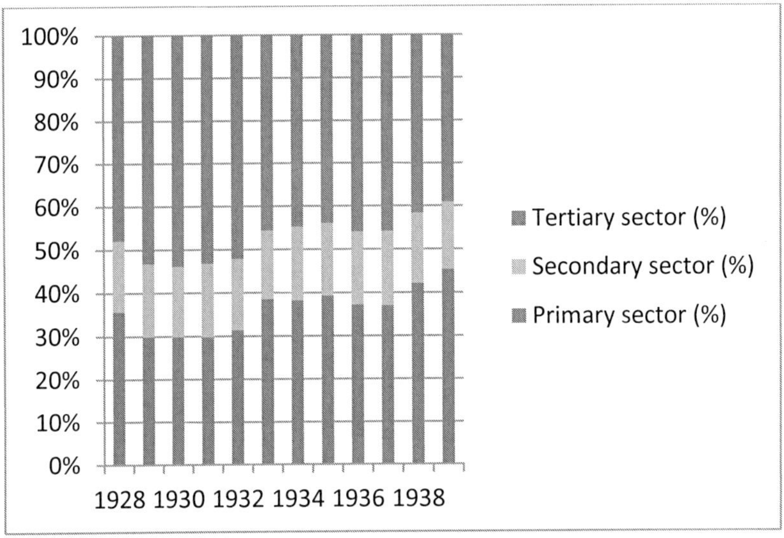

Source: Soldatos (1993)

Figure 1-5 GDP andincome per capita (1926-1939, 1926=100)

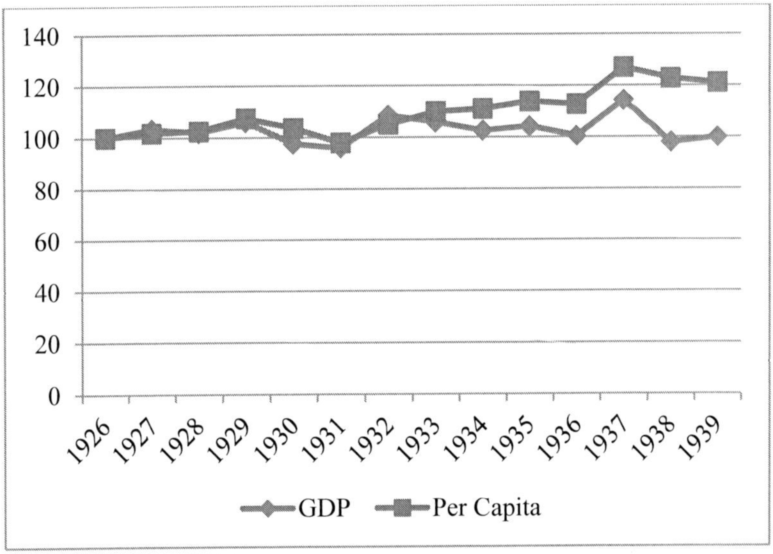

Source: Maddison (2003)

As seen in Figure 1-5, dynamic growth slowed down during the depression. The fall in the prices of primary products worsened the income level. As export revenues decreased, recovering budget deficits and foreign debt payments became extremely difficult (Kossev, 2008). Moreover, there was a clear fall in income combined with a substantial short-run income elasticity of demand for imported manufacturing goods.

When the crisis hit, a superabundance of labour (a combination of local citizens and refugees) worsened the economy. The increase in tobacco production, the increase in population living at a bare subsistence level, and a decrease in arable land per head were some of the factors aggravating the Greek economy in the period of the Great Depression. Despite the excessive amount of tobacco production in Greece, American and European consumers decreased their consumption of tobacco, since it came to be considered a luxury product during the Great Depression period. This situation resulted in a sharp decline in prices, and an increase in unemployment in this sector. The 40,000 tobacco workers felt the impact of the crisis very deeply. To decrease the harmful effects of the crisis, producers planned to reduce wages and to increase the supply of labour, by luring Anatolian Greek refugees to the main tobacco producing centres.

In fact, despite all these attempts, agrarian reforms offered almost no contribution to a market-oriented agriculture. At least initially, the above reforms had negative effects on production by reducing mechanisation, whereas they improved efficiency by promoting individualistic farming. It was clear that the primary sector, agriculture, had fallen far behind its pre-crisis level (Lazarevic, 2008).

As mentioned above, the 1930s were marked by a sharp increase in protectionist trade policies. These newly established trade barriers contributed to a major contraction in world trade in the early 1930s, beyond the economic collapse itself (Madsen, 2001). However, countries that remained on the gold standard, keeping their currencies fixed, were more likely to restrict foreign trade. Countries that abandoned the gold standard, like the UK and Greece, allowing their currencies to depreciate, saw their balances of payments strengthened. Abandoning the gold standard also freed up monetary policy. With no gold parity to defend, interest rates could be cut. No longer constrained by the gold standard, central banks had more freedom to act as lenders of last resort (Eichengreen and Douglas, 2009).

In 1932, the economy became more inward-looking and state-directed, which was, in part, a response to the actions of other countries that introduced wider controls on trade, tariffs and payments. The achievement of greater self-sufficiency, based on the use of domestic resources and less reliance on the international economy, became a main guideline in Greek economic life during this period. This aim could be seen in both industry and agriculture.

Trade balance could not improve until 1933, because of the reduction in imports by 49 million US$ due to the fall of real incomes and tariffs. Parallel to this, as protectionism spread all over Europe, exports also declined by 20 million US$. In 1934, both export and import levels were 45% lower than their 1931 levels. From this data, it can be concluded that trade imbalances reduced by almost half of their former values (Christodoulakis, 2012).

As a result of inconsistent policies in the first half of the 1930s, industrial production declined, inflation increased, real wages declined, and unemployment rose. In spite of the devaluation, uncertainties in the economy continued, which affected the labour market. Furthermore, because of the lack of capital, firms preferred to reach higher production levels by increasing working hours, instead of hiring new employees (Galbraith, 2009). Towards 1933, unemployment continued to rise and social conflicts continued, in parallel with this economic fluctuation.

2.4 Financial links of transmission of the crisis to Greece in the Great Depression

In 1925, following the British authorities' decision to return to the gold standard, a number of countries tied their national currencies to the GES, by pegging them to the sterling. Thus, the UK became the monetary zone's international centre (Bregianni, 2012). In the same period, the currency had been stabilised in Greece, and the Greek banking system was modernised through the creation of the Bank of Greece: the drachma was again tied to the GES, while the exchange rate with British sterling was fixed at 375 drachmas. Domestic discount rates were reduced until 1929, immediately after entering the GES. In the first two years of entry to the GES, Greece managed the successful implementation of fiscal and structural policies in the domestic economy. The public deficit and inflation were reduced and several structural reforms were implemented, in order to create a more liberalised economic environment and to modernise the banking system. The balance of payments improved notably and growth resumed. Public debt in dollars was reduced by almost half, in comparison to the previous decade. Actually, symptoms of a recession did not immediately appear in Greece. Because of this, the optimistic environment of the banking sector continued until the early years of the

1930s. In fact, the government launched orthodox economic policies in order to convince foreign investors, and did not consider a devaluation of the drachma. According to the banker Emmanuel Tsouderos, there was such a surplus in the domestic market that over-accumulation of capital was one of the causes of the crisis in 1930. This situation resulted in a decrease in deposit interests and a drop in discount interest rates to 9% (Mazower, 1991).

When the deep deflation waves of the 1929 crisis reached Greece, the primary impact was on the balance of payments and the drachma. According to Eichengreen and Sachs (1985), most of the countries left the GES quickly, devalued their currencies, and launched protectionist trade policies, monetary expansion and fiscal stimulus to deal with the devastating effects of the crisis. In fact, the countries remaining in the GES further tightened their monetary policy and this hit borrowing costs in Greece. For example, in May 1931, a few months before the UK left the GES, the Bank of England (BoE) raised the discount rate more than twofold, from 2.5% to 6%. As expected, the capital inflow by London investors in Greek bonds declined, and as a result the Greek economy suffered from both a credit shortage and capital outflows that worsened domestic contraction (Crafts and Fearon, 2010).

The initial effect of the crisis was a restriction on bank loans and a sharp decline in economic activity, which caused a fall in operational expenditures. Furthermore, the crisis made Greek capital investments in foreign markets non-profitable. This resulted in a decrease in deposit interests, and a drop in discount interest to 9% in the Greek banks.

On 21st September 1931, British sterling was devalued, and the UK left the gold standard. This was a great shock for other countries, as the devaluation of sterling against the US dollar was about 35%. Politically, the government lost its reputation as a strategic partner with the UK, because the UK left the GES unilaterally. The financial loss was even worse. The BoE had provided security to foreign central banks for the prevailing sterling exchange rate. Just a few months before leaving the GES, Greece, reassured by this, had increased foreign reserves in sterling by selling gold to the BoE. This transaction placed a great responsibility on the shoulders of the government, and soon afterwards the governor of the Bank of Greece was asked to resign (Eichengreen, 2012). In the same month, the government decided to suspend the Stock Exchange, which led to a reaction by investors which caused more difficulties for the government, in terms of remaining within the GES (Mazower, 1991). It was also hard to retain domestic funds. To control these funds, the Greek authorities increased the interest rates again, and discount rates rose to

12%. Not surprisingly, this rise blocked liquidity, and economic expectations became very pessimistic. The situation worsened, as the economy was heavily dependent on foreign capital inflows, and pessimistic expectations made it harder to borrow from abroad. Based on this, industries pressed commercial banks to raise liquidity, and as a result the panic, many worried investors withdrew their deposits. Commercial banks asked the Central bank for liquidity. The Central bank also tried to borrow long-term funds from abroad in order to keep the drachma stable, but it lost all of its reserves to cool down the economy.This policy cast doubt on the effectiveness of the monetary policy in general. The result of further credit expansion was the loss of foreign exchange reserves and the abondoning of the regime. The drachma came under speculative pressure, and the Central bank imposed exchange controls, which was the expected result of the suspension of convertibility.

Since there was an inflation problem accompanied with monetary expansion, currency crises and political turmoil up to 1928, the government was afraid to confront these problems by leaving the gold standard and implementing strict fiscal policies. As a result, Greece decided to stay in the GES, but pegged against the US dollar at the rate applied before the devaluation of the British pound. In this way, the government aimed to ensure monetary stabilisation, to modernise the banking system, and to open up the Greek financial system to foreign capital.

The drachma, however, came under heavy selling pressure very rapidly. Greece had to change strategy, in order to attract foreign capital. To do so, the government drove interest rates up to very high levels. There were side effects of this strategy on the real economy, and it also exhausted foreign reserves. None of the strategies for stimulating borrowing from abroad worked during the Depression period. Moreover, the government was not able to overcome Greece's economic and social problems, either during or the collapse, which is just like the contemporary situation. The devaluation of sterling in 1931 caused panic among European central banks, and as a result, Greece found itself in crisis due to the European economies' interdependence (Bregianni, 2012).

During this period, several small banks went bankrupt, others were bought out by bigger ones, and the rest preferred to merge (Alexopoulos, 2004). In 1931 and 1932, in terms of gold, the large Greek import surplus had been halved. In 1932, foreign exchange restrictions were adopted. The Central bank reacted by imposing exchange controls, marking the beginning of a de facto suspension of convertibility (Lazaretou, 2005).

Figure 1-6 The Drachma exchange rate by the US Dollar (left scale) and the British Pound (right scale)

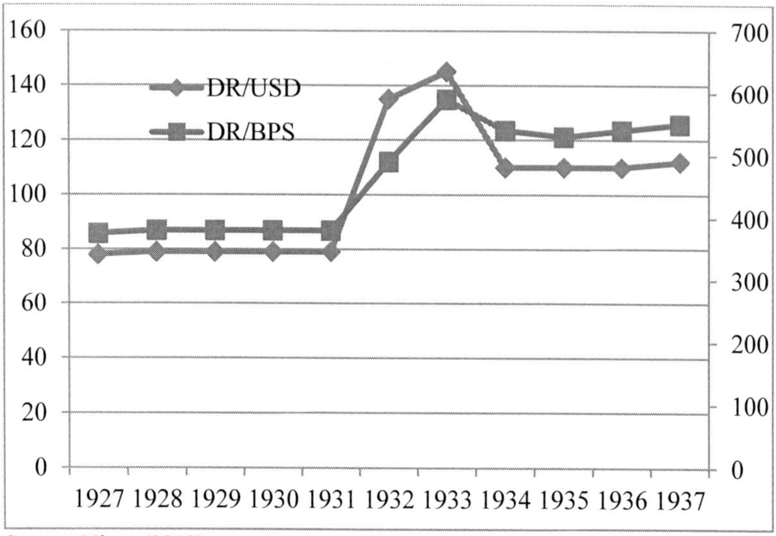

Source: Nicos (2012)

Greece was faced with a choice between internal adjustment, which would mean deflationary measures, and external adjustment, which would cause a devaluation of the currency. The latter option was chosen in April 1932, when the government devalued the drachma and abandoned the gold exchange standard (Lazaretou, 2005). The devalued drachma increased the trade competitiveness of the country. Nevertheless, protections all over the world could not raise external demand because of the erosion of real incomes. Besides, there was a great decline in both exports (32.9%) and imports (35.3%). This resulted in a lack of supply, and unemployment continued to rise and economic and social conflicts deepened. In the spring of 1932, the government declared a unilateral moratorium on the servicing of its outstanding foreign debt. The debt moratorium was a source of immediate relief on the balance of payments. The problems of the balance of payments were reflected in the restriction of monetary circulation and the diminution of the foreign exchange reserves. As seen in Figure 1-7, from 1929 through to the end of the 1930s (with the exception of 1933) the balance of payments was always in deficit.

Figure 1-7 Balance of payments (in millions of drachmas)

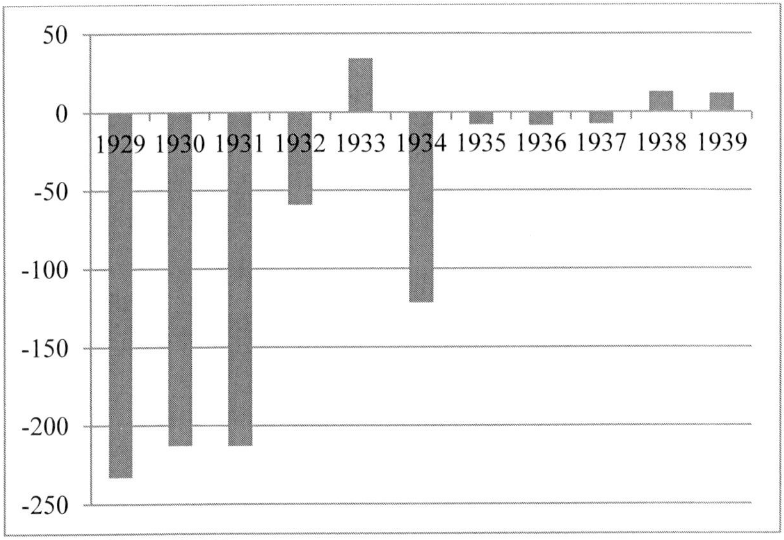

Source: Soldatos (1993)

Currency controls helped the Bank of Greece to keep currency in the country and to encourage the repatriation of any fugitive capital. The re-negotiation of Greek foreign debt closely followed these changes. The abandonment of the gold standard was followed by a period of high depreciation, and in mid-1933 the drachma dropped to about 40% of its gold parity, a level at which it remained during the decade. This currency depreciation was one of the largest among the countries leaving the gold standard, giving Greece a significant competitive advantage. In 1933, Greece attached itself to the gold block countries and started to peg the drachma against the Swiss franc. As seen in Figure 1-8, up to the abandon of GES, Greece had to keep gold reserves as high as possible. However, following the abandon the amount of gold stocks started to decline. Because of the slow recovery of the global economy, and the fact that world was on the brink of World War II, the country could not accumulate enough foreign assets.

By 1933, the country had not yet overcome its structural problems, but the crisis was over. In the preceding years, public finance problems had a significant impact on Greece's permanent monetary problems and influenced its banking activity. The Greek banking system was a highly centralised oligopoly. Through some of its activities, the Bank of Greece led banks to act as a monopoly. The banking system was a great contribution to the stability of the inter-war period, although its role in assisting economic growth was not particularly positive. Besides, the depreciation of the currency, trade restrictions and the fall in real wages resulting from the refugee inflow were the main forces behind the Greek recovery. Import volumes fell sharply in the early 1930s, while exports doubled (Aldcroft, 2006). On the other hand, the economic crisis and increasing political instability eventually led to several military coups. The Metaxas regime of 1936-1940 resembled a contemporary dictatorship, but was unable to produce "collectivist nationalism" due to the fragmentated nature of Greek society.

Figure 1-8 Foreign reserves of the Bank of Greece (1932-1939)

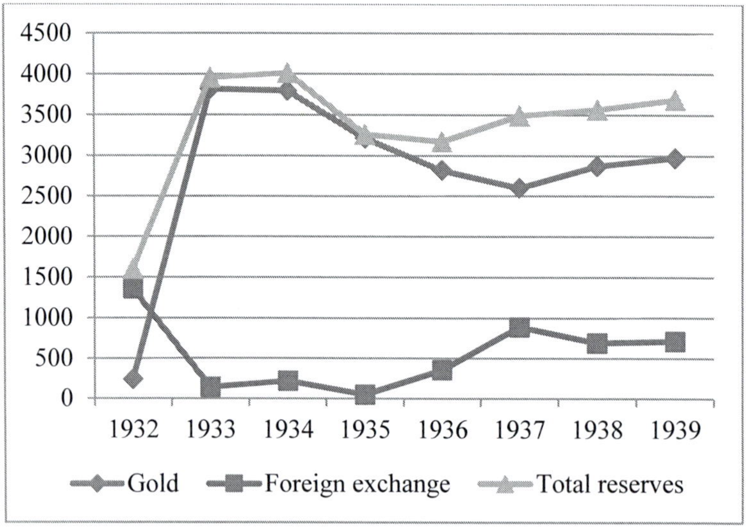

Source: Soldatos (1993)

3. The Greek economy in the last decade

3.1 General explanation of the global financial crisis

The recent global financial crisis is considered to be the worst financial crisis since the Great Depression. It has resulted in the threat of a total collapse of large financial institutions, banking bail-outs by national governments, and downturns in stock markets around the world. The crisis played a significant role in prolonged unemployment, firm bankruptcies, a decrease in consumption, and a dramatic downturn in economic activity. Between 2008 and 2010, it led to a global recession. The crisis also contributed to the European sovereign debt crisis.

Towards the end of the 1990s, following the housing construction boom in the US, various types of credit such as mortgages, credit cards, and automobile loans were easy to obtain. As banks began to give out more loans to potential home owners, housing prices began to rise. Lax lending standards and increasing real estate prices contributed to the real estate bubble. After a period of certain inflow, the housing market started to decline, and major global financial institutions that had borrowed and invested in subprime mortgage-backed securities reported significant losses. Falling prices affected house prices, and the value of houses began to fall into negative equity, i.e., a house was worth less than the mortgage. On August 7th 2007, the liquidity crisis began when BNP Paribas terminated withdrawals from three hedge funds, citing “a complete evaporation of liquidity”. Like BNP Paribas, other banks encountered the same issues, experiencing major difficulties rolling over their short-term debt. In the US, in September 2008, the bankruptcy of Lehman Brothers and fears of the insurance giant AIG (which was eventually bailed out) taking down major US and EU financial institutions caused great alarm. Panic broke out on the stock markets, market valuations of financial institutions evaporated, and investors looked for the few remaining safe havens. The crisis thus began to feed on itself, with banks forced to restrain credit and economic activity plummeting. The downturn in asset markets snowballed rapidly across the world. As commercial credit became scarce and expensive, world trade plummeted and industrial firms saw their sales drop and inventories pile up.[3]

It was also widely believed that, unlike the US economy, the European economy would be largely immune to the financial turbulence. This belief was fed by perceptions that the real economy, though slowing, was thriving on strong fundamentals such as rapid export growth and the sound financial positions of households and firms. Until 2008, the general budget deficit to GDP ratio of most EU countries (except Greece) fulfilled the Maastricht Criteria,[4] as seen in Table 1-2. On the other hand, from 2002,

---

[3] European Commission, Economic Crisis in Europe: Causes, Consequences and Responses, *European Economy* 7, 2009.

[4] Maastricht Criteria (Stability and Growth Pact) aims to keep members’ fiscal deficits below 3% of GDP and their debt-to-GDP ratios below 60% of GDP. In the case of the debt-to-GDP ratio, countries can be accepted if the debt ratio approaches to 60% critical level at a satisfactory pace. The latter criteria applied to

the public debt/GDP ratio worsened in most EU countries. As illustrated in Table 1-2, Greece, like Italy and Portugal, showed a sharp rise in debt stock between 2002 and 2011. Over this period, the level of Greek debt increased 1.5 fold (Kar, 2012).

Table 1-2 Budget balance and gross national debt over GDP (%)

General Budget Balance to GDP (%)						
	2002	2004	2008	2009	2010	2011
Greece	-4.8	-7.5	-9.8	-15.6	-10.3	-9.1
Germany	-3.8	-3.8	-0.1	-3.2	-4.3	-1
Italy	-3.1	-3.5	-2.7	-5.4	-4.6	-3.9
Portugal	-2.9	-3.4	-3.6	-10.2	-9.8	-4.2
Gross National Debt to GDP (%)						
	2002	2004	2008	2009	2010	2011
Greece	101.7	98.6	113	129.4	145	165.3
Germany	60.7	66.3	66.7	74.4	83	81.2
Italy	105.1	103.1	105.7	116	118.6	120.1
Portugal	53.8	68.3	71.6	83.1	93.3	107.8

Source: Eurostat

The indicators in the Eurozone worsened towards 2008. The crisis spread rapidly, and turned into a global crisis with the European banking failures, the decline in stock market indexes, and the sharp decline in the market value of equities and commodities. Derivatives such as credit default swaps also increased the linkage between large financial institutions. Furthermore, since assets were sold to pay back obligations, the deleveraging of financial institutions accelerated the solvency crisis and caused a decrease in international trade. In October 2008, the crisis turned into a currency crisis, with investors transferring vast capital

Greece. In 2000, Greece was welcomed into the Euro area with a debt-to-GDP ratio of near 100% (because the ratio was on a declining path) and a fiscal deficit initially reported at 3% of GDP; the latter figure was subsequently revised to 3.7% of GDP after Greece became a member of the EMU.

resources into stronger currencies, leading many emerging economies to seek aid from the IMF.

3.2 The general economic condition of Greece towards the European debt crisis

During the last four decades, the Greek economy has never stabilized, and boom-bust periods have followed each other. During the period 1979-1995, the Greek economy fell into a persistent recession and the average annual growth rate of real GDP per capita decreased to -0.07%. In spite of public debt and a large budget deficit, the Greek economy entered a pre-EMU accession period in 1994. Because of the threat of exclusion from the pre-EMU accession phase, the country launched hard budget constraints, which forced the Greek authorities to fix fiscal imbalances (Katsimi, 2010). The second half of the 1990s can be considered a recovery period: real GDP per capita increased by 3.14% and the labour factor grew by 0.75%, whereas the capital factor decreased by 1.05%. The partial recovery phase started in 1996, and continued through 2001. At the end of the recovery phase, real GDP per capita was 77.16% with respect to its trend. Moreover, real consumption expenditure per capita was 86.76% and real investment expenditure per capita was 67.99% relative to its trend (Gogos et al., 2012). This positive trend continued through the period 2001-2007, with a growth rate of 3.75%. However, as expected, in the 2007-2010 crisis period, real GDP per capita sank to -2.47%.

In January 2001, Greece was accepted as a member of the Eurozone, on the grounds that it had fulfilled the Maastricht criteria. However, this was the result of a false declaration made about its macroeconomic conditions for the period extending from 1997-2003. Right after its acceptance into the EU, the “windfall effect” of entry showed itself both in real growth rates and low interest rates. In fact, the period from 2001-2007 is important for Greece, since during this period the country used EU funds uneconomically, and this prepared the basis for the dramatic Greek debt crisis. In this period, the country’s GDP growth was 4.3%, which was better than the Eurozone average of 3.1% (IMF, 2009). Increasing private consumption (because of easier access to credit) and increasing public expenditure financed by the EU induced the growth of GDP. In spite of Greece’s relatively drastic contractionary fiscal policies and steps towards structural reform, the economic growth rate contracted by 2% in 2009, by 2.5% in 2010 and by 0.7% in 2011, with registered unemployment reaching 12.6% in 2010 (Rady and Abdel, 2012).

Table 1-3 Greece's macroeconomic performance (1980s-2000s)

Annual Average	1980s	1990s	2000s
Real GDP Growth (%)	0.8	1.9	3.6
Government Balance (% of GDP)	-8.1	-8.5	-4.9
Current Account Balance (% of GDP)	-3.9	-2.5	-9.1
Annual Inflation (%)	19.5	11.0	3.4
Exchange Rate (%vs US$)	-281	-93	35

Source: IMF

Figure 1-9 Greece and the Euro area inflation rates (2001-2010)

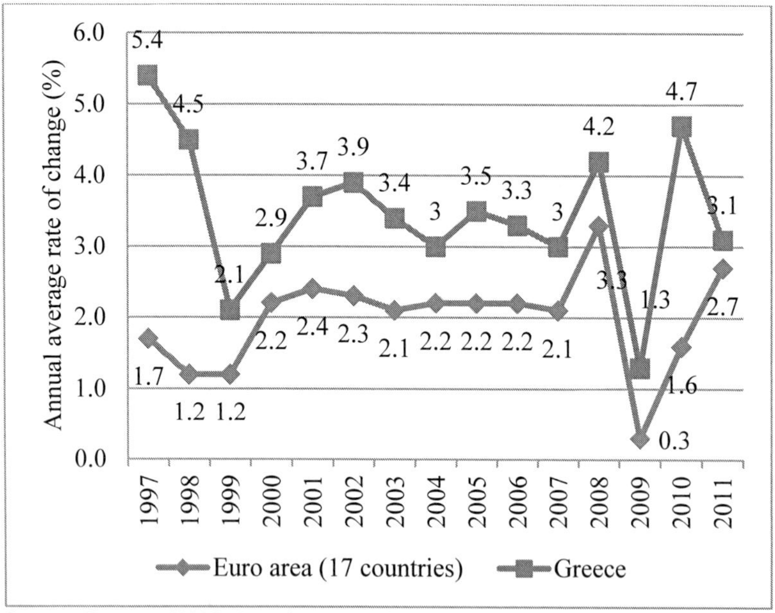

Source: Eurostat (2012, Based on annual % changes in overall Harmonised Index of Consumer Prices)

The situation was no different with respect to inflation. Until 2001, Greece had to fight high inflation and debt interest rates, which were always above 10% (Dagdelen, 2011). While inflation was around 10% between 1990 and 2000, it stood at almost 3.4% during the period 2001-2008. Briefly, being a member of the EU brought prolonged and robust growth, and relatively low inflation with respect to its historical standards. However, it should be emphasized that, as illustrated in Figure 1-9, the inflation rate was still roughly 1.5% higher on average per year than in the rest of the Euro area (Gibson et al., 2011).

3.3 Trade (real) links of the Greek crisis

Prior to the financial crisis of 2008, Greece suffered from inadequate trade policies, and entered the downturn in a weak fiscal position. In fact, between 2001 and 2009, two basic problems were growing: fiscal imbalances and the country's trade competitiveness. Both of these were partially related to the trade deficit. Increasing prices and wages at relatively high rates affected competitiveness negatively. One emphasizes relatively high wages and low productivity as a primary factor in losing competitiveness power. Nelson et al., (2011) claims that during the period 2001-2008, wages grew at an average of 5%, which was double the average rate in the Euro area. In 2008-2009, nominal wage increases reached 12%. With inflation decreasing at the end of 2008, real wage growth rose, boosting household incomes. In the period 2001-2009, competitiveness, as measured by consumer prices, dropped by around 20% and as measured by unit labour costs, decreased by almost 25%. High wage growth over the euro average had led to a deterioration in competitiveness. A major factor in boosting competitiveness is the concentration on productivity through enhancing educational outcomes. Despite progress over the past decades, educational attainment in most age groups in Greece was below the OECD average (Rady and Abdel, 2012).

Economists also emphasize over-employment and poor productivity in the public sector as among the biggest problems for the economy. As well as over-employment, the aging Greek population and its pension system (which was considered one of Europe's most generous) may have placed an additional burden on public spending. During the period 2001-2008, the Greek government faced extremely high deficits, as it indulged in high government expenditure, especially in terms of pension and health benefits (11.6 % and 5.7% of GDP on average, over the period 2001-2007).[5] This situation, coupled with low productivity, sent Greece into a spiral of declining international competitiveness.

Military expenditure is also considered to be another factor in generating high budget deficits. Despite the fact that the country's tax revenue to GDP ratio is relatively low with respect to the other Eurozone countries, the country's military expenditure is extremely high. According to data revealed by the Stockholm International Peace Research Institute

[5] OECD Factbook Statistics, 2012.

(SIPRI), between 2005 and 2009, Greece was the fifth greatest weapons importer. While military expenditure was at 7.496 million euros in 2007, it rose to 9.474 million euros in 2009 (Dagdelen, 2011).

As Perotti et al. (1997) observe, these fiscal adjustments relied too much on increasing tax revenue, instead of cutting public expenditure. From 1993 to 2000, the share of tax revenue in GDP increased by about 8%, whereas the share of government spending remained the same. Until 2008, total government spending was between 43-45% of GDP, whereas tax revenue showed a smooth declining trend, standing at 42.9% in 2000 and 39.6% in 2007. This decline is the result of company closures, decreasing production, increasing unemployment and, quite probably, tax evasion. Tax evasion and unrecorded income obstructed any improvement in Greece's fiscal position via direct tax revenue. According to a rough estimation, the ratio of unrecorded income represents 25-30% of GDP.[6] Also, complex tax codes, excessive regulations, long transactions and inefficiency in the public sector resulted in a higher level of tax evasion (Nelson et al., 2011). Unfortunately, weak revenue collection led to higher debt borrowing, representing 119% of GDP in 2009 and 144.9% in 2010.[7] Furthermore, Greece's shadow economy represented almost 25-30% of GDP (Kouretas and Vlamis, 2010). As seen in Table 1-4, indirect tax revenue is always higher than direct tax revenue. This supports the idea of government failure in collecting taxes fairly, perhaps as a result of ineffective tax law.

Although Greece was suffering from lack of productivity and revenue, the government refused to cut public expenditure. Up until 2007, the central government's expenditure increased by 87%, while revenues grew only 31%.[8] This gap resulted in large budget deficits, which were much higher than the standard 3% of GDP (Nelson et al., 2011). As seen in Table 1-5, personnel expenses were higher than the average across 16 other Eurozone countries. Social expenses were relatively high for a country suffering from budget and balance of payments deficits

From 2007 to 2010, the annual average growth rate was -5.05%. Thus, as was to be expected, the labour factor decreased to -1.03%, partially offset by a positive contribution of the capital factor of 3.61% (Gogos et al., 2012). The Greek government operated at a deficit of 10.4% of GDP in

---

[6] Country Report, Greece, March 2010.

[7] Eurostat, 2012.

[8] The Hellenic Stability and Growth Programme, Greek Ministry of Finance, January 2010.
http://www.mnec.gr/export/sites/mnec/en/economics/growth_programme_2005-8/2010_01_15_SGP.pdf

2010 and, in spite of a number of euro rescue deals agreed upon by EU leaders, market volatility persisted through to the end of 2011, and debt rose to 147.3% of GDP (Rady and Abdel, 2012).

Table 1-4 Public revenue over GDP (%)

		1996	2000	2006	2007	2008	2009
Tax Revenue	Greece	19.08	23.54	20.61	20.6	20.1	19.3
	EU–16	26.2	25.2	25.9	26.2	25.4	24.4
Indirect Taxes	Greece	12.47	13.58	12.46	12.51	12.11	11.1
	EU–16	13.3	13.4	13.5	13.5	13	12.8
Direct Taxes	Greece	6.35	9.66	7.99	7.94	7.74	7.9
	EU–16	12.6	11.5	12.1	12.4	12.2	11.3
Capital Taxes	Greece	0.26	0.31	0.15	0.15	0.25	0.2
	EU–16	0.3	0.3	0.3	0.3	0.3	0.4
Social Contributions	Greece	11.52	12.47	13.42	13.42	13.4	12.7
	EU–16	15.8	15.4	15.1	15.1	15.3	15.7
Sales	Greece	1.22	1.25	1.46	1.46	1.5	1.4
	EU–16	2.2	2.2	2.1	2.1	2.1	2.2

Source: Eurostat

There was also a trade deficit in the Greek economy. As shown in Table 1-6, Greece held a trade deficit with both the EU trade partners and non-union countries. Furthermore, the ratio of exports to imports decreased after the country entered both the EU and the EMU. During the period 2001-2010, the Greek export to import rate grew 3.8% per year. This value was only half the rate of Greek imports from other trading partners. This increased the current account deficit which fed into the budget deficit. An increase in both parameters resulted in twin deficits (Dagdelen, 2011).

Lastly, it was not only Greece but also its major trade partners in the Balkan Peninsula which suffered from the global crisis. This resulted in a great loss in trade. However, it should be noted that the recession hit Greece less than the other peninsula countries since it has a relatively small manufacturing sector (Kouretas and Vlamis, 2010).

Table 1-5 Public expenditure over GDP (%)

		1996	2000	2006	2007	2008	2009
Purchase of Good and Services	Greece	4.8	6.4	5.1	5.6	5.3	6.1
	EU–16	4.8	5	5	5	5.1	5.6
Personnel Expenses	Greece	9.7	10.4	11	11.2	11.4	12.4
	EU–16	10.4	10.4	10.2	10	10.1	10.8
Interest Expenses	Greece	10.5	7.3	4.4	4.4	4.5	4.9
	EU–16	3.9	3	2.9	3	3	2.8
Subsidies	Greece	0.4	0.1	0.1	0.13	0.1	0.1
	EU–16	1.5	1.2	1.2	1.2	1.2	1.4
Social Expenses	Greece	13.7	14.7	16.8	17.5	18.7	20.5
	EU–16	21	21.6	21.4	21	21.3	23.4
Capital Transfers	Greece	1.1	1	1.62	1.7	1.9	1.6
	EU–16	1.3	1.4	1.4	1.2	1.2	1.4
Capital Expenses	Greece	1	2.6	0.87	1.1	1.6	1.5
	EU–16	1.5	2.5	2.4	2.6	2.5	2.8
Total	Greece	**44**	**46.9**	**43.1**	**45**	**46.7**	**50.3**
	EU–16	**46.3**	**47.4**	**46.7**	**46**	**46.8**	**50.7**

Source: Eurostat

The Greek government tried to attract new foreign investment by boosting exports of goods and services, as well as focusing on the trade and investment and shipping and tourism sectors, using its geographic location. However, in 2009 Greek exports fell by 18.8%, and Greek firms became increasingly uncompetitive in both domestic and international markets. In October 2009, the Greek government unveiled three separate packages of fiscal austerity measures aimed at bringing Greece's government deficit down from an estimated 13.6% of GDP in 2009 to below 3% by 2012. In total, the measures are worth an estimated 16 billion euros, or 6.4% of GDP. In March 2010, the Parliament approved another austerity measure which aimed to increase revenues through an increase in the average value-added tax rate. On the expenditure side, most of the announced spending cuts focused on the civil service. The government decided to reduce pension funds, cut pay and non-pay expenses, and limit subsidies. They also announced a tightening of public regulations and a restructuring of Greece's public administration by consolidating local governing structures, which reduces the level of local administrative authorities (Rady and Abdel, 2012).

Table 1-6 Greece export and import volumes (in millions euro, 1999-2008)

	1999	2000	2001	2002	2003	2004	2005	2006	2007	2008
Export IntraEU	6.9	7.8	8.2	6.6	7.6	7.9	8.5	10.5	11.1	11.2
Import IntraEU	20	23.5	23.7	18.5	23	25.5	25.4	29	32.1	33.6
Export ExtraEU	3.4	4.8	4.6	4.3	4.1	4.4	5.3	5.9	6	6.2
Import ExtraEU	8.5	12.7	13.1	14.7	16.5	16.8	18.2	21.6	23.4	27.3

Source: Eurostat

3.4 Financial links of the Greek crisis

After its entry into the EU, positive effects started to be seen in the Greek economy, along with sharply reduced interest rates. The nominal interest rate on 10-year Greek government bonds decreased from about 20% in 1994 to less than 3.5% in early 2005 (Katmisi and Moutos, 2012). In other words, the borrowing costs in Greece and Germany became almost identical, as illustrated in Table 1-7 (Kar, 2012).

Furthermore, while spreads were 1,100 basis points in 1995, they fell to almost 100 basis points in 2000, on the eve of Greece's entry to the EMU. With the entry in 2001, spreads fell to 50 basis points and continued to narrow subsequently. Another decrease of between 10 to 30 basis points followed during the period 2002-2007. Actually, when the US subprime mortgage market was released at the beginning of the global crisis, there was a limited impact on the Greek financial markets. Spreads on the 10-year instrument remained almost the same as 30 basis points in its July 2007 values. After the collapse of Lehman Brothers, spreads improved to 60 and rose to 250 basis points at the beginning of 2009.

Table 1-7 Bond and interest rate convergence criteria in the EMU

	2002	2003	2004	2005	2006	2007	2008	2009	2010	2011
Greece	**5.1**	**4.2**	**4.2**	**3.5**	**4**	**4.5**	**4.8**	**5.1**	**9**	**15.7**
Germany	4.7	4	4	3.3	3.7	4.2	3.9	3.2	2.7	2.6
Italy	5	4.2	4.2	3.5	4	4.4	4.6	4.3	4	5.4
Portugal	5	4.1	4.1	3.4	3.9	4.4	4.5	4.2	5.4	10.2

Source: Eurostat

In addition, in the period 2002-2007, absolute levels of nominal interest rate rose from 3.5% to 4.5% as compared with a range of 5% to 6.5% in the year prior to entry to the EMU. Nevertheless, after the global crisis erupted in August 2007, interest rates shot upward, with the 10-year government bond yield increasing to almost 12% at the end of 2010 (Katmisi and Moutos, 2012). The 2008 global financial crisis caused capital markets to become more strained in terms of liquidity. This in turn impacted upon GDP growth and exports, and hindered Greece's progress as well as its access to financial assistance from other countries, as the crisis spread throughout the Eurozone. As a result, reliance on funds from international capital markets left Greece highly dependent on global economic conditions (Rady and Abdel, 2012). In mid-2009, a deterioration in these conditions brought real GDP growth rate down to -2%, and unemployment up to 9.5%. In November 2009, another shock affected the economy. The government owner of "Dubai World" in the Gulf Emirates asked for a six-month moratorium. This event caused a great fluctuation in the world's financial markets, and led to a sharp increase in risk aversion.

From 2001 (the year Greece joined the EMU) to 2008, the budget deficits announced by the government averaged 5% of GDP, which is 3% higher than the Eurozone average. Also, reported current account deficits over GDP were averaging 9%, compared to a Eurozone average of 1% (IMF, 2009). The decrease in debt interest payments made the Greek authorities sufficiently comfortable to get into debt. Although a global financial crisis broke out in Autumn 2008, the Greek government continued to borrow heavily on the international capital markets, in order to fund their budget and current account deficits. As a result, government debt increased dramatically (Gibson et al., 2011). Greece's gross external debt reached 149% of GDP in 2008. In October 2009, after the election, the newly elected government tried to take steps to modernise and consolidate the public administration. The government announced a budget deficit for 2009 of 12.7% of GDP, while the previous government had declared that the deficit would be no higher than 6.5% in September 2009. However, by the end of 2009, the actual budget deficit had reached 15.4% of GDP.[9] Furthermore, increasing public expenditure and an increase in borrowing in the years leading up to the crisis had already resulted in a high level of accumulated public debt. In the same year, government expenditure accounted for 50% of GDP.[10] Reliance on external financing for funding the budget and current account deficits by successive Greek governments made the economy highly vulnerable.

Figure 1-10 Fiscal deficit, total expenditure and total revenue (% of GDP)

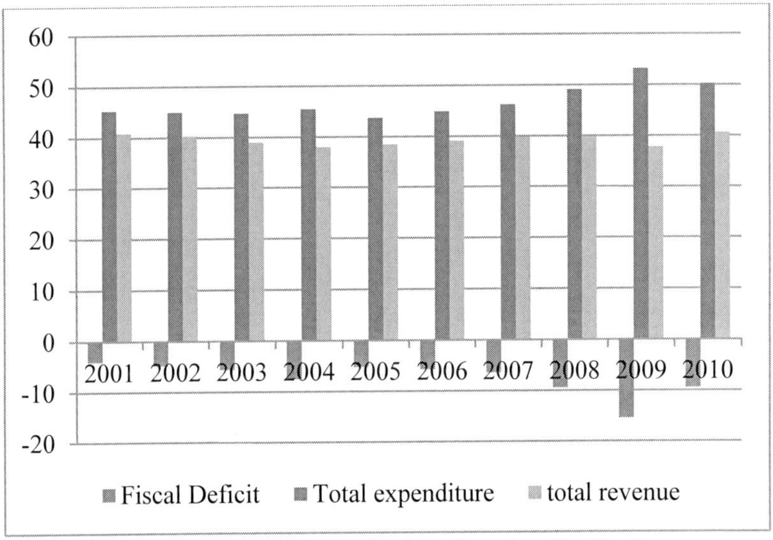

Source: European Commission, Excessive Debt Procedure Notification

On 31 December, 2009, the amount of central government debt stood at 298.5 billion euros. The debt-to-GDP ratio continued to increase in 2010, because of the 110 billion euro rescue package. In the last decade, the Greek authorities never reduced government spending. This fiscal policy led to a rise in the share of government spending, from 45% of GDP in 2001 to 50% of GDP in 2009, as expected. These maturing debt obligations reached about 54 billion euros in 2010, and the general government debt reached 147.3% of GDP. Both Greece's budget deficit

[9] Eurostat, 2009.

[10] The Hellenic Stability and Growth Programme, Greek Ministry of Finance, January 2010.

and external debt level were higher than the limits defined by the Maastricht criteria (Rady and Abdel, 2012).

As indicated in Figure 1-10, deficits were increasing consistently, and exceeding the SGP's limit of 3% of GDP. In the defined period, it is clear that total expenditure was always higher than total revenue. Increasing current account deficits affected the budget deficit. Furthermore, Greek policymakers preferred to release government spending excluding debt interest payments, since interest payments were steadily decreasing as a result of nominal convergence to the Euro area countries.

In addition to high public sector debt, the private sector's debt burden increased heavily over the same period, as a result of rapid credit expansion to households and firms. Greece focused on the service sector, which is highly dependent on global economic conditions (Rady and Abdel, 2012). As a result, the enormous differences between the first and the actual values of the budget deficits had a negative imapact upon Greece's credibility as a reliable partner in European affairs (Katmisi and Moutos, 2012).

As a result of these fluctuations in the Greek economy, the country's credit rating dropped steadily. Since 2009, credit evaluation agencies Moody's, Standard and Poor's (S&P), Fitch and R&I have agreed to decrease Greece's credit rating. A sharp reduction was observed in one year. For example, R&I graded Greece as AA in 2008, and BBB- in 2009. Similarly, Moody's graded Greece as A+ in 2008 and BB+ in 2010. Greek bonds were downgraded by three major credit rating agencies. Before the crisis, Greek 10-year-bonds were 10-40 basis points above German 10-year-bonds. Just after the crisis, in January 2010, the spread increased to an all-time high of 400 basis points[11] which led to a loss of confidence by investors in the Greek economy. Although Greece could manage to sell 8 billion euros in bonds at the end of January 2010, and 5 billion euros in bonds at the end of March 2010, the budget deficit was far from being reduced. At this time, Eurozone countries suggested providing financial assistance to Greece in concert with the IMF (Nelson et al., 2011). However, by May 2010 the Greek crisis was spreading across Europe. By this time, policymakers had finally recognised the severity of the situation, and in addition to the 110 billion euros bail-out package offered by the EU/ECB/IMF, an additional 750 billion euros package was set up on May 10 2010, in order to protect the Eurozone from the crisis. Also, the ECB provided further support by buying Eurozone bonds on the secondhand markets (Katsimi and Moutos, 2012). Related to fluctuations in the financial markets, the real economy was affected by a loss of

[11] Fiscal Woes to Dog Greek Bonds Even if Aid Offered, *Reuters*, March 22, 2010.

competitiveness. This situation deepened the "twin deficits". The rising twin deficits (accompanied by the lack of structural reforms in labour market flexibility, social security, and market competition) persuaded the Greek authorities to issue new bonds for shorter maturity periods with higher interest rates, as compared to Germany. The financial authorities started to become suspicious of Greece's ability to roll over its debt, based on a high probability of sovereign default. The maturity profile of Greek public debt was one of important reason for this mistrust. However, this period is considered to be the period in which the government was unable to pay the sovereign default. Because of such obscurities in the situation, investors required higher interest rates from the Greek authorities in order for them to lend again.

Despite all these efforts, it was impossible for the EU authorities to convince investors that the crisis would not spread throughout Europe. There was great doubt and fear among investors that the sovereign debt crisis would lead to a wider banking crisis, because of the interconnections among the national banking system in Europe (BIS, 2010).

By entering the EU, Greece lost the ability to launch its own monetary policy and its ability to change the nominal exchange rate of its own currency. By converting its local currency to the euro, as per the EU monetary policy, Greece lost the right (sovereignty) to devaluate its currency to reduce the value of debt.

To compensate for the loss of those tools, Greece needed the following economic advantages: relatively low fiscal imbalances, in order to protect the economy in case of country-specific shocks, and a flexible labour force and product markets, to sustain its competitiveness without applying changes to the domestic currency rate. However, as explained above, neither competitiveness nor fiscal balance could be managed by the Greek authorities. During the period 2001-2009, competitiveness became even worse, despite the large current account deficits. Furthermore, instead of providing the role of an automatic stabiliser, the pro-cyclical stance of fiscal policy acted as a major source of shock. Unfortunately, real time data understated the severity of the fiscal situation. This data showed that fiscal imbalances were decreasing. However, subsequent revisions to the data showed that, in fact, the economy's imbalance was growing. Nevertheless, in the period 2001-2008, the low levels of interest rate spreads brought little attention to the unsustainability of the fiscal and external imbalances (Gibson et al., 2011).

To save Greece, and to protect the rest of the Europe, the European Commission set targets to correct budget deficits widening through 2012-2013. As expected, Greece did not take effective action to fix their budgetary position. In 2010, Greece's tax revenue increased to 32.2% of GDP against an OECD average of 37.8% (Rossi and Delgado Aguiera, 2010). However, the government could not fight tax evasion strongly enough, and most of the tax revenue collected came from the middle-classes, who felt this burden on their shoulders. While in 2006, the unemployment rate was 8.9%, in 2010 it rose to 12.6%.[12] Increasing tax collection, applying reforms to decrease tax evasion and fiscal opacity would also help to reduce budget deficit (Darvas et al., 2011).

Figure 1-11 Comparison of Greece with 16-EU countries in terms of government gross debt (% of GDP)

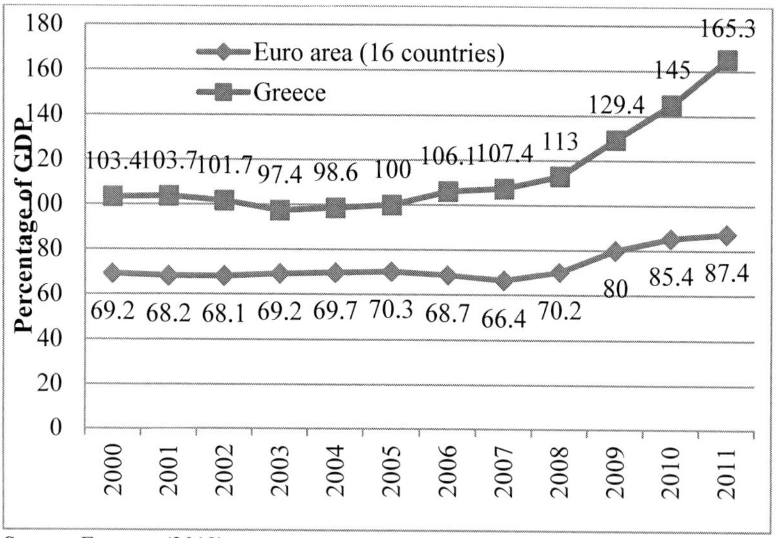

Source: Eurostat (2012)

As seen in Figure 1-11, government debt was always above the 16-country-average. After 2007, the Greek government debt curve became even steeper, while the 16-country-average curve stayed almost the same. In parallel, the current account deficit also rose over the years, standing at 7.5% in 2005, rising to 14.4% in 2007 and to 14.8% in 2008. With the austerity programmes and the rescue packages, it dropped to 11.1% in 2009 (Bank of Greece, 2009).

European authorities criticised the Greek economy for being an inefficient public administration with a costly pension and healthcare

[12] Eurostat, 2010. http://epp.eurostat.ec.europa.eu/guip/themeAction.do.

system, characterised by tax evasion and corruption, and of displaying insufficient good will in maintaining fiscal discipline. All these problems contributed to increasing public debt (Nelson et al., 2011).

As is well known, the EU is a monetary but not an economic union with a federal budget. With the entry to the EMU, Greece accepted the euro as its national currency. As such, the Union has a common monetary policy at a supranational level, but member countries have separate economic policies such as budgetary, wage and social policies or credit regulations. This means that while the monetary policy of Greece was in the European authorities' hands, economic policies were controlled by the local authorities. This two-headed system resulted in an irregular management by Greece as a country base, and a lack of adjustment mechanisms to deal with such a crisis at a supranational level. This policy change is considered to be one of the reasons for Greek debt accumulation. The heavyweights of the EU, Germany and France, the ECB, and investors, preferred to view the reliability of Eurozone member countries with a heightened degree of confidence. This is why, like the other Eurozone members, Greece could borrow at a more favourable interest rate and service their existing debt. At first glance, this opportunity looked like an advantage for Greece. However, this sense of comfort contributed to the accumulation of its debt. Since the launching of the euro, most countries have complained about the limits set by the SGP. Besides, the lack of enforcement of the SGP encouraged countries like Greece to accumulate high level of debt (Nelson et al., 2011). Table 1-8, which illustrates the countries' government debt risks, provides an opportunity to compare the macroeconomic situation in Greece with the other EU members who suffered from the crisis. In 2010, when the global crisis erupted, Greece found itself in the unique situation of suffering from twin deficits. Therefore, despite the irrefusable responsibilities and mistakes of successive Greek governments in managing the Greek debt crisis, ignoring the EU as a controller can also be classed as another important mistake. Furthermore, many authorities were suspicious about the risk of contagion to other countries in the Eurozone.

Table 1-8 Comparison of government debt risks in 2010

	Budget Deficit/ GDP	Debt/ GDP	External Debt (% of Total Debt)	Short-term Debt/GDP	Current Account/GDP
Greece	**-12.2**	**124.9**	**77.5**	**20.8**	**-10.0**
Portugal	-8.0	84.6	73.8	22.6	-9.9
Ireland	-14.7	82.6	57.2	47.3	-1.7
Italy	-5.3	116.7	49.0	5.7	-2.5
Spain	10.1	66.3	37.0	5.8	-6.0
UK	-12.9	80.3	22.1	3.3	-2.0
US	-12.5	93.6	26.4	8.3	-2.6

Source: European Commission, World Bank, IMF

4. Similarities and differences between two crises

Although its size and extent are exceptional, the global crisis that struck in 2007 is considered similar to the Great Depression, with its financial stress which drove recession, and its harmful effects for both industrial and emerging countries. Inter-war crises occurred under the GES. This situation caused the transmission, of the crisis for two basic reasons: firstly, most of the countries were linked to each other via gold parity fixed exchange rates and free flow of goods and capital; secondly, the crises mostly hit during periods of deflation. As Bordo and Wheelock (1998) emphasize, in the long-run deflation drove the price for the gold standard, with an excess demand for monetary gold creating an environment of monetary stringency and financial distress. Furthermore, a gold standard imposed discipline on all economies in the system, but monetary and fiscal policies were used to defend the gold standard instead of being used to increase output.

Like the global crisis, the Great Depression originated in the US, and was transmitted to Europe via advanced countries such as the UK, which was the international centre of the Continent. Moreover, just like the global crisis, the intensity of the transmission was so deep that the turmoil was even more devastating for periphery countries than source countries. Because the periphery countries were far too dependent on the advanced ones during the Great Depression (just like today), such countries were affected both financially and commercially. In the Great Depression, the year-on-year reduction in imports in the industrial countries, and the collapse of international lending, placed developing countries in situatinos of great difficulty. In particular, a regular flow of dollars was inevitable for debtor countries, since the dollar was used to buy goods and services and to discharge their debt payments. When the flow dried up, those countries had to confront their balance of payments and debt-repayment problems. In response to this economic environment, primary producers had to reduce imports and boost their exports as the terms of trade moved sharply against them. To reduce the gold and foreign exchange losses, producers used restrictive monetary and fiscal policies to deflate their economies. To support this strategy, public spending and wages were cut. Despite all these precautions, it was impossible for the developing countries to earn sufficient foreign currency or, at least, to attract international loans.

The situation was not very different for Greece, being an emerging periphery country, which was dependent on the UK. It had tied its economy to the UK in 1925, since the UK was the international centre of the monetary zone. After the UK left the GES, the capital inflow of London investors for Greek bonds decreased, and the Greek economy therefore suffered from both a credit shortage and from capital outflows, which worsened the domestic squeeze. Furthermore, just a few months before the UK left the GES, Greece had increased its foreign reserves in sterling by selling gold to the BoE. This decision made the situation even worse. In 1931, the government and the Central bank, with the assistance of the League of Nations, placed the banking system under strict control, but these measures were taken too late.

Many scholars also emphasize the fact that central banks like the FED were too passive during the Depression years. They did not halt the panic in the banking system. Intervention at decisive moments (for instance, the failure of the Bank of the United States in late 1930 or Austria's Credit Anstalt in spring 1931) could have changed history. Instead, increasing unemployment and falling prices fed on each other and worsened the situation. Debtors could not repay loans, leading to more bank failures and a reduction in credit and deposit losses. Unlike the Great Depression, governments and central banks were active during the global crisis.

To protect local economies, many countries launched protectionist trade policies. The 1930 Smoot-Hawley tariff enactment, aimed at boosting farm incomes by protecting them from foreign competition in agricultural products, caused a great rise in protectionist trade policies in the US and Europe. Those policies reduced trade in the global economy and may have contributed to the dramatic decline in the world price of raw materials. This in turn caused severe balance of payments problems, in particular in emerging countries, deepening the harmful effects of the Great Depression. As expected, in Greece, particularly firms linked to the

UK and Germany by trade, investment and financial transactions were adversely affected by this global policy.

Despite all this tragedy, the Great Depression can be considered as the best benchmark, in terms of its financial triggers. It has served as a great lesson. In the present crisis, the EU governments and central banks were well aware of the need to avoid policy mistakes. Large-scale bank runs have been avoided, monetary policy has been eased aggressively, and governments have released substantial fiscal stimulus measures. Despite criticism, the banks were bailed out. Money was injected into credit markets to preempt a downward spiral.

In its early stages, the global crisis revealed an acute liquidity shortage among financial institutions, and the solvency of financial institutions was increasing. This perception dramatically changed when Lehman Brothers, a major US investment bank, defaulted in September 2008. This event destroyed market confidence, and investors liquidated their positions in panic. The transmission of financial distress to the real economy evolved at record speed, due to the credit crunch. After these events, the EU economy entered the steepest downturn since the 1930s. Losing confidence hit investments and demand. Cross-border transmission was also extremely rapid, due to the tight connections within the financial system. The strongly integrated supply chains in the global product markets also fed this transmission. Job losses and social conflicts became very common during the crisis.[13]

However, it should be accepted that southern and eastern countries in the Eurozone (like Greece, Spain and Portugal) were affected more deeply by the crisis, due to weak macroecomic conditions. For example, on entering the EU, Greece lost the ability to launch its own monetary policy and the ability to change its own exchange rate. By converting its local currency to the euro, it lost the right to devaluate its currency and to reduce the value of foreign debt or to improve competitiveness. Therefore, Greece's debt crisis called in question the idea of a common monetary policy with different fiscal policies. Some economists argue that the decision to adopt the euro was partly dictated by non-economic rather than economic factors. It is a fact that if Greece defaults, because of high trade and financial links amongst economies, the crisis could spillover into the rest of the Eurozone. Portugal, Spain and Ireland were already affected by the crisis with their risky debt to international markets, and a high level of government debts. Nevertheless, the longer the solution process of the

---

[13] European Commission, Economic Crisis in Europe: Causes, Consequences and Responses, *European Economy* 7, 2009.

crisis for the affected Eurozone countries, the higher the risk of contagion to the rest of the EU (Kibritcioglu, 2011).

The global recession has shown that international economic downturns were like the Great Depression. However, in contrast with the Great Depression, the global integration of both finance and trade and the global trade policy was not protectionist, and so allowed international trade to continue during the global crisis. In this crisis, countries all over the world took a more coordinated approach to the economic crisis. Industrialised and developing countries implemented different forms of economic stimulus. Furthermore, countries worked together to reach agreements to keep the international markets open to trade and investment. By seeking international cooperation and not taking protectionist action, governments created an environment in which the international economy could start to recover (Shomali and Giblin, 2010).

Greece's debt crisis has implications for the US, because the US and the EU have strong economic ties. These implications involve a loss of confidence in the Eurozone, as the value of the euro weakens. This lowers US exports to and increases US imports from the Eurozone, thus widening the US trade deficit. Furthermore, widespread financial instability in the EU affects trade and growth in the region, which in turn impacts upon the US economy, as it has a large financial stake in the EU. In this framework, the sovereign debt crisis that started in Greece threatens the future of the EU, both because of slow decision making, and non-acceptance of responsibility for the problems which have been created.

References

Aldcroft, D. 2001, *European Economy 1914-2000*, London: Routledge, 4th Edition.

Ahtik, M., Z. Erenet-Sunko and O. Pilipović 2009, "The Great Depression and Rise of Auhoroterian Regimes in Balkans in 1930s". http://www.iseg.utl.pt/aphes30/docs/progdocs/OZREN%20PILIPOVIC.pdf

Alexopoulos, G.C. 2004, *Financial Co-operatives and Rural Development in Greece*, PhD Thesis, University of Leicester.

Balakrishnan R., S. Danninger, S. Elekdag and I. Tytell, 2009, "The Transmission of Financial Stress from Advanced to Emerging Economies", *IMF Working Paper,* 09/133.

Bank of Greece, *Various Publications*.

Bernanke, B.S. 2000, *Essays on the Great Depression*, Princeton, NJ: Princeton University Press.

—. 1994, "The Macroeconomics of the Great Depression: A Comparative Approach", *NBER Working Paper,* 4814.
Bemanke, B. and H. James 1991, "The Gold Standard, Deflation, and Financial Crisis in the Great Depression: An International Comparison", in Hubard, R.G. *Financial Markets and Financial Crises,* Chicago: University of Chicago Press, p. 33-68.
BIS 2010, *Quarterly Review*, Basel, December.
Bordo, M.D., C. Goldin and E.N. White (eds) 1997, *The Defining Moment: The Great Depression and the American Economy in the Twentieth Century,* Chicago: University of Chicago Press.
Bordo, M.D. and H. James 2009, "The Great Depression Analogy", *NBER Working Paper,* 15584.
Bordo, M.D. and A.P. Murshid 2000, "Are Financial Crises Becoming Increasingly More Contagious? What is the Historical Evidence on Contagion?", *NBER Working Paper,* 7900.
Bordo, M.D. and D.C. Wheelock 1998, "Price Stability and Financial Stability: The Historical Record", *Federal Reserve Bank of St. Louis Journal Review,* September-October, p.41-62.
Boyce, R. 2009, *The Great Interwar Crisis and the Collapse of Globalization,* Hampshire: Palgrave Macmillan.
Bregianni, C. 2012, "The Gold-Exchange Standard, the Great Depression and Greece: Lessons from the Interwar Greek Default", http://www.euro.uni-bayreuth.de/en/research/publications/Euro-Symposium-2012/Catherine_Bregianni
Christodoulakis, N. 2012, "Currency Crisis and Collapse in Interwar Greece: Predicament or Policy Failure?", *Hellenic Observatory Papers on Greece and Southeast Europe, GreeSE Paper,* 60.
Corsetti, G., P. Pesenti, N. Roubini and C. Tille 1999, "Competitive Devaluations: A Welfare-Based Approach", *NBER Working Paper,* 6889.
Crafts, N. and P. Fearon 2010, "Lessons from the 1930s Great Depression", *Oxford Review of Economic Policy* 26-3, p. 285-317.
Dagdelen I. 2011, "Bütünleşme Sürecinde Yunanistan'ın Borç Krizi", *Ankara Avrupa Çalışmaları Dergisi* 10-2, p. 1-26.
Darvas Z., J. Pisani-Ferry and A. Sapir 2011, "A Comprehensive Approach to the Euro Area Debt Crisis", *Bruegel Policy Brief,* 2011-02.
Dornnbusch, R., Y.C. Park and S. Claessens 2000, "Contagion: Understanding How It Spreads" *World Bank Research Observer* 15-2, p. 177-197.

Dornbusch, R., C.V. Rijckeghem and B. Weder 1999, "Source of Contagion: Finance or Trade?", *IMF Working Paper,* 99-146.

Eichengreen, B. 2012, "When Currencies Collapse: Will We Replay the 1930s or the 1970s", *Foreign Affairs* January-February.

Eichengreen, B. and D.A. Irwin 2009, "The Slide to Protectionism in the Great Depression: Who Succumbed and Why?", *NBER Working Paper,* 15142.

Eichengreen, B., A. K. Rose and C. Wyplosz 1996, "Contagious Currency Crises", *NBER Working Paper,* 5681.

Eichengreen, B. and J. Sachs 1985, "Exchange Rates and Economic Recovery in the 1930s", *The Journal of Economic History* 45-4, p. 925-946.

European Commission 2009, "Economic Crisis in Europe: Causes, Consequences and Responses", *The European Economy Series,* 7.

Fratzscher, M. 2003, "On Currency Crises and Contagion" *International Journal of Finance & Economics* 8, p. 109-129.

Fremling, G.M. 1985, "Did the United States Transmit the Great Depression to the Rest of the World?", *The American Economic Review* 75-5, p. 1181-1185.

Friedman, M. and A. J. Schwartz 1971, *A Monetary History of the United States, 1867-1960,* Princeton, NJ: Princeton University Press.

Galbraith, J.K. 2009, *The Great Crash of 1929*, New York: Houghton Mifflin Harcourt.

Gibson, H.D., S.G. Hall and G.S. Tavlas 2011, "The Greek Financial Crisis: Growing Imbalances and Sovereign Spreads", *Journal of International Money and Finance* 31-3, p. 498-516.

Gogos, S.G., N. Mylonidis, D. Papageorgiou and V. Vassilatos 2012, "Greece 1979-2001: A (First) Great Depression Seen from the Basic RBC Model", *Athens University of Economics and Business, Working Paper Series,* 01-2012.

IMF 2009, *World Economic Outlook,* April.

Khan, H., W.K. Wong and S.K. Yeo 2005, "Has Trade Increased the Risk of Contagion? An Empirical Investigation", *U21 Global Working Papers,* 006-2005.

Kaluza, M. 2010, "Financial Crisis in Eastern Europe– Do Impact and Transmission Links Differ for EMU Members?", *Georg Simon Ohm University of Applied Sciences Nurmberg, Research Papers in International Finance and Economics,* 01-2010.

Kar, M. 2012, "Kriz ve Krizi Derinleştiren Faktörler", in Metin-Ozcan K. (ed) *SDE Analiz: AB Krizi ve Türkiye'ye Olası Yansımaları,* Ankara.

Katmisi, M. and Moutos, T. 2010, "EMU and the Greek Crisis: The Political Economy Perspective", *European Journal of Political Economy* 26-4, p. 568-576.

Kavonius, I.K. 2009, "Fiscal Policies in Europe and the United States during the Great Depression", *Government Institute for Economic Research VATT Working Paper,* 13.

Kibritcioglu A. 2011, "Sovereign Debt Crisis in Eurozone Countries", *MPRA Paper,* 33528.

Kirkegaard J.F. 2009, "Greece's Unlikely Disciplinarians: The European Commission and Europe's Bond Market Vigilantes", *Peterson Institute for International Economics RealTime Economic Issues Watch,* 12.

Kouretas G.P. and P. Vlamis 2010, "The Greek Crisis: Causes and Implications", *Panoeconomicus* 57-4, p. 391-404.

Kossev, K.D. 2008, "The Banking Sector and the Great Depression in Bulgaria, 1924-1938: Interlocking and Financial Sector Profitability", *Bank of Greece Working Paper,* 76.

Kostis, C. and S. Petmezas 1998, "Growth and Stagnation in the Greek Economy, 1830–1940", presented in the *Colloquium "Two Centuries of Long Run Economic Change in the Mediterranean Basin"*, Istanbul, June.

Lampe, J.R. and Marvin R.J. 1982, *Balkan Economic History, 1550-1950: From Imperial Borderlands to Developing Nation,* Bloomington: Indiana University Press.

Lazaretou, S. 2010, "Money Supply and Greek Historical Monetary Statistics: Definition, Construction, Sources and Data", *Economies et Sociétés* 41, p. 47-68.

—. 2005, "Greek Monetary Economics in Retrospect: The Adventures of the Drachma", *Economic Notes* 34-3, p. 331-370.

Lazarevic, Z. 2008, "Banking Performance in South-Eastern Europe During Interwar Period", *Bank of Greece Eurosystem Working Paper,* 79.

Maddison, A. 2003, *The World Economy: Historical statistics*, Paris: OECD Publishing.

Madsen, J.B. 2001, "Trade Barriers and the Collapse of World Trade during the Great Depression", *Southern Economic Journal* 67-4, p. 848-868.

Mazower, M. 1991, *Greece and the Inter-War Economic Crisis,* Oxford: Oxford University Press.

Moser, T. 2003, "What is International Financial Contagion?", *International Finance* 6, p. 157-178.

Nelson, R.M., P. Belkin and D.E. Mix, 2011, "Greece's Debt Crisis: Overview, Policy Responses, and Implications", *Congressinonal Research Service Report for Congress,* August.

OECD 2012, *Factbook Statistics*.

Pentzopoulos, D. 1962, *The Balkan Exchange of Minorities and its Impact upon Greece*, Paris, The Hague: Mouton.

Perotti, R., R. Strauch and J. von Hagen 1997, "Sustainability of Public Finances", *CEPR Discussion Papers,* 1781.

Person, K.G. 2010, *An Economic History of Europe, Knowledge, Institutions and Growth, 600 to the Present*, Cambridge: Cambridge University Press.

Rady, M. and D. Abdel 2012, "Greece Debt Crisis: Causes, Implications and Policy Options", *Academy of Accounting & Financial Studies Journa*l 16-si.

Reuters 2010, "Fiscal Woes to Dog Greek Bonds Even if Aid Offered", March 22.

Rigobon, R. 2002, "Does Contagion Exist?", in Figlewski, S. and R.M. Levich, *Risk Management: The State of the Art*, New York: Springer, p. 163-166.

Rijckeghem, C.V. and B. Weder 1999, "Sources of Contagion: Finance or Trade?",*IMF Working Paper,* 99-146.

Rossi V. and R.D. Aguilera 2010, "No Painless Solution to Greece's Debt Crisis", *Chatham House Programme Paper,* IE PP 2010-03.

Rothermond, D. 1996, *The Global Impact of the Great Depression, 1929-1939,* London: Routledge.

Shomali, H. and G.R. Giblin 2010, "The Great Depression and the 2007-2009 Recession: The First Two Years Compared", *International Research Journal of Finance and Economics* 59, p. 15-22.

Soldatos, G.T. 1993, "The Inter-war Greek Economy: Income Inequality and Speculation", *European History Quarterly* 23-3, p. 359-379.

The Economist Intelligence Unit 2010, *Country Report: Greece,* February.

Triantis, S.G. 1951, "Cyclical Changes in the Balance of Merchandise Trade of the Countries Exporting Chiefly Primary Products", *The American Economic Review* 42-1, p. 69-86.

World Bank, *Various Publications*.

CHAPTER TWO

PUBLIC DEBT CRISES IN THE EUROZONE AND POSSIBLE EFFECTS ON SOVEREIGN CREDIT RANKINGS

ATA OZKAYA
GALATASARAY UNIVERSITY AND GIAM

1. Introduction

In a recent paper, Reinhart and Rogoff (2011) note that since the problems of external default, domestic default and inflation are all integrally related, the overt default on (or repudiation) and rescheduling of public debt are hidden behind high inflation, banking crises, currency crashes and debasements which often go hand in hand with default. Large public deficits and high levels of public debt over GDP are important factors affecting the budget process of the public sector. According to the findings of Polackova-Brixi et al. (2001), even though the stock may initially be manageable, if public liabilities persistently augment, they may present a threat to future fiscal policy, solvency and sustainability. These factors have come to the forefront of the stabilisation policy in recent years. The questions of whether a given level of public debt is sustainable and/or whether large and persistent deficits will lead a government to default have become common concerns for both developed and less-developed countries.[1] Without balanced budgets, accumulating deficits

[1] Corsetti and Roubini (1991) and Chalk and Hemming (2000) focus on fiscal sustainability in the OECD economies, and announce rather mixed results. Following the Stability and Growth Pact and the Maastricht Treaty fixing maximum values for the deficit (3% of GDP) and net public debt (60% of GDP), the budgetary policy in Europe has been a matter of concern (Buiter, 2003). The sustainability of fiscal policy as well as the solvency of the governments in the less developed countries have received great attention from the IMF and the World

lead to an unstable rise in public debt stock (Reinhart and Rogoff, 2008). Over recent decades, many European countries have suffered from increasingly high public deficits.[2] This trend still represents a serious problem, from an economic and political point of view, especially for members of the EMU.

The related theoretical literature emphasizes the government's intertemporal budget constraint, as well as the flow-budget constraint, and focuses on whether current fiscal policy can be followed without disturbing government solvency. At an empirical policy analysis level, "fiscal sustainability" remains highly ambiguous, and nearly every empirical study attempts to develop its own definition of the concept and to derive its conclusions accordingly.

For the most part, the literature focuses on three different motives for debt repayment (Eaton, 1989; Dreher et al., 2006): "Illiquidity"; "unwillingness-to-pay" (insufficient incentive to repay), and "insolvency" (inability-to-pay).

Based on these causes, different theoretical models have been developed in order to explain the occurrence of debt problems of countries. The illiquidity approach holds that the debt crisis is temporary, and should be met through different financing arrangements designed to gain time until the process evolves (Sachs, 1984; Krugman, 1985). Secondly, the debtor country may be able to pay its debt but unwilling to do so. In this case, new lending may therefore be constrained by repudiation risk. That is, it is likely that long before the debtor country is unable to service its debt, it will choose not to do so (Eaton and Gersovitzs, 1981; Cohen and Sachs, 1986). Finally, under the solvency (ability-to-pay) approach, the debtor country does not repay the debt since it is unable to pay. In other words, the indebted country repays its debt as long as it is able to pay. Here, the only requirement is that the debtor has the future resources to service its debt without needing to borrow forever in order to meet its interest payments.

From an empirical analysis perspective, the applied literature with regards to the "ability-to-pay" approach can be considered to have followed two main paths. First, according to the country risk (or debt servicing capacity) models, a country's prospects of repaying the funds borrowed are evaluated using a variety of economic indicators, usually in the form of aggregate ratios such as primary surplus/GDP, debt/GDP,

---

Bank. Among others, see Buiter and Patel (1992)for India, Gerson and Nellor (1997) for Philippines, Bascard and Razin (1997) for Indonesia, and Agénor (2001) on Ghana and Turkey.

[2] See a recent survey by Arghyrou and Tsoukalas (2011).

debt/exports and debt-service/exports (Blanchard, 1990; Cuddington, 1997; Croce and Juan-Ramon, 2003).

The second path in the applied literature, the econometric approach for sustainability, focuses on the sustainability of debt policies in the long-run. All that is required, i.e., the solvency condition, is that the present value of the flow of future primary surplus is not less than the net current indebtedness. The non-stationarity analysis in particular provides useful tools for gaining deep insight into the long-term implications of a government's or a country's intertemporal solvency. By using the intertemporal budget constraint, the tests determine whether a government or country is able to sustain its budget or external deficits without defaulting on its debt. Such tests are first introduced in the literature relating to a government's solvency (or the sustainability of fiscal deficits) by Hamilton and Flavin (1986), and developed by Wilcox (1989), Trehan and Walsh (1991), Hakkio and Rush (1991), Buiter and Patel (1992), Tanner and Liu (1994), Liu and Tanner (1995), Tanner (1995), Bohn (1995), Wu (1998), and Makrydakis et al. (1999). Regarding the econometric approach to sustainability, we see that this notion is assimilated to that of stationarity. Thus, public debt stock will be considered sustainable if it is stationary. In the case where debt stock is not stationary, we should consider the causes of non-stationarity. Two possible explanations are reported in the related literature: either the "transversality" condition fails to be satisfied, or the sum of the present values of anticipated deficits is not stationary. Trehan and Walsh (1991) show that the convergence of the present value of the deficit is equivalent to the satisfaction of the transversality condition. For the present value of the deficit to converge, the total budget balance has to be stationary. Secondly, Hakkio and Rush (1991) suggest that a necessary and sufficient condition for sustainability is the existence of at least one co-integration relation between total revenue and total expenditure, with a co-integrating vector of a particular type. Finally, Bohn (1995) proposes a test for sustainability based on a co-integration relationship between primary balance and debt stock.

In this paper, we focus on the studies by Trehan and Walsh (1991), Hakkio and Rush (1991) and Bohn (1995), which have received considerable attention in economics. Firstly, these three different motives on public debt and fiscal policy sustainability are re-examined and linked, in order to form a compact step-wise test algorithm. This step-wise econometric test procedure enables us to perform a deeper analysis for public debt sustainability. Secondly, the period that we consider covers the recent global financial crisis process and, especially, its effects on European countries' public finance policy, and this may generate possible non-linearities in the observed data. Thus, we aim to strengthen our findings for the sustainability of debt policy. We also intend to make a smaller contribution to the literature that goes beyond linear estimation techniques in that area, and tries to find structural breaks, thresholds, or possible non-linearities (see Bajo-Rubio et al., 2004; Martin, 2000; Payne et al., 2008; Westerlund and Prohl, 2010; Fincke and Greiner 2011, among others). Therefore, we present a different simple method which enables us to visualise the path for debt dynamics, i.e., moving from some initial stable "equilibria" and diverging through unsustainable values. To do this, we revisit dynamical systems literature, more specifically Takens' theorem for phase-space reconstruction (Takens, 1981 and Eckman et al., 1987). Our motive for introducing phase-space reconstruction in a sustainability analysis is that the fiscal policy may exhibit a deterministic character for most of its duration (Fincke and Greiner, 2011), and the above-mentioned econometric approach focuses on long-run implications, having possible drawbacks in terms of the potential to distinguish between more vulnerable[3] countries in the short- and medium-term. Phase-space examination of time-evolution characteristics of debt dynamics is based upon an economic intuition: if the government's debt policy remains stable, depending on some pre-determined benchmark scenario, then we are able to observe that public debt to GDP ratio values move closer to some "attracting"[4] set. This movement shows us whether the path for debt dynamics is sustainable or not, respectively corresponding to the convergence or divergence of those values on phase-space. In its policy approach to determining whether a fiscal position is sustainable, the IMF is seen to apply the following steps:[5] (i) based on the available data, a projection with a five-year horizon is made, assuming that the current fiscal policy is to be continued. This is regarded as the benchmark scenario. (ii) From this projection, a path for debt dynamics is generated and its sustainability is assessed. It is possible that different criteria are used for sustainability, but an increasing debt ratio is usually regarded as a cause for concern. (iii) If the path for debt dynamics is indicated as "unsustainable", an alternative scenario is prepared, making necessary corrections on fiscal policy variables, which will typically define a "stable path" over the medium-term.

---

[3] We use the term "vulnerable" in the sense of a deterioration of both fiscal policy and the budget process.

[4] Attracting set definitely refers to the attractor on phase-space, corresponding to unique or multiple "equilibria".

[5] See Chalk and Hemming (2000) and Agénor and Montiel (1999, chap.13). The IMF's official programming model is known as the Polak model (Polak, 1997).

We should note that we do not consider the central bank when dealing with the question of the conditions under which a given path of public debt is sustainable. This is because central banks are independent, and governments should not rely on central banks to reduce public debt when making decisions about debt and deficits.

Fiscal policy, sustainability and solvency have come to the forefront of stabilisation policy in recent years, as the main factor determining the credit rating of a country. Sovereign ratings are among the crucial determinants of the borrowing costs facing a country on the financial markets. Their assignments may have a constraining impact on the ratings assigned to domestic banks or companies. Moreover, some institutional investors have lower limits for the risk that they can assume in their investments, and probably choose their bond portfolio composition taking into account the credit risk perceived by the rating notations. Therefore, for both governments and financial markets, it is essential to understand the criteria set determined by rating agencies and how they evaluate the various elements in attributing a rating score (Fitch, 2011). The literature mainly focuses on estimating which quantitative indicators are weighed most heavily in the determination of ratings, and on evaluating the predictive power of ratings to explain a cross-section of sovereign bond yields. More specifically, most of these empirical studies concern an estimation of the determinants of the ratings that S&P and Moody's announce (Cantor and Packer, 1996; Afonso, 2003). The studies examining the rating determinants utilise two main approaches: regression analysis techniques and ordered response models. Although obtaining ratings determinants using linear estimation techniques has, in general, a good predictive power, it faces some critiques. The other strand of the literature applies to ordered response models, (Hu et al, 2002; Bissoondoyal-Bheenick, 2005; Depken et al., 2007 among others). Although an ordered probit should be considered the preferred estimations procedure, the ordered probit model's asymptotic properties do not generalise for small samples, and so an estimate using only a cross-section of countries may be problematic. Indeed, the generalisation of ordered probit to panel data is not simple, because of the country-specific effects (Afonso et al., 2011). Our study differs from other existing studies at various levels. First, we do not intend to approximate an exact linear model which can be considered for implementation by rating agencies. Therefore, we do not estimate the weights of selected variables (determinants) which are considered in order to explain ratings. Instead, we propose a more simple ordering (ranking) methodology, based on countries' performances in terms of selected fundamentals. Since these fundamentals are chosen according to their diagnostic power for showing the evolution of the recent financial crisis through the public financing process, we aim to shed light on possible rating revisions that could be performed in the near future by rating agencies. Secondly, we take into account the rating agencies' announcements on forecasts of these countries' fundamentals. This is also consistent with our aim of increasing the accuracy of the results, and distinguishes our study from those focusing on regression models.

The rest of the paper is organised as follows. Section 2 presents the data. Section 3 describes the theoretical background. We develop a step-wise algorithm for econometric analysis in this section. Section 4 presents the results of the econometric analysis performed for selected countries. Section 5 introduces the theoretical background for phase-space examination, and presents the results. In section 6, we measure the relative credit ratings of selected OECD countries, including the Eurozone members subject to previous sections. Our measurement method is based on GDP per capita, change in consumer prices (CPI), and GDP ratios of the following: General government budget balance, General government primary balance, General government gross debt stock, Current account balance, and Public foreign currency debt stock. Finally, section 7 summarises the central findings.

2. Data

The countries[6] we consider in our study are France, the UK, Greece, Ireland, Italy, Portugal, Poland, Turkey and Spain. The UK, France and Italy are included because they are among the largest economies in Europe. We also include Greece, Ireland, Portugal, and Spain because they belong to the so-called PIIGS countries that have been recently characterised by large deficits and debt to GDP ratios, and questions have been raised about the sustainability of their debt policies. Greece is even backed by other Euro area member countries and the IMF to avoid bankruptcy in early 2010. Among European economies, we take Turkey into account because, following on from its greatest financial crisis in 2000-2001, Turkey is steadily respecting the Maastricht Treaty Criteria. The 9 countries' gross debt stock to GDP ratio are analysed in terms of sustainability. The common period chosen for quarterly data is 1999Q1-2010Q1. The data is obtained from the Eurostat Public Finance database. Turkish data is obtained from the Turkish Statistical Association. The debt

[6] These countries have to stick to the Convergence Criteria of the Maastricht Treaty of the EU and to the Stability and Growth Pact, which limits public deficit to 3% of GDP and public debt to 60% of GDP.

stock data begins from 1999Q1 for all EU countries. On the other hand, for some of the other variables, the data of some countries go back to 1989Q1, i.e., expenditure and revenue for the UK, France and Italy. However, the analysis that includes debt stock as a variable begins from 1999Q1. In order to account for the size of the different countries in the EU, public debt is usually expressed in terms of ratios, mostly relative to GDP. This measurement is also expressed in terms of the Convergence Criteria of the EU Maastricht Treaty.

3. Theoretical background and methodology for econometric approach

The approach in the empirical debt stock sustainability literature is based on the equation of evolution over time of public debt, hence on general budget identity.

$$B_T = (1 + i_T).B_{T-1} + G_T - T_T \tag{2.1}$$

where B_T is the volume of public debt at the end of period T, i_T is the nominal ex post interest rate during period T, G_T is the volume of public spending excluding interest payments, and T_T is volume of taxes. To simplify the argument, we have explicitly not taken into account seignorage revenue, so that they find themselves in the expost interest rate. Let P_T denote the price level during period T, and be defined as given in Eq. (2.2), and let $GDPA_T^r$ denote the real annual GDP, and be defined as given in Eq. (2.3).

$$P_T = (1 + \pi_T).P_{T-1} \tag{2.2}$$

where π_T denotes the rate of change in price-level.

$$GDPA_{T+1}^r = (1 + \eta_{T+1}^r)GDPA_T^r \tag{2.3}$$

where η_{T+1}^r is real growth rate.

By forward induction, we can rewrite Eq. (2.1) as shown by Eq. (2.4).

$$\frac{B_{T+k}}{\prod_{j=1}^{k}\left(1+i_{T+j}\right)} = B_T + \sum_{n=1}^{k}\frac{G_{T+n} - T_{T+n}}{\prod_{j=1}^{n}\left(1+i_{T+j}\right)} \tag{2.4}$$

where $\prod_{j=1}^{k}\left(1+i_{T+j}\right)^{-1}$ is k-period ahead discount factor. Let us denote the discount factor by $\rho_{T,k} = \prod_{j=1}^{k}\left(1+i_{T+j}\right)^{-1}$, and then Eq. (2.4) can be rewritten as given in Eq. (2.5).

$$B_{T+k}.\rho_{T,k} = B_T + \sum_{n=1}^{k}\left(G_{T+n} - T_{T+n}\right).\rho_{T,n} \tag{2.5}$$

The variables in Eq. (2.5) are in nominal terms. Let us rewrite Eq. (2.5) in real terms. First, divide Eq. (2.5) by price-level $\left(P_T\right)$, given by Eq. (2.2) and obtain Eq.(2.6).

$$B^r_{T+k}.\rho^a_{T,k} = B^r_T + \sum_{n=1}^{k}\left(G^r_{T+n} - T^r_{T+n}\right).\rho^a_{T,n} \tag{2.6}$$

where $\rho^a_{T,k} = \prod_{j=1}^{k}\left(1+i_{T+j} - \pi_{T+j}\right)^{-1}$.

Thus, all variables with upper indice r are defined in real terms. The discount parameter $\rho^a_{T,k}$ then signifies the nominal interest rate adjusted by inflation, and hence the real expost interest rate. Secondly, divide Eq. (2.6) by real annual GDP, $GDPA^r_T$ defined by Eq. (2.3).

$$D_{T+k}.\rho^b_{T,k} = D_T + \sum_{n=1}^{k}\left(g_{T+n} - \tau_{T+n}\right).\rho^b_{T,n} \tag{2.7}$$

In Eq. (2.7), D_T , g_T and τ_T respectively denote real debt stock per real GDP, real non-interest expenditure per real GDP, and real spending per real GDP. Finally, $\rho_{T,k}^{b} = \prod_{j=1}^{k}\left(1 + i_{T+j} - \pi_{T+j} - \eta_{T+j}^{r}\right)^{-1}$ denotes the real ex post interest rate adjusted by the rate of real growth or nominal ex post interest rate, also adjusted by the nominal rate of growth.

In order to complete the analysis, we have to consider the limiting case of Eq. (2.5). As period horizon goes to infinity,

$$B_T = \lim_{k\to\infty} B_{T+k}.\rho_{T,k} - \sum_{n=1}^{k=\infty}\left(G_{T+n} - T_{T+n}\right).\rho_{T,n} \qquad (2.8)$$

3.1. The stochastic behaviour of primary surplus

If the real ex post interest rate or real ex post interest rate, adjusted by real rate of growth, is positive for all periods T, then the debt stock will grow without limit with a primary deficit. To prevent this case, the government must generate a primary surplus. The preceding argument leads us to seek a statistical tool to examine the third case, under which $\rho < 0$ for some periods and $\rho > 0$ for some others.

Let $E_T\left\lfloor X_{T+j}\right\rfloor$ denote the conditional expected value of variable X at period $T + j$ based on the information set at period $T, I(T)$.

In their study, Trehan and Walsh (1991) assume that:

- i_T is stochastic with $E\left(i_{T+j-1}\middle|I(T)\right) = i$ for all $i \geq 0$ and $j \geq 1$.
- $R_T = \left(1 + i_T\right)$ is realised gross rate of return and $E\left(R_T\right) = R$ $= \left(1 + i\right)$.
- $B_T \subset I(T)$ and $i_T, \left(G_T - T_T\right) \not\subset I(T)$.

Furthermore, if we assume that all possible agents are Bayesian decision makers, then by taking expectations of Eq. (2.1), conditional on $I(T)$ and substituting future values of debt into Eq. (2.1), we obtain the following value function for debt stock. For any given period k in the future, the value of debt stock today is

$$B_{T-1} = \lim_{j\to\infty}(1+i)^{-(j+1)} E\left(B_{T+j} \middle| I(T-1)\right) - \sum_{k=0}^{j\to\infty}(1+i)^{-(k+1)} E\left(G_{T+k} - T_{T+k} \middle| I(T-1)\right) \qquad (2.9)$$

Eq. (2.9) signifies governmental intertemporal budget constraint. The first term of the RHS of Eq. (2.9) signifies the discounted value of expected future debt stock. Under the hypothesis of the present value budget balance, the first term of RHS must equal zero, which implies Eq. (2.10).

$$\lim_{j\to\infty}(1+i)^{-(j+1)} E\left(B_{T+j} \middle| I(T-1)\right) \to 0 \qquad (2.10)$$

Eq. (2.10) also implies that $\lim_{j\to\infty} E\left(B_{T+j} \middle| I(T-1)\right) < \infty$.

If the relation given by Eq. (2.10), which is known as the transversality condition, is satisfied, then the discounted value of expected future debt stock converges to zero as the period horizon goes to infinity. Therefore, current outstanding (real or nominal) stock of debt must equal the present discounted value of current and expected future primary surpluses, which is signified by the second term of RHS of Eq. (2.9).

For an intertemporal budget balance to be satisfied, Trehan and Walsh (1991) propose testing three cases. All arguments stated below are valid through the variables in both nominal and real terms. Equivalently, one can easily adopt Eqs. (2.9) and (2.10) to the debt stock over GDP, and the following arguments still remain valid. The variables shown below are denoted in their nominal terms.

- If the primary surplus is stationary I(0), then the evolution of debt stock given by Eq.(1) should follow the I(0) process so that the budget balance be satisfied.

- On the other hand, if primary surplus is non-stationary, $(1-\lambda L)(G_T - T_T)$ is I(0) with zero mean $E[(1-\lambda L)(G_T - T_T)] = 0$ and $0 \leq \lambda < 1+i$ then Eq.(2.10) holds if and only if the debt stock is non-stationary and furthermore there exists at least one co-integration relationship between B_{T-1} and $(G_T - T_T)$.

- As a special case, if $\lambda = 1$, then primary surplus follows the I(1) process, notably different stationary. Then, in order for the intertemporal budget balance to be satisfied, Eq.(2.10), the budget balance should follow the I(0) process.

3.2. Relationship between expenditure and revenue

Again we consider Eq. (2.1), in which variables are in nominal terms. The assumptions employed by Hakkio and Rush (1991) can be tabulated as shown below:

- All government bonds have one-period of maturity. Then Eq. (2.1) signifies government's one-period budget constraint.

- i_T is a one-period interest rate and $i_T \sim$ I(0) with $E(i_T) = i$. This also implies that we cannot analyse the government's budget constraint in nominal terms.

The variables in Eq. (2.1) can be nominal, real or deflated by population or real GDP. The interpretation of the interest rate in Eq. (2.1) depends on how government expenditure and revenue are measured.

By solving Eq.(2.1) going forward, the single-period budget constraint can be combined to yield the government's intertemporal budget constraint. As usual, let R_T be the nominal discount factor, the solution is given by Eq.(2.11):

$$B_0 = \lim_{n \to \infty} R_n . B_n - \sum_{T=1}^{\infty} R_T (G_T - T_T) \tag{2.11}$$

where $R_T = \prod_{s=1}^{T} \beta_s$ and $\beta_s = \frac{1}{(1+i_s)}$

In Eq. (2.11), all the variables are in nominal terms. In contrast to Trehan and Walsh (1991), Hakkio and Rush (1991) do not take into account expectations during the first step. However, both Trehan and Walsh (1991) and Hakkio and Rush (1991) point out that when the first term of RHS of Eq. (2.11) equals zero, the outstanding stock of bonds, equals the present value of the government's primary surpluses. As reported by Hamilton and Flavin (1986), Barro (1987) and McCallum (1984), the limiting value of discounted future debt stock must equal zero in order to rule out the possibility of the government financing its deficit by issuing new debt. If the limit term does not converge to zero, the government is bubble-financing its expenditure, that is, old debt that matures is financed by issuing new debt, implying the Ponzi scheme. Finally Hakkio and Rush (1991) propose the test equation either (both) in real, in real per real GDP or (and) in real per real GDP per capita.

$$T_T^r = \alpha + \beta\left(G_T^r + (i_T - \pi_T)B_{T-1}^r\right) + \varepsilon_T \tag{2.12}$$

Eq. (2.12) denotes the so-called relation in terms of real variables, and upper indice (r) denotes that the variable is in real terms. The null hypothesis is $\beta = 1$ and ε_T ~I(0). In other words, if expenditure and revenue are non-stationary, then the null is that $\beta = 1$ and expenditure and revenue are co-integrated. If expenditure is non-stationary while revenue is stationary, then it is easy to conclude that the government violates its intertemporal budget constraint, implying that $\hat{\beta} = 0$ holds. When both expenditure and revenue are non-stationary, co-integration is a necessary condition for the government to obey its present value budget constraint. However, $\hat{\beta} = 1$ is not a required condition, but is probably necessary. We prefer to test government variables shown in Eq. (2.12) in terms of real per real GDP. We divide both sides of Eq. (2.12) by real annual GDP (see Eq. 2.3). Eq. (2.13) clarifies this issue. Then the interest rate should be measured in terms of real interest rate adjusted by the growth rate of real GDP.

$$\frac{T_T^r}{GDPA_T^r} = a + b\left(\frac{G_T^r + (i_T - \pi_T)B_{T-1}^r}{GDPA_T^r}\right) + \varepsilon_T \qquad (2.13)$$

where $\varepsilon_T \sim$ I(0) and i_T is nominal ex post interest rate.

3.3. Relationship between primary balance and debt stock

In contrast with the two models briefly presented above, Bohn (1995) introduces a stochastic economy model based on Lucas (1978)—a type of government endowment economy in order to examine the general constraints on government borrowing in a stochastic setting. Bohn's (1995) main results show that the government has to satisfy an intertemporal budget constraint and an associated transversality condition, regardless of the level of safe interest rate. Policies that satisfy these constraints will be called sustainable. In contrast with the models by Trehan and Walsh (1991) and Hakkio and Rush (1991), the discount factors on future government spending and on future government revenue are determined by the distribution of revenue and spending across states of nature, and are in general not related to the interest rate on government bonds.

Finally, Bohn (1995) proposes a test equation, so that the intertemporal budget constraint and the transversality conditions both hold. The main idea of this equation is to test whether there is at least one co-integration relationship between primary balance and debt stock. All the government variables that Bohn uses in his test equation are in per capita terms. However, since we prefer to use government variables in terms of real per real GDP, we arrange the test equation proposed by Bohn (1995) as given in Eq. (2.14).

$$\frac{(G_T^r - T_T^r)}{GDPA_T^r} = \beta_0 + \beta_1 \frac{B_T^r}{GDPA_T^r} + \mu_T \text{ where } \mu_T \sim \text{I}(0) \qquad (2.14)$$

If the average maturity is assumed to affect interest rates directly, then Bohn's model captures it. Following Bohn (1995), we state that the government has to satisfy an intertemporal budget constraint and an associated transversality condition, regardless of the level of safe interest rate. Secondly, Hakkio and Rush (1991) assume that in all, government bonds have one-period of maturity.

3.4. Test algorithm

Sections 3.1, 3.2 and 3.3 enable us to establish a compact econometric test algorithm. The test algorithm that we follow can be summarised as shown below. Following on from sections 3.1, 3.2 and 3.3, the variables used in algorithm are in real terms.

Step 1: The stationarity (unit root) test is applied for debt stock over annual GDP in real terms. If it is estimated to be stationary, then the algorithm ends. If it is estimated to be non-stationary, then the algorithm goes to step 2.

Step 2: Based on Trehan and Walsh (1991)

a) First, we test the stationarity of primary surplus over GDP, and if it is stationary, then we conclude that the debt stock is not sustainable and the algorithm moves on to Step 3.

b) If primary surplus over GDP is non-stationary, then we seek at least one linear combination of primary surplus over GDP and debt stock over GDP that is stationary. If there is at least one, then we conclude that debt stock is sustainable. In particular, if the primary surplus over GDP series is I(1), then the algorithm moves on to Step 4.

c) If there is no linear combination, then we test the stationarity of the budget balance over GDP. If it is stationary, then we conclude that sustainability exists. Otherwise, sustainability does not exist and the algorithm goes to Step 3.

Step 3: Based on Hakkio and Rush (1991), we estimate Eq.(2.13).

a) If there is at least one co-integration relationship between total expenditure over GDP and total revenue over GDP, then we conclude that debt stock may be sustainable, depending on the value of the estimated co-integrating vector. That is, with a co-integrating vector (1.b) under the condition that $0<b<1$.

Step 4: The test proposed by Bohn (1995) is applied and Eq. (2.14) is estimated.

a) If there is at least one co-integration relationship between primary balance over GDP and debt stock over GDP, then we conclude that the debt stock is sustainable, implying that both the intertemporal budget constraint and transversality conditions apply.

b) Otherwise we conclude that there is no sustainability.

To analyse the stochastic behaviour[7] of a given series, we use three different test methods: The Augmented Dickey-Fuller (ADF) test, the Phillips-Perron (PP) test, and the KPSS[8] test.

To analyse the multivariate process generated by revenue and public spending, we have chosen to use the method proposed by Johansen (1991). The advantages of this method, as compared with Engle and Granger's (1987) is that it allows us to test for the number of co-integration relationships, it does not impose an arbitrary normalisation on a co-integrating vector, and it allows us to test for constraints on the coefficients of the co-integration relationship.

4. Results of econometric analysis

We employ the test algorithm we introduced in section 3.4. Three types of unit root tests are deployed: ADF, PP and KPSS test statistics. The results of the analyses are depicted in Table 2-A1, shown in the Appendix. Each column consists of three inputs; ADF, PP and KPSS test results respectively. The variables shown in Table 2-A1 and Table 2-1 are in real terms. The overall results (decisions) are given in Table 2-1.

In Table 2-1, the non-stationarity of some data is determined according to two affirmative and one negative test result, and some others by three affirmative test results. The "steps" column in Table 2-1 defines the steps proposed in section 3.4. The second column in Table 2-A1 and Table 2-1 indicates debt stock over GDP, while the third, fourth and fifth columns refer to primary surplus/deficit, budget balance, expenditure and revenue over GDP, respectively. The "No of Coint" column depicts the estimated co-integration relationships based on Johansen and Juselius (1990) values. The sign shown in the "No of Coint" column indicates the sign of the estimated coefficient vector. The last column in Table 2-1 shows the state determined: "Sus" refers to sustainable while "Unsus" refers to unsustainability of debt stock over GDP data.

For Ireland, we look for co-integration between primary surplus/deficit and debt stock. Both the Trace test and the Max.eigenvalue test results indicate 1 co-integration relationship with a positive coefficient vector. Even though there exists a co-integration relationship, expenditure is I(1),

---

[7] The estimation of lags are performed by both SIC, Hannan-Quinn and Akaike criteria. Where two methods give different lag values to each other, we choose the one estimated by SIC. Both E-views 5.00 and Stata 10 are used for the analysis. In order to conserve space, we do not locate the details of estimation results here. They can be supplied upon to request.

[8] Kawiatowski, Phillips, Schmidt and Shin (1992).

and revenue is estimated to be I(0). It is straightforward that Ireland is bubble-financing its expenditure—the Ponzi scheme. Therefore, we conclude that the debt stock over GDP is not sustainable.

For Greece, Spain and Italy, we look for a co-integration relationship between primary surplus/deficit and debt stock. Both the Trace test and the Max.eigenvalue test results indicate 1 co-integration relationship with a positive coefficient vector. For Italy, we conclude that debt stock over GDP is sustainable. We have to note that Spain's ADF and KPSS statistic values for both budget balance and expenditure are very close to critical threshold, and if we work with a 90% confidence interval then we accept that both their budget balance and expenditure are non-stationary, implying the unsustainability of debt stock to GDP ratio. For Greece, since primary surplus/deficit over GDP exhibits a non-stationary character and, in particular, is I(1), we do not look at whether budget balance is stationary or not. Instead, we seek a co-integration relationship between primary surplus/deficit over GDP and debt stock over GDP. We find that neither the Trace test nor the Max. eigenvalue test indicates a co-integrating relationship between primary surplus/deficit and debt stock. We conclude that the Greek debt policy is certainly unsustainable.

For the UK, we look for a co-integration relationship between total expenditure and total revenue. Both the Trace and Max. eigenvalue tests indicate one co-integration relationship with a positive coefficient vector, indicating that a one-unit increase in revenue results in a less-than-one unit increase in expenditure. Therefore, we conclude that debt stock over GDP is sustainable.

For France, budget balance, expenditure and revenue are all I(0). Therefore, we conclude that debt stock over GDP is sustainable.

For Poland, budget balance, expenditure and revenue are all I(0). Therefore, we conclude that debt stock over GDP is sustainable.

For Portugal neither budget balance nor expenditure is I(0). Therefore, debt stock over GDP is not sustainable. We conclude that Portugal is bubble-financing (Ponzi scheme) its expenditure, implying violation of the transversality condition.

For Turkey, we look for a co-integration relationship between expenditure and revenue. We find that there exists one co-integration relationship with a co-integrating vector (1-b) under the condition that $0<b<1$. We conclude that debt policy is sustainable for the given period.

The drawback in most of the studies focusing on public debt sustainability, in the aftermath of the global financial crisis, is that they omit the possibility of non-linearity. During the crisis period, fiscal stimulus packages placed a heavy burden on public finances while the low economic growth rates led to further disruption of the debt dynamics. In this sense, debt dynamics may follow a non-linear path, and even chaotic behaviour. Therefore, we present a different and simple method, which enables us to visualise the path for debt dynamics, i.e., moving from some initial stable "equilibria" and diverging through unsustainable values. Our motivation for introducing phase-space reconstruction in the sustainability analysis is that the fiscal policy may exhibit a deterministic character for most of its duration (Fincke and Greiner, 2011) and that the above-mentioned econometric approach focuses on long-run implications, and thus has possible drawbacks in terms of distinguishing between the more vulnerable[9] countries in the short- and medium-term.

Table 2-1 Results of the step-wise algorithm for the sustainability of debt stock over GDP

Country	Debt stock/ GDP	PS/ GDP	BB/ GDP	Exp/ GDP	Rev/ GDP	Steps	No of Coint	State
Ireland	I(1)	I(1)	I(1)	I(1)	I(0)	1;2.b;4	1(+)	Unsus
Greece	I(1)	I(1)	I(0)	I(1)	I(1)	1;2.b;4	No	Unsus
Spain	I(1)	I(1)	I(0)	I(0)	I(0)	1;2.b;4	1(+)	Sus
France	I(1)	I(0)	I(0)	I(0)	I(0)	1;2.a;3	No need	Sus
Italy	I(1)	I(1)	I(0)	I(0)	I(0)	1;2.b;4	1(+)	Sus
Poland	I(1)	I(0)	I(0)	I(0)	I(0)	1;2.a;3	No need	Sus
Portugal	I(1)	I(0)	I(1)	I(1)	I(0)	1;2.a;3	No need	Unsus
UK	I(1)	I(0)	I(0)	I(1)	I(1)	1;2.a;3	1(+)	Sus
Turkey	I(1)	I(0)	I(0)	I(1)	I(1)	1;2.a;3	1(+)	Sus

[9] We refer to the term "vulnerable" in sense of deterioration of both fiscal policy and budget process.

5. Theoretical background for phase-space examination of the debt stock GDP ratio

Let us denote the dynamical system, $f : R^n \rightarrow R^n$, with the trajectory,

$$x_{t+1} = f(x_t) + \varepsilon_t \text{, } t = 0,1,2,...., \tag{2.15}$$

The dynamical system itself may be assumed to be contaminated by noise, or the observed time series z_t given in Eq. (2.17), may be assumed to convey noise. The Lyapunov exponents for such a dynamical system are measures of the average rate of divergence or convergence of a typical trajectory or orbit. The trajectory is also written in terms of the iterations of f. For an *n*-dimensional system as above, there are *n* exponents which are customarily ranked from largest to smallest:

$$\lambda_1 \geq \lambda_2 \geq ..... \geq \lambda_n \tag{2.16}$$

One rarely has the advantage of observing the state of the system at any period *t*, x_t, and the actual functional form f that generates the dynamics. The most widely used model is the following: associated with the dynamical system in Eq.(2.15), there is a measurement function $h : R^n \rightarrow R$ which generates the time series,

$$z_t = h(x_t) \tag{2.17}$$

It is assumed that all that is available to observe is the sequence $\{z_t\}$. The observed data can be assumed to be contaminated by noise.[10]

Assume that the target system is a dynamical system, as given in Eq. (2.15), and that the observed time series is obtained through a measurement function as given in Eq.(2.17). Then, following Takens's famous theorem (Takens, 1981), the reconstructed trajectory is an embedding of the original trajectory when the value of the embedding dimension *m* is sufficiently large. If any attractor has appeared in the original dynamical system, another attractor, which retains the phase

[10] See Nychka et al. (1992) and Kantz (1994).

structure of the first attractor, will appear in the reconstructed phase-space. In order for such a reconstruction to achieve embedding, it has been proven that the dimension m should satisfy $m \geq 2n+1$. However, this is a sufficient condition and upper-worst case (Gencay and Dechert, 1992). Depending on the data, embedding can be established even when m is less than $2n+1$. In the embedding method, there are two parameters, the embedding dimension and time delay. Abarbanel (1995) offers a good suggestion for how to select these two parameters. Time delay does not strongly affect reconstruction of phase-space and the estimation of Lyapunov exponents. One approach to estimating the value of time delay is to select the frequency (1/time scale) that corresponds to a dominant power spectral feature.

From the observed time series $\{z_t\}$, one can generate the data vector $y_t = \left(z_{t+(m-1).d}, z_{t+(m-2).d}, \ldots, z_t\right)$ where d is the time delay; this vector indicates a point of m-dimensional reconstructed phase-space R^m, where m is called the embedding dimension. Therefore, a trajectory can be drawn in the m-dimensional reconstructed phase-space by changing t.

Let us rewrite the observed time series as $z_1, z_2, \ldots, z_N$, where N is the length of the observed sequence $\{z_t\}$. While embedding this data in the m-dimensional phase-space, the time delay d can be used to obtain $\left(N-(m-1).d\right)$ points in phase-space. Therefore, a point on the orbit shown by y_i is obtained as given in Eq.(2.18).

$$y_i = \left(z_i, z_{i+d}, \ldots, z_{i+(m-1).d}\right) \quad \text{for all } i \in \left(N-(m-1).d\right) \qquad (2.18)$$

If this is applied for all i, such that $i \in \left(N-(m-1).d\right)$, then we obtain the orbit. From now on, the time delay d is taken to be equal to 1, corresponding to our observation interval on the time-domain.

5.1. Results of the phase-space analysis

In order to perform the analysis, we employ Eq. (2.18) to the debt stock to GDP ratio series of each country. The debt stock to GDP ratio data for Poland, Portugal, Ireland, Greece, the UK and Turkey are embedded in a 3-dimensional[11] phase-space. Our reasons for choosing these countries is that in the period under examination, the primary balances of Poland, Portugal, Ireland, Greece, and the UK economies deteriorate and exhibit negative trend, while the debt stock to GDP ratio of each increases. This observation clearly indicates that the reaction of each government to increasing debt stock to GDP ratio does not constitute an increase in primary surplus. Turkey is included for comparison, in the sense that it steadily reduces public debt stock over GDP ratio and increases primary surplus to GDP ratio.

The results are depicted from Figure 2-A1 to Figure 2-A6 in the Appendix. In each graph, the *z-axis* shows the quarterly debt stock over GDP series, the *y-axis* shows a one-quarter lagged debt stock over GDP series, and the *x-axis* shows a two-quarter lagged series. The similarity of debt stock to GDP ratio phase-evolution of Greece, Portugal, the UK and Ireland is interesting. Greece, Ireland and the UK's debt stock over GDP exhibit almost the same path. These countries' initial states of debt stock over GDP seem stable around some equilibria, implying stable public finance policies in the 1999Q1-2003Q1 period. However, the values diverging on phase-space show that such equilibria have not been sustainable. For Portugal, the movement is slightly slower than that of Greece, implying a slower divergence. Polish debt stock to GDP ratio exhibits distributive behaviour on phase-space. In Figure 2-A1, we see that there is no equilibria set for the dynamic values of debt stock to GDP ratio, implying a steadily changing public finance policy. Moreover, the data shows us that the movement is not cyclical, but mostly linear and ascending. It reaches 60%.

Greek debt stock to GDP ratio wastes most of the space-time on two equilibria sets shown in Figure 2-A2. The initial equilibria set of debt stock over GDP is settled at approximately 100-110%. However, there is a second equilibria set which is between 110-115%, implying the non-synchronisation of coordination of expectations around 100-110%. This could be due to a type of market correction on interest rates. For detailed analysis, one should take into account phase-space construction for real ex post interest rates. However, Figure 2-A2 is sufficient to see a major shift, from 110-115% to 145%.

[11] The method of recurrence plots (RP) was firstly introduced by Eckmannn et al. (1987) to visualise the time dependent behaviour of the dynamics of systems (the recurrence of states in a phase-space), which can be pictured as a trajectory in the *m*-dimensional phase-space.

For Portugal, the structure of multiple equilibria slightly differs from that of Greece. We see from Figure 2-A3 that until 80% is reached, minor shifts exist, and debt stock to GDP ratio exhibits high instability. Market expectations seem to partially coordinate some equilibria, but this is not permanent and is quickly disrupted. The minor shifts toward 100% imply that common knowledge of disruption may enable traders to expect debt repudiation. However, as Detragiache (1996) points out, instead of not-lending, the traders prefer to lend to government to roll over debt.

The outcome of an econometric test algorithm for the UK's debt stock to GDP ratio leads us to believe that public debt is sustainable. On the other hand, in Figure 2-A4, we observe that the debt stock exhibits a divergent character, implying a major shift from the initial equilibria set. Moreover, it slows down slightly around 78%, another equilibria set around which public finance policy seems settled. When the divergence is compared with that of Poland, we see that the UK's public finance is disturbed more quickly, possibly because of its steadily increasing primary deficit. The behaviour of the latter is relatively slow. However, the debt stock to GDP ratio for the UK, Greece, and Ireland all exhibit similar divergence on phase-space. We know that international credit rating institutions do not estimate the public debt crisis for the UK (see Fitch, 2011). Figure 2-A7 shows the time evolution of the UK primary surplus over GDP. We can easily see that at the beginning of 2001Q2, there is a negative trend. We consider that the disrupted structure of the UK's primary surplus explains why the debt stock over GDP series enjoys a quick shift to instability. According to the phase-space analysis, the UK will probably have a liquidity crisis.

Figure 2-A5 shows that Ireland's debt stock over GDP series quickly escapes an initial equilibria set around 1999Q1-2003Q1. It is easy to see that the financial policy loses its stability. The initial equilibria set of debt stock over GDP is settled at approximately 40-50%. The quick shift probably shows us the insufficient repayment capacity of the economy to the value of 50%. However, one needs a more detailed examination to shed light on why the Irish economy jumped into debt crisis and why, as yet, the UK's has not done so.

Beginning in 2002Q1, Turkish debt stock to GDP ratio exhibits deterministic characters on phase-space. In Figure 2-A6, we see that there is no equilibria set for the dynamic values of debt stock to GDP ratio. Moreover, the data shows us that the movement is not cyclical but descending, which is the difference between the Polish and Turkish cases. We observe divergence in the 2001-2002 debt stock values. A 45-50% figure is reached, and is not settled around a pre-determined equilibria set.

It seems that the Turkish government's debt management and public finance policies focus on a maximum decrease in debt stock over GDP (see Medium Term Macroeconomic Program 2012-2014).

6. Sovereign credit rating mechanism

The main international credit rating agencies (Moody's, S&P, Fitch and JCR) announce that an understanding of sovereign ratings—what they mean and the criteria behind them—is more relevant now than ever before. Accordingly, another primary contribution of this paper is to help better understand the recent revisions to sovereign ratings by the rating agencies. Sovereign ratings are assessments on the relative likelihood of default. The rating agencies examine a wide range of elements, from solvency factors affecting the capacity to repay the debt to socio-political factors that might influence the willingness to pay the borrower (Afonso, 2003). Ratings agencies' sovereign ratings are supported by a qualitative and quantitative investigation of sovereign credit risk. Sovereigns are assigned two default ratings: a local-currency default rating, reflecting the likelihood of default on debt issued (and payable) in the currency of the sovereign, and a foreign-currency default rating, which is an assessment of the credit risk associated with debt issued in foreign currencies. Most sovereigns collect their tax revenue in local currency; the exceptions are commodity producers and dollarized economies. Therefore, they must purchase foreign currency on the foreign-exchange market (or from the central bank)[12] or borrow it. The government's access to foreign currency therefore depends on the economy's rather than the sovereign's capacity to generate foreign currency as well as the agents' willingness to exchange it for local currency. For sovereigns, such as members of the Eurozone and fully dollarized economies, the foreign and local-currency ratings are the same (see the instructions reported by S&P, 1998; JCR, 2000; Moody's 2001; Fitch, 2011; Moody's, 2006; S&P, 2011). Although the agencies use different symbols, the symbol used by each has its counterpart in the others' rating scale. This correspondence allows a comparison of the sovereign ratings assigned by the main credit rating agencies (Cantor and Packer, 1996). Fitch reports (2011) that sovereign risk analysis is a synthesis of quantitative and qualitative judgments, capturing the willingness as well as the capacity to pay. Moreover, given the significance of the government and public sector as a whole to the national

[12] The Turkish domestic borrowing structure throughout the mid-1990's is a good example. For detailed analysis, see Boratav and Akyuz (2003).

economy, the activities and policy actions of the sovereign state have a profound impact on and are influenced by the performance of the economy as a whole. As such, the sovereign rating analysis incorporates a wider range of factors than just the sovereign state's financial strength.

Fitch's sovereign credit rating analysis focuses on the following common factors: (i) Macroeconomic performance and prospects; (ii) Structural features of the economy that render it more or less vulnerable to shocks, including the risks to macroeconomic stability and public finances posed by the financial sector, as well as political risk and governance factors; (iii) Public finances, including the structure and sustainability of public debt as well as fiscal financing; (iv) External finances, with a particular focus on the sustainability of international trade balances, current account funding, capital flows, and the level and structure of external public and private debt. However, it is evident that we could not establish a linear relationship between sovereign ratings and all metrics used by rating agencies in their analysis (Afonso et al., 2011). On the one hand, this reflects the multivariate property of the analysis. On the other hand, it reflects qualitative factors influencing the ability and willingness of a sovereign to fulfill its financial obligations. These intangible effects (Depken et al., 2007), on sovereign creditworthiness in particular, reveal the reason why developed countries are able to sustain a much higher debt burden, even after taking per capita income into account. Given that qualitative factors have an important bearing on the rating assessment, each of the rating agencies has a proprietary sovereign rating model that generates a score, calibrated against the foreign-currency long-term default rating. These models are tools that take into account the rating consistency across regions and time. However, rating agencies already declare that no model can fully capture all the relevant influences on sovereign creditworthiness, and the actual rating determined by the sovereign rating committees can and does differ from that implied by the rating model.

6.1. Re-constructing credit ratings of the selected 25 countries

Keeping the set of criteria taken into account in perspective, the literature reports the usage of various fundamentals. An earlier study by Cantor and Packer (1996) suggests that, to a large extent, Moody's and S&P rating assignments can be explained with reference to a small number of well-defined criteria, to which the two agencies appear to accord similar weight. The authors concluded that the ratings can be largely explained by the following small set of variables: per capita income, GDP growth, inflation, external debt, level of economic development, and default history. Further studies have incorporated some other macroeconomic variables, such as the unemployment rate or the investment-to-GDP ratio (Bissoondoyal-Bheenick, 2005). The studies focusing on currency crises show the important role played by several external indicators, such as foreign reserves, current account balance, exports or terms of trade (Monfort and Mulder, 2000). Indicators of how the government conducts its fiscal policy, in particular budget balance and government debt, can also be relevant, as well as variables that assess political risk, such as corruption or social indexes (Depken et al., 2007). By basing the information on complex criteria utilised by international rating agencies, (briefly described in section 2 above), we determine a narrower subset which is consistent with those reported by Cantor and Packer (1996), Afonso (2003), Brooks et al. (2004) and Afonso et al. (2011). The credit ratings of the 25 selected countries are reconstructed according to the following set of criteria: GDP per capita, change in Consumer prices, GDP ratios of General government budget balance, General government primary balance, General government debt stock, Current account balance and Public foreign currency denominated debt stock. The seven inter-related criteria are examined over three non-overlapping periods: 2005-2010, 2011, and 2012-2013. The average values are taken into account and future value estimations are obtained from the OECD, the IMF, Eurostat, Fitch, S&P and Moody's. For each of the criteria, the countries are classed from best to worst (from 1 to 25). For seven criteria and three periods, 21 different classifications are performed on 25 countries. Then, for each country, an average ranking order[13] is computed. This relative ranking is mapped with actual credit rankings. The relative ranking methodology has been implemented in governments' debt management reports (Vincent, 2010). Some sort of conversion between qualitative information and cardinal variables is always needed before performing an empirical analysis. In order to get appropriate data in order to implement empirical estimations, it is necessary to carry out a numerical transformation of the rating notches into numbers. Like most analysts who transform bond ratings into data for regression analysis purposes, beginning with Horrigan (1966) and continuing through to Billet (1996) and Afonso (2003), we assign numerical values to the agencies' ratings: the results are depicted in Table 2-A2, shown in the Appendix. In Table 2-A2, the column "Country" signifies the 25 countries; "Avg. rank" signifies the order in accordance with proposed criteria; "Cre. Rating" signifies the actual credit ratings by

[13] A very similar ranking methodology has been proposed in "La note d'analyse—La France et l'Europe face a la crise économique" by Vincent in 2010. We are grateful to Prof. Thomas Jobert who informed us of this document.

Fitch and S&P, such that the greater is taken into account. "Rank" signifies the numbers (from 1 to 14) assigned to "Cre. Ratings". In contrast to the above mentioned studies, we assign numbers 1 to 14 to the relative credit ratings which are limited with our set of countries. According to the criteria that we employ, Switzerland is in the best situation, matching its actual AAA rating. However, the US's position does not merit its actual AAA rating, i.e., it is worse than Italy's, given that Italy is ranked as an AA–, and both the US and Italy are worse than Turkey's. Greece is the worst, and its actual credit ranking matches its estimated average rank perfectly. Figure 2-1 depicts the re-ordering of the countries versus their actual ranks. The *x-axis* shows "Avg.rank" while the *y-axis* shows both "Cre.Rating" and "Rank" together, where "Rank" numerically signifies "Cre.Rating". The figure explicitly depicts the "mismatching" of actual credit rankings and the current situation of some countries. The matching case can be obtained by drawing appropriate[14] $y = x$ line(s). Then, the points which remain below the line(s) show that the associated sovereign rating(s) has been overestimated by international ranking institutions.

Figure 2-1 Composite indicator of sustainability vs credit ratings

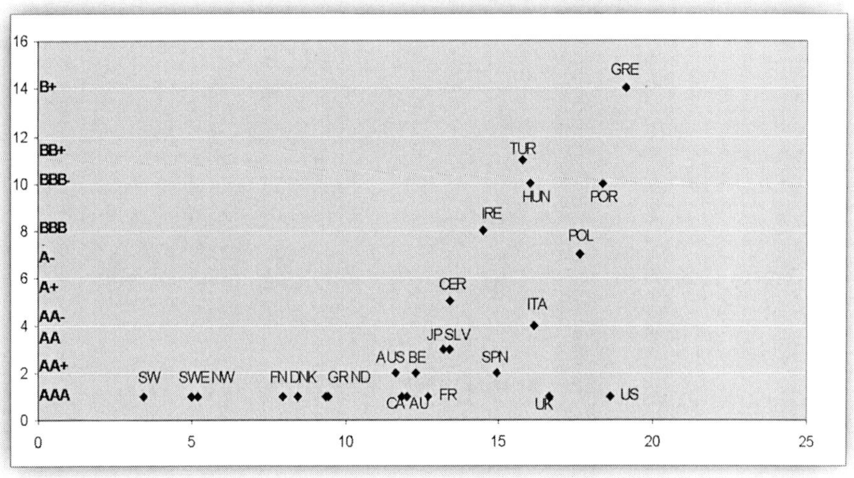

During the last few months, S&P and Fitch have performed "corrections" on credit ratings. The US credit rating has been noted as

[14] One may define only one $y = x$ curve as well as 14 curves, each of which maps actual credit ratings to an estimated rank.

AA+; Italy is an A+ and Turkey is a BBB-. It is also probable to expect a further downgrade in the credit ratings of the UK, France and Spain.[15] For a detailed analysis of public debt sustainability and budget deteriorations in the UK, see Ozkaya (2012). On the other hand, we might expect an upgrade for Australia. Even though the Turkish economy enjoys a relatively good performance in terms of its public sector's economic structure, based on international rating agencies "stable growth" criteria and a possible near-future overheating[16] of the economy plus some risks of macroeconomic imbalances emerging (which can be originated from capital inflows), these factors may be the main constraints upon upgrading its investment grade.

In section 2, we explained that in addition to the data on the public sector's economic performance, the rating agencies take into strict account the current account balance data. In 2012Q1-Q2, given the high rate of increasing private external debt, Turkey's economic performance and its external balances were a cause for concern, and inflation has fluctuated (Turkish Statistical Institute). When combined, both of the above factors may rekindle an "old illness", namely the risk of exchange rate volatility. Since net export figures have turned negative, expectations on an increase in interest rates may result in a decreasing growth rate in future periods. For the rating agencies, such a scenario is a high probability risk. This in turn implies that Turkey's long-term rating will not change in the near future, or may jointly fluctuate, along with that of similar economies. The intuition behind relative ranking enables us to further interpret Turkey's situation, which has lower grades despite its successful public budget policy. That is, the agencies' ratings also serve as a regulation mechanism managing capital inflows across countries and economic zones. Therefore, in conclusion, any change in a country's rating may correspond to a similar change in another country's (zone) rating, thus implying joint analysis.

7. Concluding remarks

We have analysed whether selected European countries and Turkey have followed sustainable debt policies over the last 12 years. For this purpose, by using the methodologies proposed in Trehan and Walsh

---

[15] As of 03.09.2012, based on public debt processes data, Moody's announced a negative revision for the credit rating of the EU, including the UK (see Global Credit Research, www.moodys.com).

[16] Rating agencies use the following proxies in order to detect overheating: capital inflows, broad money (M2), bank credit growth to the private sector, and inflation.

(1991), Hakkio and Rush (1991) and Bohn (1995), we have developed a compact step-wise test algorithm. We have analysed the time series properties of the primary surplus to GDP ratio; budget balance to GDP ratio; primary balance to GDP ratio; total revenue to GDP ratio and total expenditure to GDP ratio from an econometric perspective. Moreover, out of necessity, as pointed out by our algorithm, we have also employed co-integration tests. Our initial results suggest that Ireland and Portugal have pursued unsustainable debt policies over the period considered in our estimation. Moreover, Greece has clearly conducted an unsustainable debt policy, culminating in the Greek debt crisis of early 2010. Spanish fiscal policy can be considered unsustainable if we take into account 90% confidence intervals in our estimations. We have also found that France, Italy, Poland and Turkey have pursued sustainable debt policies.

On the other hand, we observed that during most of the period under consideration, the primary balances of Poland, Portugal, Ireland, Greece, and the UK economies deteriorated and exhibited a negative trend, while the debt stock to GDP ratio of each increased. This observation clearly indicates that in the short- and medium-term, governments do not react to increasing debt stock to GDP ratios by increasing the primary surplus. Therefore, we found it more useful to introduce phase-space representations of debt stock to GDP ratio for Poland, Portugal, Ireland, Greece, the UK and Turkey, embedded in a 3-dimensional phase-space. We included Turkey in our analysis, since the Turkish government has followed a sharper debt policy, and has reacted to decreasing debt stock to GDP ratio with an increasing primary surplus. We found that Greece's, Ireland's and the UK's debt stock over GDP series exhibits nearly the same movement path. The initial states of debt stock to GDP ratio of these countries seem stable, at around certain equilibria, implying a stable public finance policy in the 1999Q1-2003Q1 period. This may be due to the results of stabilisation policies in Europe in the late 1990s with the upcoming Monetary Union. However, according to phase-space, such an equilibria set did not remain sustainable for long. For Portugal, the movement is slightly slower with respect to that of Greece, implying slower movement towards a state of crisis. On the other hand, the debt stock to GDP ratio behaviours of Poland and Turkey imply steadily changing public finance policies. Even though Poland's debt policy deteriorates, and that of Turkey's remains stable, we see that, as yet, there exists no equilibria sets for both countries.

The econometric analysis of the UK debt stock to GDP ratio leads us to conclude that debt stock is sustainable. On the other hand, phase-space analysis suggests that a debt stock to GDP ratio process has exhibited divergent characteristics which have been slowing down slightly, at around 78% in recent quarters. There is a major shift from the initial equilibria set, and the finance policy seems to be on the search for another path in order to settle down. The econometric analysis, together with phase-space examination, implies that the rise in the debt to GDP ratio can be compatible with a sustainable debt policy in the long-run, but not over a specific time period. Moreover, the disrupted structure of the UK primary surplus, which explains the quick shift in their debt stock over GDP series to a position of instability, suggests that remedying this instability will take longer. Thus, we do not draw a clear-cut conclusion, in the case of the UK.

With respect to credit ratings, comparing our study with other literature studies (for a survey see Afonso, 2005), one realises that earlier studies performing a time series analysis with respect to the series of public debt or discounted debt tended to favour the conclusion that debt policies in Europe are not sustainable. More recent studies, in particular those that test how the primary surplus reacts to public debt, tend to conclude that debt policies are sustainable. Finally, from a methodological point of view, the novelty of our paper consists mainly in the implementation of a compound sustainability analysis. Developing a step-wise econometric test procedure leads us to perform a long-term sustainability analysis from a broader perspective, and resorting to phase-space analysis enables us to obtain short- and medium-term debt policy behaviours for the countries under consideration.

The main finding of the study is that a well-defined set of fundamentals, which is considered to be a measure for the effects of the recent financial crisis on public financing and which constitutes a narrower subset of more complicated quantitative measures employed by rating agencies, can be used to explain recent rating revisions. This may be due to the fact that the fundamentals utilised to diagnose the deterioration of the public budget process, originating from the worldwide financial crisis, provide information on short- and medium-term economic performance and on its main structural features. In contrast with regression analysis, which basically makes a backward-looking analysis through estimated weights of determinants, we also point out that a sovereign rating analysis requires forward-looking evaluations of risk default over a short to medium-term horizon. Therefore, we take medium-term forecasts by rating agencies into account. Finally, by proposing a simple ranking order methodology and applying it to a set of selected world economies, we shed light on recent revisions that are taking place, and that may occur in the near future. There are no qualitative criteria amongst those used in the analysis of recent revisions. Yet, qualitative factors such as stable and flexible political systems, strong external and fiscal financing flexibility, law and property rights, institutions (and so on) play an important role in credit ratings. However, the seven criteria used in this paper have been important in contemporary rating decisions and, based on these, the rating agencies have decreased the rating grades of Italy, France, and the US. We make the conjecture that in the near future, a further negative revision is due for the UK. Therefore, given the situation emerging from the global financial crisis, these seven criteria may be used to explain the recent credit rating revisions.

References

Abarbanel, H.D.I. 1995, *Analysis of Observed Chaotic Data*, New York: Springer.

Afonso, A. 2005, "Fiscal Sustainability: The Unpleasant European Case", *Finanzarchiv* 61, p. 19-44.

—. 2003, "Understanding the Determinants of Sovereign Debt Ratings: Evidence for the two Leading Agencies", *Journal of Economics and Finance* 27-1, p. 56-74.

Afonso, A., P. Gomes andP. Rother 2011, "Short-run and Long-run Determinants of Sovereign Debt Credit Ratings", *International Journal of Finance & Economics* 16-1, p. 1-15.

Agénor, P.R. 2001, "Fiscal Policy, Public Debt Sustainability, and Solvency", *World Bank Lecture Notes.*

Agénor, P.R. and P.J. Montiel 1999, *Development Macroeconomics*, Princeton, NJ: Princeton University Press, 2nd Edition.

Arghyrou, M.G. and J.D. Tsoukalas 2011, "The Greek Debt Crisis: Likely Causes, Mechanics and Outcomes", *The World Economy* 34-2, p. 173-191.

Bajo-Rubio, O., C. Diaz-Roldan and V. Esteve 2004, "Searching for Threshold Effects in the Evolution of Budget Deficits: An Application to the Spanish Case", *Economic Letters* 82, p. 239-243.

Bascard, G. and A. Razin 1997, "Indonesia's Fiscal Position: Sustainability Issues", in Hicklin, J., D. Robinson, and A. Singh (eds), *Macroeconomic Issues facing ASEAN Countries,* Washington: IMF, p. 58-90.

Bean, C.R. 1991, "The External Constraint in the U.K.", in Algoskoufis, G., L. Papademos and R. Fortes (eds), *External Constraints on Macroeconomic Policy: The European Experience,* Cambridge: Cambridge University Press, p. 193-218.

Bissoondoyal-Bheenick, E. 2005, "An Analysis of the Determinants of Sovereign Ratings", *Global Finance Journal* 15-3, p. 251-280.

Blanchard, O. 1990, "Suggestions for a New Set of Fiscal Indicators", *OECD Working Paper,* 79.
Bohn, H. 1995, "The Sustainability of Budget Deficits in a Stochastic Economy", *Journal of Money, Credit and Banking* 27-1, p 257-271.
Buiter, W.H. 2005, "Two Naked Emperors? Concerns about the Stability and Growth Pact and Second Thoughts about Central Bank Independence", *Fiscal Studies* 25-3, p. 249-277.
Buiter, W.H. and U.R. Patel 1992, "Debt, Deficits, and Inflation: An Application to the Public Finances of India", *Journal of Public Economics* 47, 171-205.
Cantor, R. and F. Packer 1996, "Determinants and Impact of Sovereign Credit Rating", *Economic Policy Review* 2-2, p. 1-15.
Chalk, N. and R. Hemming 2000, "Assessing Fiscal Sustainability in Theory and Practice", *IMF Working Paper,* 00-81.
Cohen, D. and J. Sachs 1986, "Growth and External Debt under Risk Debt Repudiation", *European Economic Review* 30-3, p. 529-560.
Corsetti, G. and N. Roubini 1991, "Fiscal Deficits, Public Debt and Government Solvency: Evidence from OECD Countries", *Journal of Japanese and International Economy* 5-4, p. 354-380.
Croce, E. and V.H. Juan-Ramon 2003, "Assessing Fiscal Sustainability: A Cross-Country Comparison", *IMF Working Paper,* 03-145.
Cuddington, J.T. 1997, "Analysing the Sustainability of Fiscal Deficits in Developing Countries", *Mimeo,* Georgetown University.
Dickey, D.A. and W.A. Fuller 1979, "Distribution of the Estimators for Autoregressive Time Series with Unit Root" *Journal of the American Statistical Association* 74, p 427-432.
Dolado, J.J. and J. Vinals 1991, Macroeconomic Policy, External Targets and Constraints: The Case of Spain, in Algoskoufis, G., L. Papademos and R. Fortes (eds), *External Constraints on Macroeconomic Policy: The European Experience,* Cambridge: Cambridge University Press, p. 304-341.
Dreher, A., B. Herz and V. Karb 2006, "Is There a Casual Link between Currency and Debt Crises", *International Journal of Finance & Economics* 11-4, p. 305-325.
Eaton, J. 1989, "Foreign Public Capital Flows", in Chenery, H. and T.N. Srinivasan (eds.), *Handbook of Development Economics,* North Holland, p. 1305-1386.
Eaton, J. and M. Gersovitzs 1981, "Debt with Potential Repudiation: Theoretical and Empirical Analysis", *Review of Economic Studies* 48, p. 289-309.

Eckmann, J.P.S., S.O. Kamphorst and D. Ruelle 1987, "Recurrence Plots of Dynamical Systems", *Europhysics Letters* 4-9, p. 973-977.
Engle E.F. and C.W.J. Granger 1987, "Co-integration and Error Correction: Representation, Estimation and Testing", *Econometrica* 55, p. 251-276.
Fincke, B. and A. Greiner 2011, "Debt Sustainability in Selected Euro Area Countries: Empirical Evidence Estimating Time-Varying Parameters", *Studies in Nonlinear Dynamics & Econometrics* 15-3, p. 1-23.
Fitch Ratings 2011, "Sovereign Review and Outlook", *Special Report,* 30.
Gencay, R. and W.D. Dechert 1992, "An Algorithm for the n Lyapunov Exponents of an n-Dimensional Unknown Dynamical System", *Physica D* 59, p. 142-157.
Gerson, P. and D. Nellor 1997, "Philippine Fiscal Policy: Sustainability, Growth and Savings, in Hicklin, J., D. Robinson, and A. Singh (eds), *Macroeconomic Issues facing ASEAN Countries,* Washington: IMF, p. 91-129.
Hakkio, G.S. and M. Rush 1991, "Is the Budget Deficit too Large?", *Economic Inquiry* 29, p. 429-445.
Hamilton, J.D. and M.A. Flavin 1986, "On the Limitations of Government Borrowing: A Framework for Empirical Testing", *The American Economic Review* 76, p. 808-819.
Herz, B. and H. Ton 2003, "The Interactions between Debt and Currency Crises –Common Causes or Contagion?", *University of Bayreuth Discussion Papers in Economics,* 17.
Horrigan, J. 1966, "The Determination of Long-Term Credit Standing with Financial Ratios", *Empirical Research in Accounting* 4, p. 44-62.
Hu Y.T., R. Kiesel and W. Perraudin 2002, "The Estimation of Transition Matrices for Sovereign Credit Ratings", *Journal of Banking & Finance* 26-7, p. 1383-1406.
Husted, S. 1992, "The Emerging U.S. Current Account Deficit in the 1980s: A Cointegration Analysis", *Review of Economics and Statistics* 74, p. 159-166.
JCR 2000, *Sovereign Rating Methodology Multi-Stage Evaluation System.*
Johansen, S. 1991, "Estimation and Hypothesis Testing of Cointegration Vectors in Gaussian Vector Autoregressive Models", *Econometrica* 59, p. 1151-1181.
Johansen, S. and K. Juselius 1990, "Maximum Likelihood Estimation and Inferences on Cointegration with Approach", *Oxford Bulletin of Economics and Statistics* 1, p. 169-209.

Kantz, H. 1994, “A Robust Method to Estimate the Maximal Lyapunov Exponent of a Time Series”, *Physics Letters A* 185-1, p. 77-87.
Kawiatowski, D., P.J.B. Phillips, P. Schmidt and Y. Shin 1992, “Testing the Null Hypothesis of Stationarity against the Alternative of a Unit Root”, *Journal of Econometrics* 54-1, p. 159-178.
Krugman, P.R. 1985, “International Debt Strategies in an Uncertain World”, in Smith, G.W. and J.T. Cuddington (eds), *International Debt and the Developing Countries*, Washington, A World Bank Symposium, p. 213-235.
Liu, P. and E. Tanner 1995, “Intertemporal Solvency and Breaks in the U.S. Deficit Process: A Maximum-Likelihood Cointegration Approach”, *Applied Economics Letters* 2, p. 231-235.
MacKinnon, J.G. 1991, “Critical Values for Cointegration Tests, in Engle, R.F. and C.W.J. Granger (eds), *Long Run Economic Relationships: Readings in Cointegration,* New York: Oxford University Press.
Makrydakis, S., E. Tzavalis and A. Balfoussias 1999, “Policy Regime Changes and Long Run Sustainability of Fiscal Policy: An Application to Greece”, *Economic Modelling* 16, p. 71-86.
Martin, G.M. 2000, “US Deficit Sustainability: A New Approach Based on Multiple Endogenous Breaks”, *Journal of Applied Econometrics* 15, p. 83-105.
McCallum, B.T. 1984, “Are Bond-Financed Deficits Inflationary? A Ricardian Analysis”, *Journal of Political Economy* 92-1, p. 123-135.
Monfort, B. and C. Mulder 2000, “Using Credit Ratings for Capital Requirements on Lending to Emerging Market Economies –Possible Impact of a New Basel Accord” *IMF Working Paper,* 00-69.
Moody’s 2006, “A Guide to Moody's Sovereign Ratings”, *Special Comment.*
Moody’s 2001, *Country Credit Statistical Handbook.*
—. 1995, “Sovereign Supernationals Credit Opinions”, September.
Payne, J.E., H. Mohammadi and M. Cak 2008, “Turkish Budget Deficit Sustainability and the Revenue-Expenditure Nexus”, *Applied Economics* 40, p. 823-830.
Phillips, P.C.P. 1987, “Time Series Regressions with a Unit Root”, *Econometrica* 55-2, p. 277-301.
Phillips, P.C.P. and P. Perron 1988, “Testing for a Unit Root in Time Series Regressions”, *Biometrika* 75, p. 335-346.
Polackova-Brixi, H., H. Ghanem and R. Islam 2001, “Fiscal Adjustment and Contingent Liabilities: Case Studies of the Czech Republic and the Former Yugoslav Republic of Macedonia”, *World Bank Economists’ Forum* 49-77.

Polak, J. 1997, "The IMF Monetary Model at Forty", *IMF Working Paper,* 97-49.
Sachs, J.D. 1984, "Theoretical Issues in International Borrowing", *Princeton Studies in International Finance,* 54.
Said, S.E. and D.A. Dickey 1984, "Testing for Unit Roots in Autoregressive Moving Average Models of Unknown Order", *Biometrica* 71, p. 599-608.
Standard and Poor's 2011, *Sovereign Government Rating Methodology and Assumptions.*
—. 2009, "Understanding Standard & Poor's Rating Definitions Credit Market Services", August.
Standard and Poor's 1998, *Sovereign Credit Rating: A Primer.*
Standard and Poor's 1994, "Sovereign Rating Criteria, Emerging Markets", 124-7, October.
Takens, F. 1981, "Detecting Strange Attractors in Turbulence", in Rand A. and L.S. Young (eds), *Dynamical Systems and Turbulence, Lecture Notes in Mathematics*, Berlin: Springer-Verlag, p. 366-381.
Tanner, E. 1995, "Intertemporal Solvency and Indexed Debt: Evidence from Brazil, 1976-1991", *Journal of International Money and Finance* 14-4, p. 549-573.
Tanner, E. and P. Liu 1994, "Is the Budget Deficit 'too large': Some Further Evidence", *Economic Inquiry* 32, p. 511-518.
Trehan B. and C.E. Walsh 1991,"Testing Intertemporal Budget Constraints: Theory and Applications to U.S. Federal Budget and Current Account Deficits", *Journal of Money, Credit and Banking* 23, p. 206-223.
Turkish State Planning Organization 2011, *Medium Term Program Main Macroeconomic and Fiscal Targets.*
Vincent, C. 2010, "La France et l'Europe face à la Crise Economique", *Centre d'Analyse Stratégique La Note d'Analyse,* 191.
Westerlund, J. and S. Prohl 2010, "Panel Cointegration tests of the Sustainability Hypothesis in Rich OECD Countries", *Applied Economics* 42, p. 1355-1364.
Wilcox, D.W. 1989, "The Sustainability of Government Deficits: Implications of Present-Value Borrowing Constraint", *Journal of Money, Credit and Banking* 21-3, p. 291-306.
Wu, J.L. 1998, "Are Budget Deficits too Large? Evidence from Taiwan", *Journal of Asian Economics* 9-3, p. 519–528.

Appendix

Figure 2-A1 Poland's gross debt stock to GDP ratio

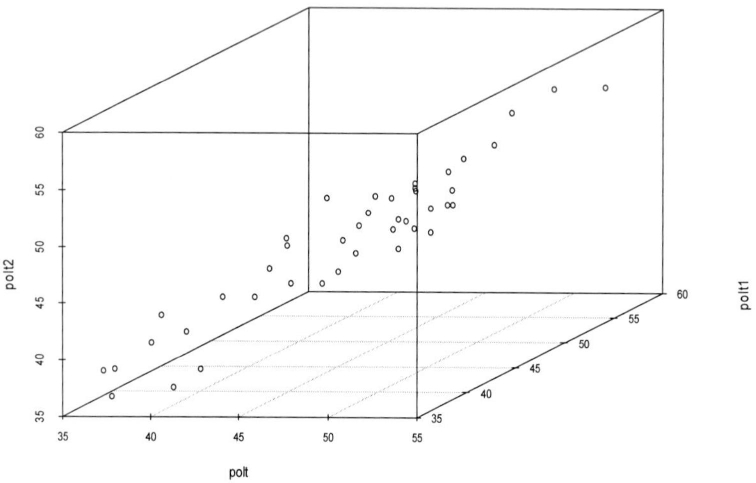

Figure 2-A2 Greece's public gross debt stock to GDP ratio

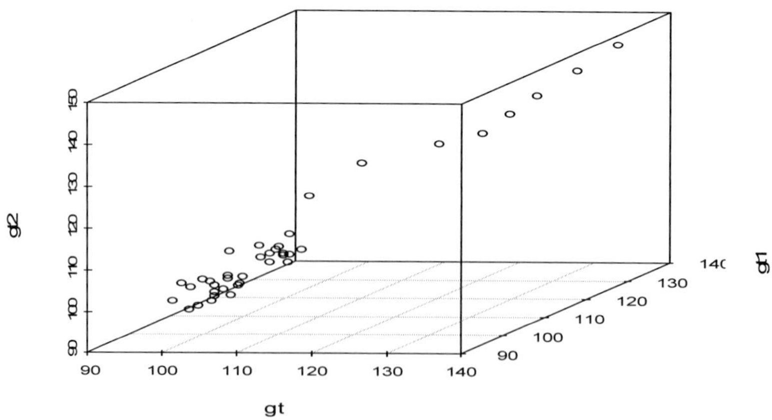

Figure 2-A3 Portugal's public gross debt stock to GDP ratio

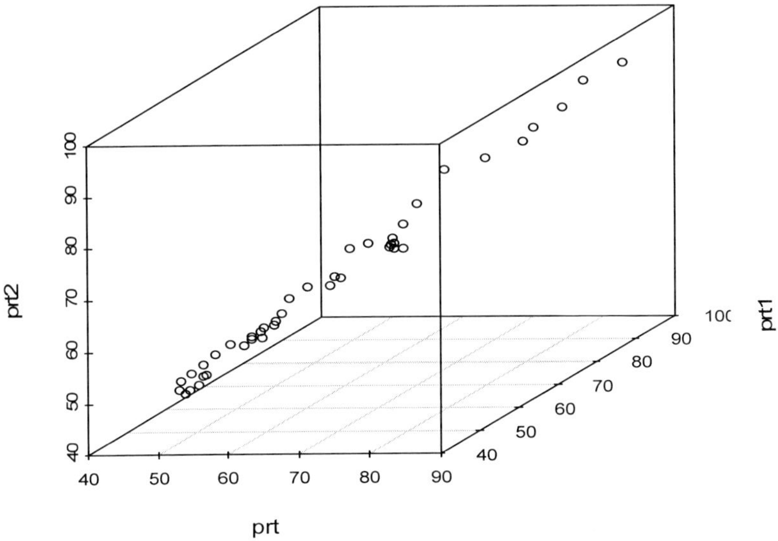

Figure 2-A4 The UK's public gross debt stock to GDP ratio

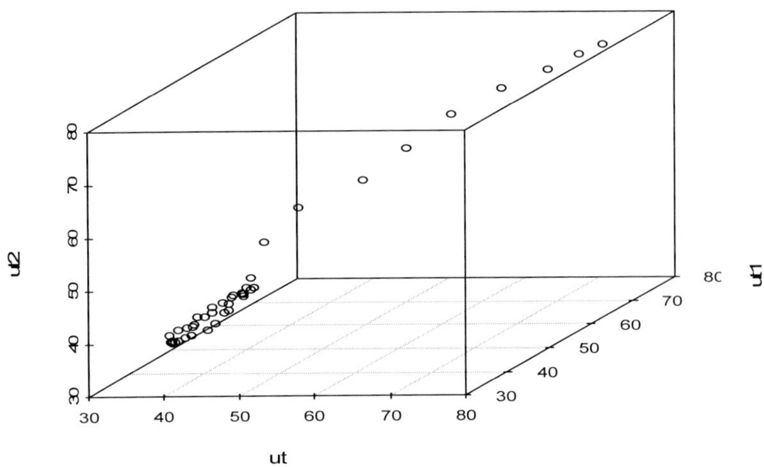

Figure 2-A5 Ireland's public gross debt stock to GDP ratio

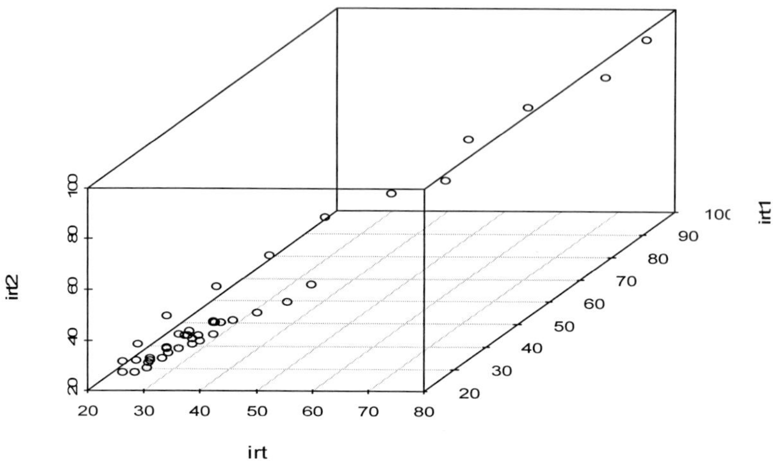

Figure 2-A6 Turkey's gross debt stock to GDP ratio

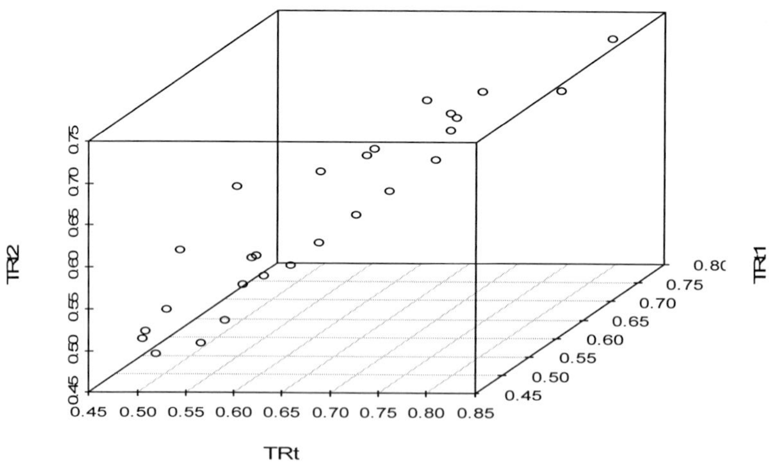

Figure 2-A7 The UK primary surplus over GDP

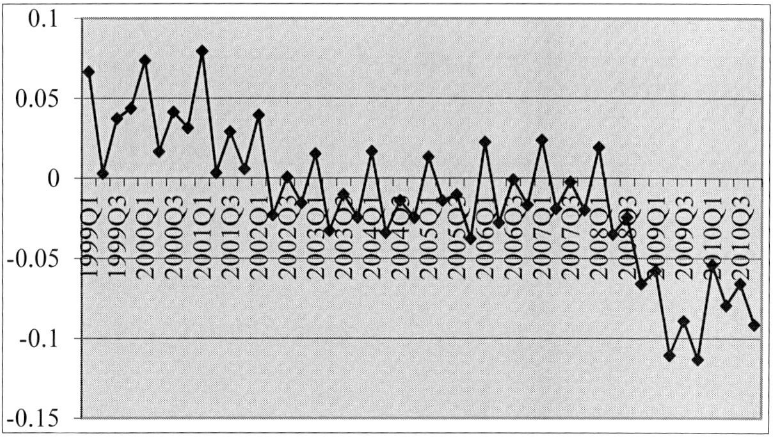

Table 2-A1 Sustainability analysis of public debt stock to GDP ratio for 9 countries

Country	Debt stock/ GDP	PS/GDP	BB/GDP	Exp/GDP	Rev/GDP
Ireland	I(1);I(1); I(1)	I(1);I(0); I(1)	I(1);I(0); I(1)	I(1);I(1); I(1)	I(0);I(0); I(0)
Greece	I(1);I(1); I(1)	I(1);I(1); I(0)	I(1);I(0); I(0)	I(1);I(1); I(0)	I(1);I(0); I(1)
Spain	I(1);I(1); I(1)	I(1);I(0); I(1)	I(0);I(0); I(1)	I(0);I(0); I(0)	I(1);I(0); I(0)
France	I(1);I(1); I(1)	I(1);I(0); I(0)	I(1);I(0); I(0)	I(1);I(0); I(0)	I(0);I(0); I(0)
Italy	I(1);I(1); I(0)	I(1);I(0); I(1)	I(1);I(0); I(0)	I(1);I(0); I(0)	I(1);I(0); I(0)
Poland	I(1);I(1); I(0)	I(1);I(0); I(0)	I(1);I(0); I(0)	I(1);I(0); I(0)	I(0);I(0); I(0)
Portugal	I(1);I(1); I(1)	I(0);I(0); I(1)	I(1);I(0); I(1)	I(1);I(0); I(1)	I(1);I(0); I(0)
UK	I(1);I(1); I(1)	I(1);I(0); I(0)	I(1);I(0); I(0)	I(1);I(1); I(1)	I(1);I(0); I(1)
Turkey	I(1);I(1); I(1)	I(0);I(0); I(0)	I(0);I(0); I(1)	I(1);I(1); I(0)	I(1);I(1); I(0)

For Ireland, Greece, Spain, and Italy "Step 2.b and Step 4" are performed. Steps 2.b and 4 consider given that primary surplus/deficit over GDP is non-stationary and is in particular I(1), then we should seek at least one co-integration relationship between primary surplus/deficit and debt stock. The results are presented in Table 2-1. For France, Portugal, Poland, Turkey and the UK "Step 2.a. and Step 3" are performed. These steps basically say that where primary balance over GDP exhibits I(0) behaviour, and where there is at least one co-integration relationship between total expenditure over GDP and total revenue over GDP, (thus indicating a one-unit increase in revenue results in a less-than-one unit increase in expenditure), then debt policy is sustainable.

Table 2-A2 Reconstructed credit ratings of 25 selected world economies

Country	Avg.rank	Cre. Rating	Rank
Switzerland	3,428571429	**AAA**	1
Sweden	5	**AAA**	1
Norway	5,214285714	**AAA**	1
Finland	7,928571429	**AAA**	1
Denmark	8,428571429	**AAA**	1
Germany	9,357142857	**AAA**	1
Netherlands	9,428571429	**AAA**	1
Australia	11,64285714	**AA+**	2
Canada	11,85714286	**AAA**	1
Austria	12	**AAA**	1
Belgium	12,28571429	**AA+**	2
France	12,71428571	**AAA**	1
Slovenia	13,21428571	**AA**	3
Japan	13,42857143	**AA**	3
Czech Republic	13,42857143	**A+**	5
Ireland	14,5	**BBB+**	8
Spain	14,92857143	**AA+**	2
Turkey	15,78571429	**BB+**	11
Hungary	16	**BBB-**	10
Italy	16,14285714	**AA-**	4
UK	16,64285714	**AAA**	1
Poland	17,64285714	**A-**	7
Portugal	18,35714286	**BBB-**	10
United States	18,64285714	**AAA**	1
Greece	19,14285714	**B+**	14

PART II:

CONSEQUENCES

CHAPTER THREE

THE EFFECTS OF THE GLOBAL CRISIS ON EMERGING ECONOMIES

JEAN-PIERRE ALLEGRET
ECONOMIX - CNRS AND PARIS WEST NANTERRE UNIVERSITY

1. Introduction

The subprime crisis and its consequences have led to the most severe financial crisis since the Great Depression (IMF, 2009). In this paper, we focus our attention on two main questions. First, we analyse the transmission of the current financial crisis to emerging economies. Two main features distinguish the current episode from the crises of the late 1990s and early 2000s. On one hand, the main trigger of the crisis was a shock which originated in the financial sector of advanced countries. After an initial period of resilience, the financial turmoil in advanced economies hit emerging markets, in late 2008. On the other hand, this crisis is characterised by an exceptional synchronisation at a worldwide level. In other words, the subprime crisis has led to a global crisis, affecting financial systems across the globe and economic activity in virtually all countries. Emerging markets have been hit by two major shocks in external drivers: the "sudden stop" of capital inflows, and the collapse in export demand. Second, taking into account the fact that many financial crises have sustained long-term damages to the path of economic growth (Cerra and Saxena, 2008; Furceri and Zdzienicka, 2011), this paper studies the responses of policymakers in emerging markets to the financial crisis. We stress that the ability of emerging countries to mitigate the impact of the crisis has been linked to their economic situation prior to the crisis. In sharp contrast with past crises, the majority of emerging markets have been better equipped to respond to the current crisis.

The remainder of the paper is organised as follows. Section 2 considers the transmission of the financial crises in developed countries to emerging markets, by distinguishing two main transmission channels: finance and trade. Section 3 analyses the monetary policy responses in emerging countries to the current financial crisis. Section 4 concludes with some policy implications.

2. The transmission of the financial crisis in developed countries to emerging economies

The IMF has built a financial stress index allowing a study of the extent to which financial stress in developed countries leads to contagion in emerging economies. Balakrishnan et al. (2011) define financial stress as a period when the financial system is under strain, impairing its ability to intermediate funds from savers to borrowers. More precisely, four main characteristics are associated with financial stress: large shifts in asset prices, a sudden increase in risk perception, liquidity shortages, and concerns about the health of the banking system. From this definition, it is possible to build a financial stress index, including indicators such as stock market volatility, sovereign debt spreads, the exchange market pressure index (exchange rate depreciations and declines in international reserves) and the stability of the banking system.

Figure 3-1 exhibits the financial stress index for emerging markets. It fits the main episodes of financial turbulences that hit these countries over the period.

More precisely, four systemic financial stress episodes can be identified. The first is the intensification of the Asian crisis during the last quarter of 1997. The second occurs from the middle of 1998, with the default of Russian external obligations (August 1998) and the collapse of Long-Term Capital Management (LTCM) (September 1998), to the Brazilian currency crisis in January 1999. The third tension in the financial stress indicator appears in the aftermath of the ICT bubble crash, at the beginning of 2000. The fourth increase focuses more on Latin America during the Argentine default in 2002. Finally, it is important to underline that the subprime crisis has led to a strong synchronisation of financial stress tension. In addition, it is important to note that at the end of the considered period (mid-2010), financial stress in Emerging Europe slightly increases under the impact of the Euro area sovereign debt crisis.

Figure 3-1 suggests the presence of a strong co-movement of financial stress across emerging economies. This means that common factors play a role. One of these factors could be financial stress in advanced economies, as exhibited in Figure 3-2. This figure shows the relationship between the financial stress in developed countries and the financial stress in emerging economies.

The relationship between the two indexes is strong, especially during the current financial crisis. In fact, Balakrishan et al. (2011) shows that on average, close to 70% of stress in developed economies is transmitted to emerging economies. In addition, they find that the transmission is fast: it takes only one to two months to reach emerging economies.[1]

Figure 3-1 Financial stress in emerging countries by region (Monthly data, 1996M11-2010M07)

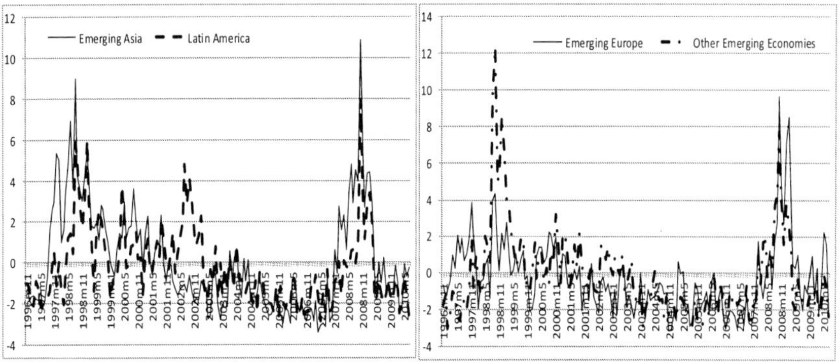

Emerging Asia: China, India, Indonesia, South Korea, Malaysia, Pakistan, Philippines, Sri Lanka, Thailand
Emerging Europe: Czech Republic, Hungary, Poland, Romania, Russia, Slovak Republic, Slovenia, Turkey
Latin America: Argentina, Brazil, Chile, Colombia, Mexico, Peru
Other Emerging Economies: Egypt, Israel, Morocco, South Africa
Source: Balakrishnan et al. (2011).

Dooley and Hutchison (2009), among others, distinguish three phases in the transmission of the subprime crisis to emerging markets. During the first phase, from February 2007 to May 2008, emerging markets are decoupled from industrial countries. Thus, equity market performances tend to diverge between the two groups of countries (Figure 3-3) while emerging market currencies appreciate against the dollar (carry trade as investors chased high yields in emerging markets) (Figure 3-4).

The second phase covers the period from May 2008 to the Lehman Brothers collapse on September 15, 2008. During this phase, revised expectations about the real effects of the crisis on output in industrial

[1] The co-movement parameters, however, vary substantially across countries, ranging from close to zero for Pakistan, Hungary, and China, to more than one for Chile and Turkey.

countries and emerging markets occur. Commodity and oil prices begin to drop sharply, after a long period of increase. In phase 2, we also see a rise in default spreads, both in the US and in emerging markets. All these changes reflect expectations that the financial crisis in the US and Europe could also turn into a long and deep decline in economic activity.

Figure 3-2 Financial stress in developed countries and emerging economies (1997-2009)

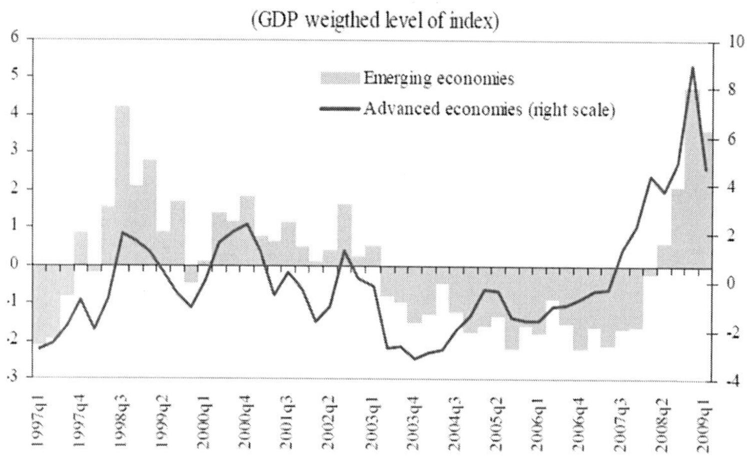

Source: Balakrishnan et al. (2011)

The third phase starts with the Lehman collapse, and ends at the beginning of 2009. As exhibited in Figure 3-3, emerging markets and developed countries' equity markets fall together, to levels sharply below their pre-crisis levels. As seen in Figure 3-4, emerging market currencies decline against dollar. Indeed, the crisis of confidence leads to a sudden halt in carry trade practices. In addition, the safe heaven characteristic of the dollar, and the appetite of investors for riskless assets, induce a sharp reversal in capital inflows to emerging and developing countries (Figure 3-5). Once again, we see that the Euro area sovereign debt crisis has been accompanied by a significant slowdown of capital inflows to emerging and developing countries.

Figure 3-5 exhibits a striking feature: the main fall in capital inflows concerns both portfolio and other financial flows. Among these others, international banking credit activities are especially important. Figure 3-6 shows that international banks have contracted their cross-border positions more vis-à-vis developing countries, relative to their external positions vis-à-vis developed countries.

Figure 3-3 Equity markets performances in developed and emerging countries (Daily data, January 02 2006=100)

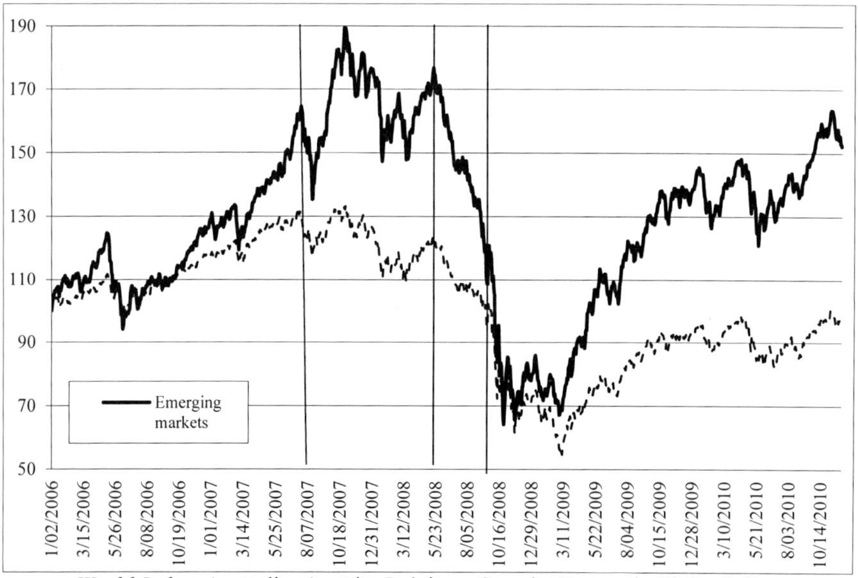

World Index: Australia, Austria, Belgium, Canada, Denmark, Finland, France, Germany, Greece, Hong Kong, Ireland, Italy, Japan, Netherlands, New Zealand, Norway, Portugal, Singapore, Spain, Sweden, Switzerland, United Kingdom, United States

Emerging Markets: Brazil, Chile, China, Colombia, Czech Republic, Egypt, Hungary, India, Indonesia, Israel, South Korea, Malaysia, Mexico, Morocco, Peru, Philippines, Poland, Russia, South Africa, Taiwan, Thailand, Turkey.

Source: MSCI Barra

In their econometric studies on fourteen emerging markets[2] over the sample period January 1, 2007-February 19, 2009, Dooley and Hutchison (2009) find that sovereign CDS spreads in these countries are strongly influenced by news about the financial crisis and real economic activity emanating from the US, especially during the third phase. In other words, external factors exert a strong influence on risk premia in emerging

[2] Argentina, Brazil, Chile, Colombia, Mexico, China, South Korea, Malaysia, Czech Republic, Poland, Hungary, Russia, South Africa and Turkey.

markets. Figure 3-7 stresses this point, in showing the relationship between the VIX index and the EMBI spreads.

The VIX index measures market expectations of near term volatility conveyed by stock index option prices. Since volatility often signifies financial turmoil, VIX is often referred to as the "investor fear gauge". VIX tends to be high during times of financial turmoil and investor fear. During tranquil periods, VIX levels tend to drop. As a result, this index is an indicator of investor's perception of risk.

EMBI measures yield spreads (over safe or risk free assets that bear minimal credit risk) on emerging market countries' debt instruments. The spread is the extra return required to compensate the investor for the additional risks faced when investing in emerging economies, rather than in a safe asset (such as a US government bond). EMBI measures the sovereign risk. Spreads increase with the deterioration—effective or expected—of fundamentals in the countries issuing bonds; they also increase in periods of international financial strains. EMBI is a proxy for market and foreign investor sentiment, and it also gauges contagion from global or other emerging markets crisis.

Figure 3-4 Emerging markets: exchange rate against USD (2002:1=100, increase=depreciation)

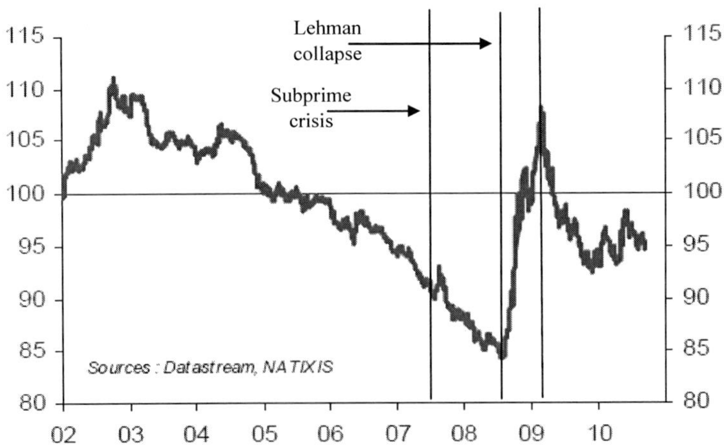

Source: Natixis (2010)

Figure 3-7 shows clearly that during the crisis—and more especially after the Lehman collapse—the relationship between VIX and EMBI seems very strong. Indeed, we see that the widening in spreads has been highly synchronised across emerging markets, and appears to be correlated with the fluctuations in the VIX index. Testing Granger causality between the two variables, we find that during the period January 1 2002-December 31 2007, the VIX index does not cause EMBI change, while over the period January 1 2008-August 21 2009, Granger causes it. In the two periods, contemporaneous correlations between the VIX index and EMBI are 0.73 and 0.89 respectively.

The trade channel is strongly linked to the evolution of the world economy. The subprime crisis has led to a dramatic worldwide activity slowdown, reversing the primary commodity prices boom that occurred from 2004 (Figure 3-8).

For primary commodity-producing countries, the decrease in prices induced a major negative shock in terms of trade. For instance, terms of trade deteriorated sharply in Latin American countries: about 25% between their peak of July 2008 and December 2008 (Izquierdo and Talvi, 2009). In some commodity-exporting countries, notably Chile and Russia, exports fall by more than 40% in the first quarter of 2009.

Figure 3-5 International capital flows to emerging and developing countries (net, USD billions)

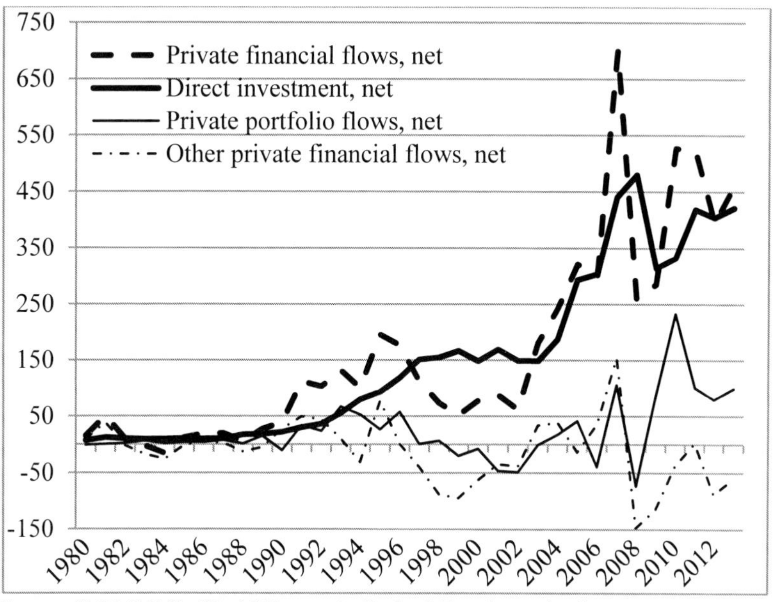

Source: IMF (2012), *World Economic Outlook Database*, April

Figure 3-6 External positions of reporting banks vis-à-vis all sectors, Assets (Quarterly changes, %)

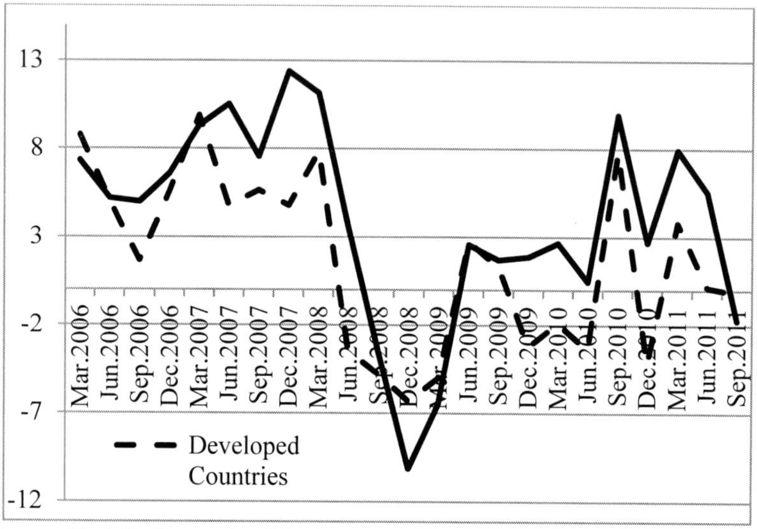

Source: Bank for International Settlements

Figure 3-7 The VIX index and the EMBI spreads

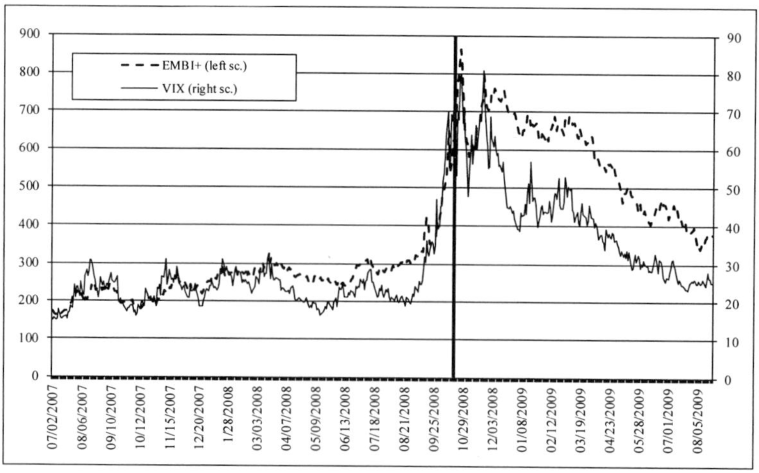

Source: Chicago Board Options Exchange and Argentinean Ministry of Economy and Public Finance

Figure 3-8 Primary commodity prices (2005=100, Monthly data, 1992M01-2012M03)

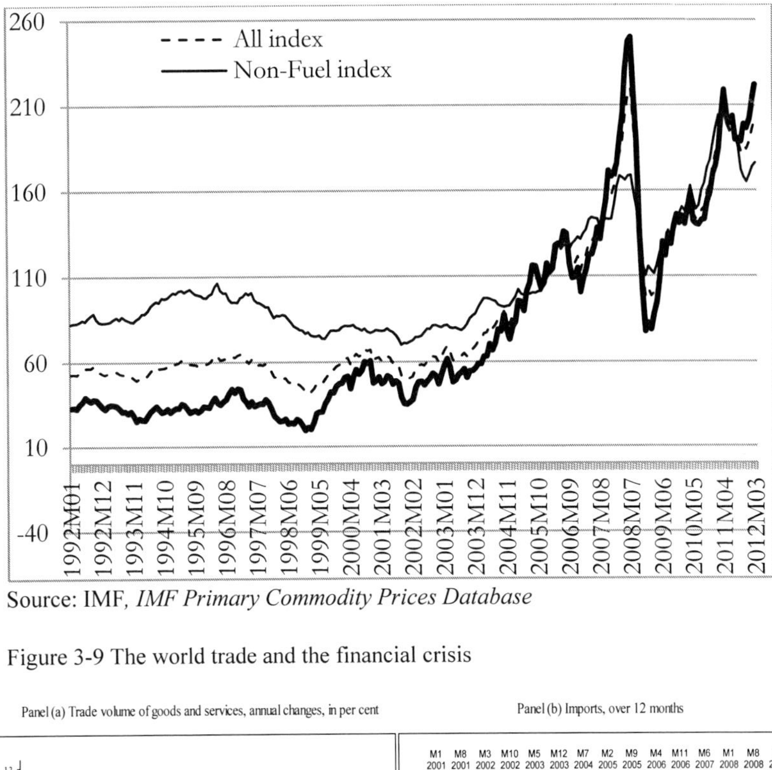

Source: IMF, *IMF Primary Commodity Prices Database*

Figure 3-9 The world trade and the financial crisis

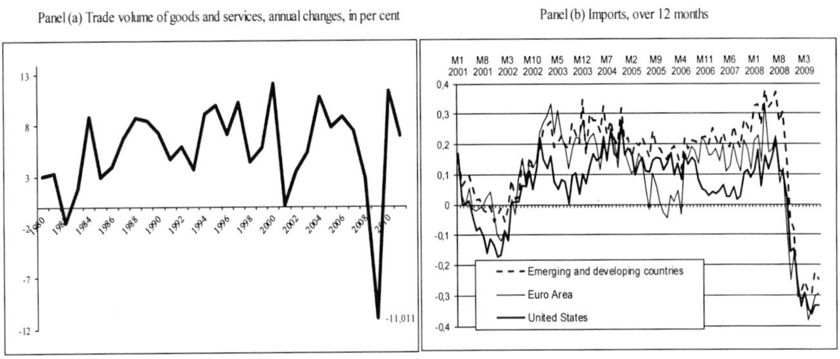

Source: IMF, *International Financial Statistics Database*

The primary commodity prices are a part of the trade channel. As shown in Figure 3-9, the financial crisis has been accompanied by an unprecedented drop in international trade, largely driven by a sharp decrease in imports at a worldwide level, especially in both the US and the Euro area. This widespread collapse in world trade is due to three main factors: (i) the recession in developed countries; (ii) the seizing-up of the international credit markets; and (iii) the global integration of production chains.

The recession in developed countries led to a sharp reduction in economic activity in emerging markets in the fourth quarter of 2008, with double digit declines in exports and industrial production. The decline in trade was particularly strong where exports were concentrated in high-end manufacturing and destined for US markets. Economies with the highest share of exports to GDP suffered the most, namely Hong Kong, South Korea, Malaysia, the Philippines, Singapore and Thailand.

Figure 3-10 Public financing conditions in selected Euro area countries (Daily data)

a. Spreads 10-Year Government Bonds Rates, in percent

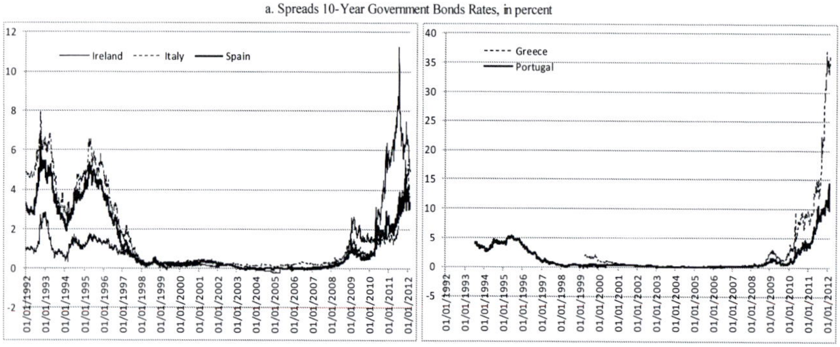

b. Sovereign CDS Premium, basis points

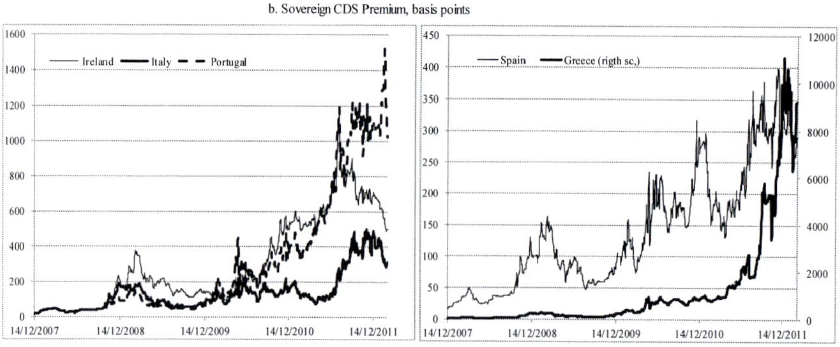

Source: Datastream

Figure 3-11 Spillovers from the sovereigns to banks and from banks to sovereigns

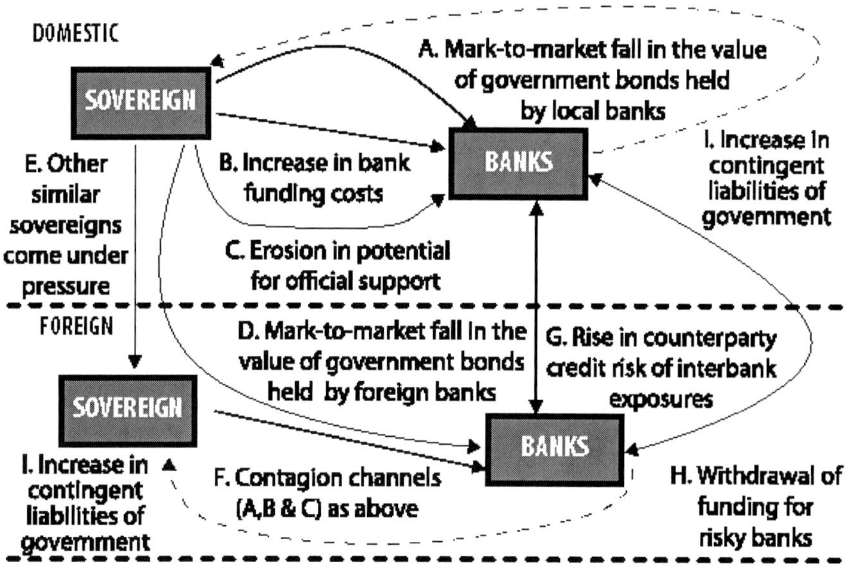

Source: IMF (2010)

The financial crisis dramatically deteriorated the public finance situation in advanced countries, especially in the Euro area. Some of these economies suffered from worsening financing conditions (Greece, Ireland, Italy, Portugal, and Spain: see Figures 3-10a (Spreads 10-year government bond rates) and 3-10b (Sovereign CDS 5-years spreads)), leading to the emergence of the sovereign debt crisis at the beginning of 2010.

If it is too early to assess the contagion effects from the European sovereign debt crisis,[3] it is nevertheless the case that some developments suggest that a worsening debt crisis may lead to significant spillover effects in emerging countries, especially in Emerging Europe. Figure 3-11 portrays potential spillovers from the sovereigns to the banks and, in turn, spillovers from banks to sovereigns.

Figure 3-11 shows that a worsening debt crisis may destabilise the banking sector, insofar as banks hold public bonds in their portfolios. Broadly speaking, a significant increase in long-term interest rates may

[3] Aizenman et al. (2012) report mixed results on the contagion of the sovereign debt crisis to equity and bond markets in developing countries.

cause capital losses for banks and, in turn, may trigger a banking crisis via contagion effects, due to loss of confidence. In turn, banking rescue packages may lead to a negative retroaction effect on public finance. The transmission to the non-financial sectors, which may rest on the Euro area banks deleveraging, is explained as the result of the following two main forces: rising banking funding costs, and the rules imposed by banking supervision.

The effects of the sovereign debt crisis on banks depend on their degree of exposure to sovereign bonds. According to OFCE (2011), on average, European banks hold at least 50% of public debt from advanced countries. This average hides a significant disparity among European banks: for instance, French banks hold 77% of the public debt, while this share amounts to 97% for Spanish banks. If we focus on countries encountering the strongest difficulties—Greece, Ireland, Italy, Portugal, and Spain—the French banking system appears as one of the main exposed (18.9% of GDP, if we take into account both public and private assets). In terms of GDP, German banks assets vis-à-vis these countries amount to 10%.

Since the beginning of the sovereign debt crisis, some indicators clearly show that banks, especially in the Euro area, are suffering. First, as shown in Figure 3-12, we observe tensions on the interbank funding markets. Interestingly, even if tensions have been especially strong in euro markets, the sovereign debt crisis has affected the dollar and pound interbank markets to a lesser extent

Figure 3-13 shows the increase in banking sector CDS beyond European banks, suggesting the presence of contagion effects.

In a similar way, the VIX index has encountered new tensions since the beginning of the sovereign debt crisis (Figure 3-14). In other words, the Euro area crisis has a potentially systemic dimension.

Tensions have been observed on sovereign CDS in the emerging markets since 2010, as suggested by Figure 3-15.

Bank deleveraging leads to a reduction in credit to emerging countries. Figure 3-16 exhibits the banking external positions vis-à-vis all sectors in different emerging country regions. After a significant international credit contraction, in the aftermath of the Lehman collapse (September 2008), the European sovereign debt crisis has been accompanied by a significant slowdown in international banking activities. The greatest effects are observed in Emerging Europe: Figure 3-19 shows a reduction in lending to the residents in this region.

Figure 3-12 Tensions on interbank funding markets and sovereign debt crisis

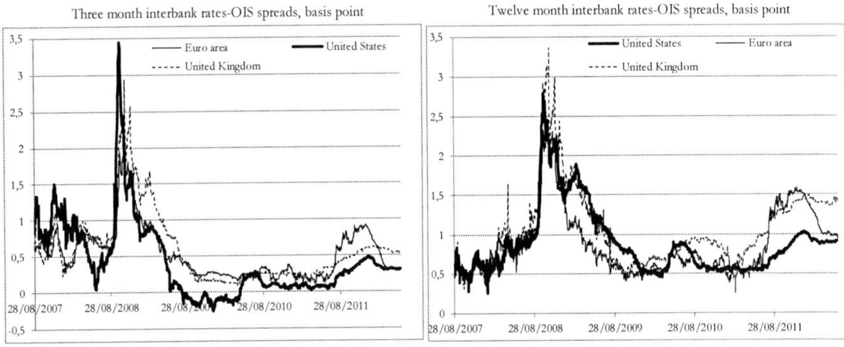

Source: Datastream

Figure 3-13 Banking sector CDS spreads (Basis points, Daily data)

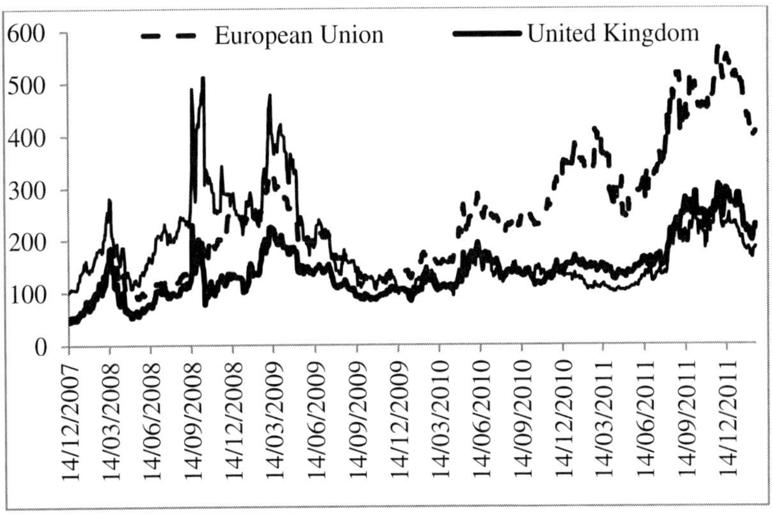

Source: Datastream

Figure 3-14 The VIX index (Daily data)

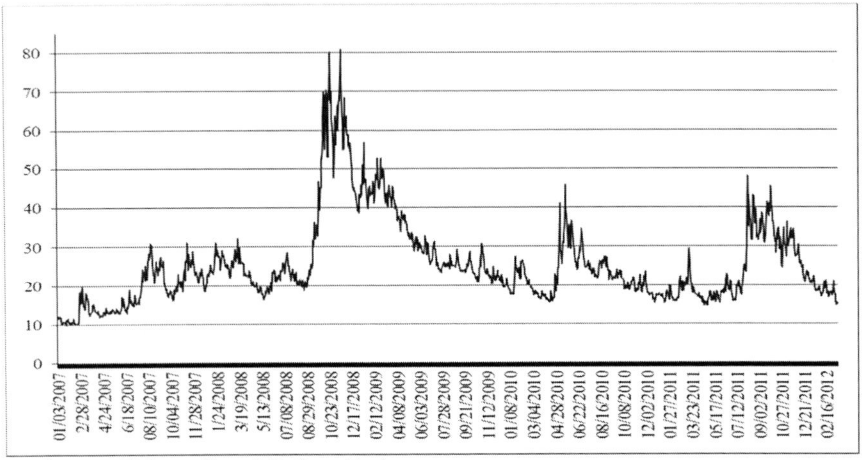

Source: Chicago Board Options Exchange

Figure 3-15 Sovereign CDS spreads in selected emerging markets (Daily data, Basis points. Simple average by region)

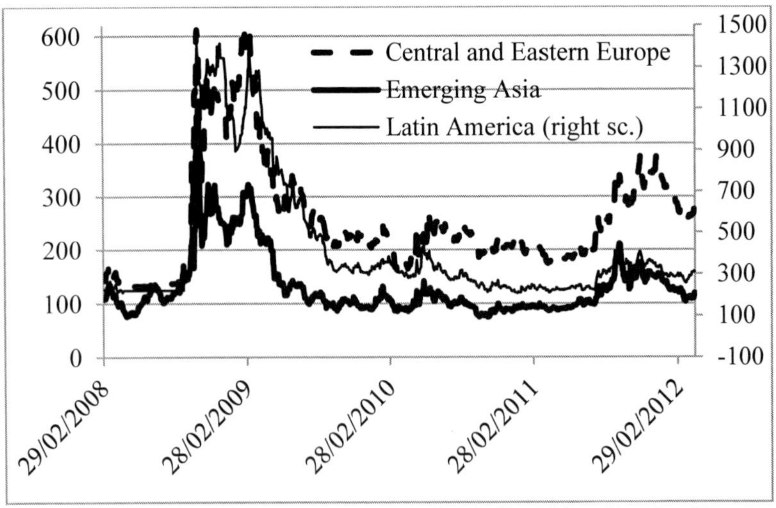

Central and Eastern European countries: Czech Republic, Croatia, Hungary, Lithuania, Poland, Serbia, Turkey, Romania, Russia
Emerging Asia: China, Hong Kong, Korea, Philippines, Thailand,
Latin America: Argentina, Brazil, Chile, Peru
Source: Datastream

Figure 3-16 External positions of reporting banks vis-à-vis all sectors, Assets (Quarterly changes in %)

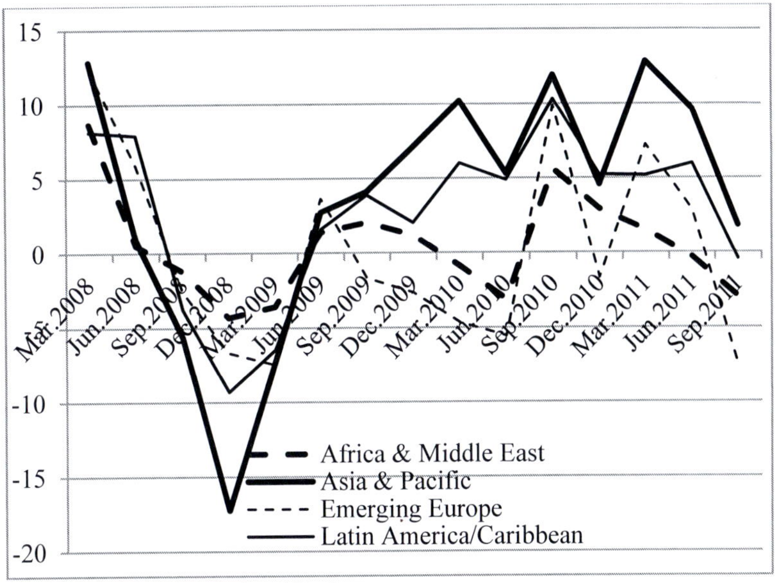

Source: Bank for International Settlements

The IMF (2012) has shown that non-Euro area banks have reduced their credits to emerging markets more gradually than to those in the Euro area. Finally, Figure 3-17, which depicts Euro imports from the rest of the world, suggests that the negative impact of the debt crisis on the Euro area's economic activity has led to a significant slowdown of European imports from all parts of the world. Taking into account the interdependences between countries, the sovereign debt crisis may induce a negative impact on the world economic activity.

Figure 3-17 Imports of the Euro area (Growth rate M/M-12 of the volume indices, %)

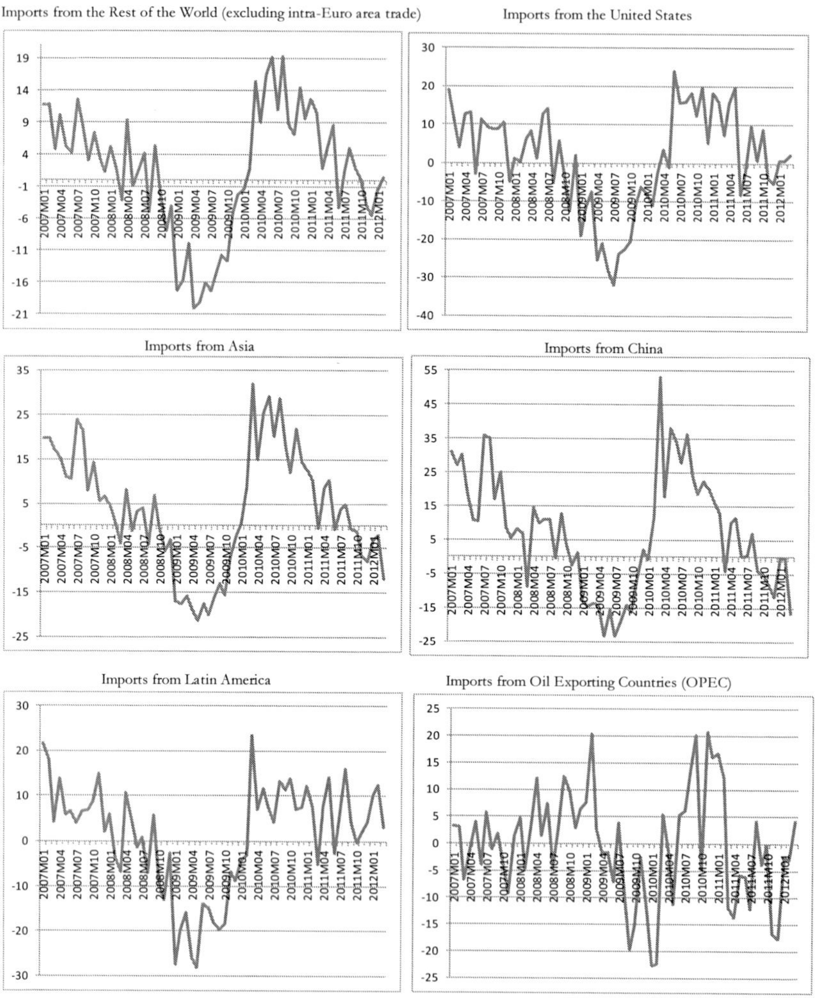

Source: Eurostat

3. The responses of policymakers in emerging countries to the financial crisis

To understand how emerging countries have reacted to the crisis, it is necessary to take their pre-crisis vulnerability into account. Indeed, an important lesson drawn from the crisis is that those countries which entered the crisis with better fundamentals were able to respond with more counter-cyclical policy easing.[4] In other words, countries with sizeable domestic and external imbalances have been constrained in their ability to face to the crisis.

3.1. The emerging markets vulnerabilities

The financial crisis in developed countries has led to a sharp reversal in capital flows. An important question concerns the extent to which emerging countries are vulnerable to shocks affecting capital flows. Emerging Europe is particularly vulnerable to the financial channel. Indeed, Emerging Europe has accumulated large and sustained external deficits, while many countries in Asia, the Middle East, and the Commonwealth of Independent States (CIS) have shifted to surpluses, partly because of the commodity prices boom (Figure 3-18).

Liabilities to advanced economies banks and portfolio exposures to advanced economies show that Emerging Europe is more vulnerable to external bank crises, while emerging Asia is more sensitive to external securities-market disturbances. At the same time, Western European banks have increasingly dominated banking flows, whereas North America has been the main source for portfolio investments in emerging and developing economies. As a result, Western Europe has become the most likely source of common-lender effects, and the US and Canada have become more important sources of securities-market disturbances.

In addition, in some emerging countries, households and firms borrow in foreign currencies, leading to currency mismatch insofar as their assets are often denominated in domestic currency. Foreign currency borrowings rely on two main mechanisms: first, lending interest rates tend to be lower in international financial centres; secondly, exchange rate risks seem low when authorities peg their currency against the US dollar (Asian countries

---

[4] See, for instance, IMF (2010) and Gallego et al. (2010). Pre-crisis conditions refer to both financial (ratio of international reserves to short-term external debts, credit booms), fiscal (ratio of primary balances to public debt levels), external (current account deficits and composition of capital inflows) and monetary (exchange rate regimes, initial level of inflation) vulnerabilities.

Figure 3-18 Current account balances (% of GDP)

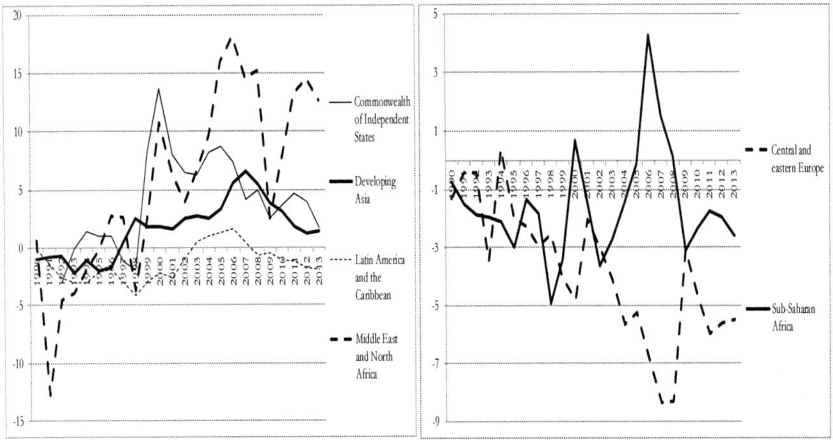

Source: IMF (2012), *World Economic Outlook Database*, April

Figure 3-19 Loans denominated in foreign currency as a share of GDP, Selected countries in Emerging Europe, 2007 and 2011 (%)

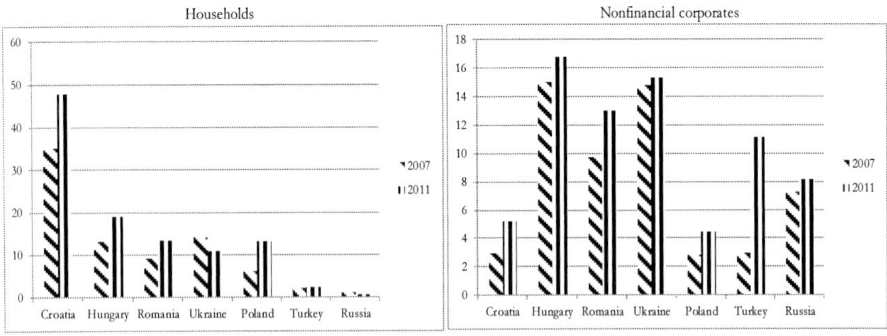

Source: IMF (2012)

in the 1990s) or euro (Emerging Europe now). These countries are vulnerable to a sudden and large devaluation of their currency against an anchor currency. Any devaluation increases the cost of the debt, inducing a negative balance sheet effect. While Emerging Europe as a whole increased the currency mismatch (Figure 3-19), the impressive improvement in fundamentals in Latin American countries allowed them to undergo a de-dollarization process, as both the share of foreign-currency denominated debt in total public debt stock and liability dollarization in the domestic banking systems decreased after 2002 (Figure 3-20).

Figure 3-20 The De-dollarization process in Latin America

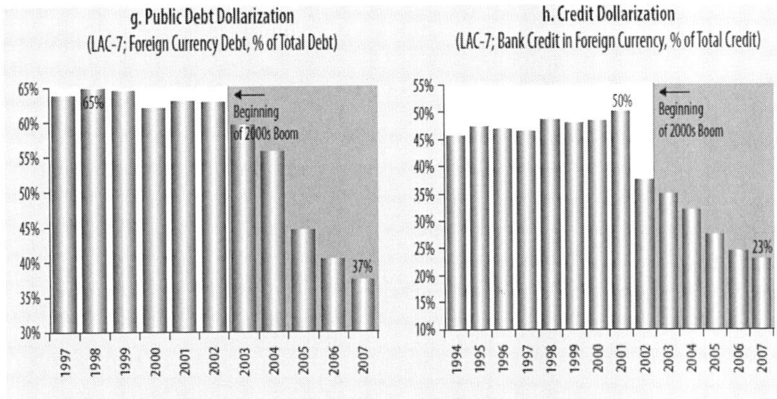

LAC-7 is the simple average (*sum) of the seven major Latin American countries, namely Argentina, Brazil, Chile, Colombia, Mexico, Peru and Venezuela. These countries represent 91% of Latin America's GDP. For bank credit figures LAC-7 excludes Brazil, Colombia and Venezuela.

Source: Izquierdo and Talvi (2009)

3.2. Monetary and exchange rate policies

Central banks in emerging markets have more room for manoeuvre than before to conduct an expansionary monetary policy in response to the financial crisis. Firstly, emerging markets are not the epicentre of the crisis. As a consequence, they can decrease their interests without provoking a loss of confidence. The situation was very different in the 1990s, when emerging markets were at the centre of financial turbulence. Secondly, in the majority of emerging markets, inflation is under control. Some of these markets adopted an inflation targeting framework, and this improved their credibility (Coulibaly, 2012; Takáts, 2012). Finally, since the end of the 1990s, we have seen a shift in exchange rate regimes towards more flexible ones. More flexibility in exchange rate management allows central banks to assign their interest rates to their internal balance. They can conduct a more independent monetary policy.

Despite these improvements, there has been no immediate response to offset tighter financing conditions on international financial markets by lowering policy rates. Indeed, until late 2008 or early 2009, there were continuing concerns in many emerging markets about inflationary pressures.

Figure 3-21 compares the evolution of policy rates in countries with low vulnerability (panel a) and high vulnerability (panel b). High vulnerability refers mainly to currency mismatch and to dependence on capital inflows. The main lesson of this figure is that countries with high vulnerability have responded later to the financial crisis. More precisely, panel b shows that when the shock happened, monetary authorities either increased their policy rates (see for instance the sizeable interest rate hike in October 2008 in Hungary and Russia) or did not change them (Latvia, Lithuania).

Figure 3-21 Discount rates in some emerging countries

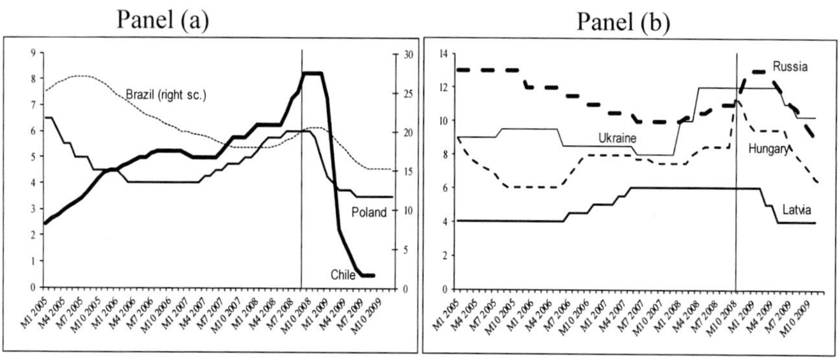

Source: IMF, *International Financial Statistics Database*

Since late 2008, policy rates have fallen sharply in many emerging markets such as Brazil or Chile. It is clear that countries with pegged exchange rates have been more constrained in their ability to lower policy rates. At the same time, countries that had more room for lowering interest rates also allowed more exchange rate depreciations (Figure 3-22).

This policy reaction in Latin American countries is in stark contrast with the one enacted in the aftermath of the Russian crisis of 1998. While in the former, Latin American currencies depreciated and policy interest rates decreased, in the latter pegged exchange rates limited the size of the depreciation and interest rates were dramatically increased (Figure 3-23).

Figure 3-22 Nominal effective exchange rates in some emerging countries (2005=100)

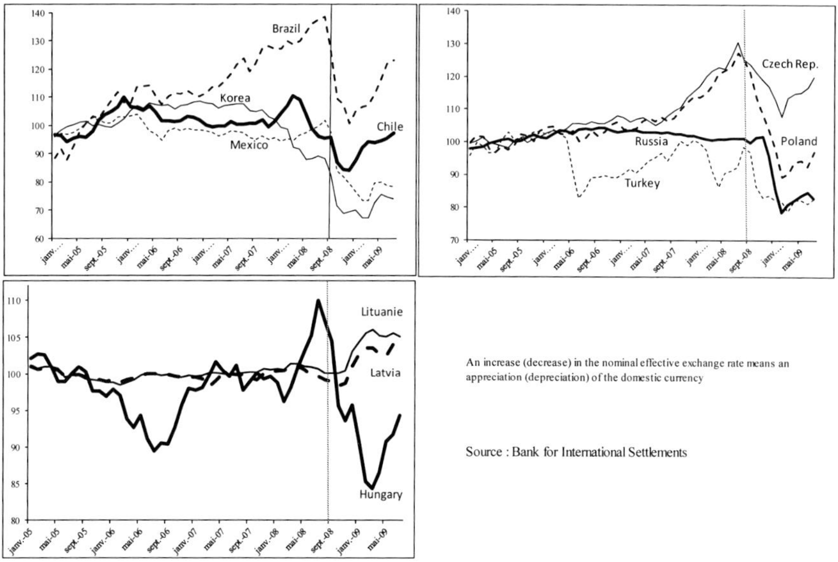

Source: Bank for International Settlements

Figure 3-23 Policy responses in Latin American countries

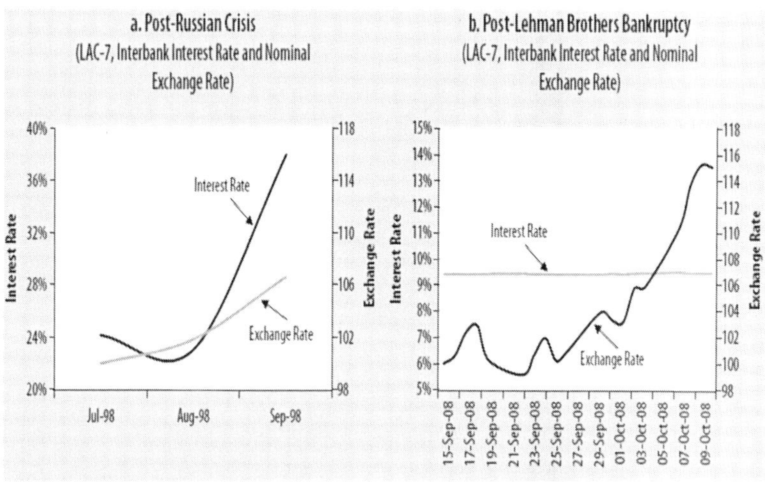

Source: Izquierdo and Talvi (2009)

Figure 3-24 The ratio of foreign liabilities to money and the money market interest rates (2004M1-2010M12, %)

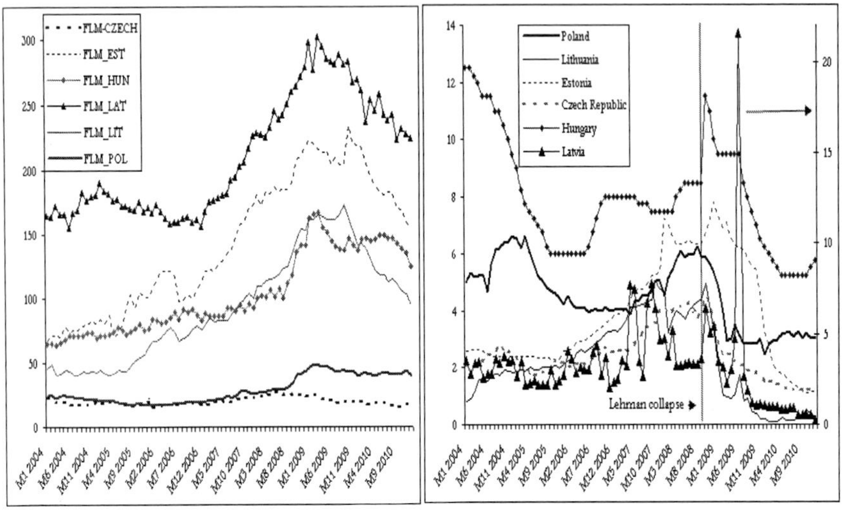

Source: Allegret et al. (2013)

Allegret et al. (2013) analyse adjustment mechanisms and exchange rate regimes of new EU members that stayed outside the Euro area during the subprime period. Two sub-groups of Emerging European countries are distinguished, according to their exchange rate regimes—fixed regimes group ("fixers" including Estonia, Lithuania, and Latvia) vs. flexible regimes group ("floaters" including Poland, Czech Republic, and Hungary)—in order to gauge the extent to which these countries differ, in terms of responses to the crisis. Using country specific VAR models over the period January 2004-December 2010, they find that countries with rigid exchange rate regimes had weaker real exchange rate adjustment in the aftermath of the Lehman collapse, relative to other economies. In addition, their results suggest that nominal exchange rate shocks tend to have a higher influence on real exchange rate variance in floater countries, relative to that of fixers. In other words, real exchange rate depreciation in the latter group is very costly, since it occurs with an internal depreciation, in other words, with a decrease in real wages.

The responses of the nominal exchange rate in new EU members to the current crisis confirm the main findings of Cavallo and Izquierdo (2009), relative to Latin American countries. They show that more dollarization liability triggers fear of floating, and then constrains the ability of the monetary policy to respond to external shocks. Indeed, fear of floating implies that policymakers are reluctant to let the nominal exchange rates depreciate after negative shocks. Figure 3-24 estimates the extent of dollarization-euroization in the six studied countries. To this end, we use the same methodology as Levy Yeyati et al. (2010), calculating the ratio of foreign liabilities to money.[5] The left hand side of Figure 3-24 exhibits these ratios, while the right hand side shows the money market interest rates. The most striking lesson to be learnt from this figure is that the higher the foreign liabilities to money ratio (the Baltic countries here), the weaker the immediate monetary policy response to the crisis. In other words, in high vulnerability countries—characterised by both currency mismatch and dependence on capital inflows—once the shock happened, monetary authorities increased their policy rates.

4. Conclusion

From the past experiences of emerging countries, the main lesson drawn from the subprime crisis is that, except in Emerging Europe, the improvement in fundamentals at the beginning of 2000 has allowed emerging countries to respond better to the crisis. Such an evolution is in stark contrast to previous episodes of financial turbulence. As a consequence, in the majority of emerging countries, the impact of the financial crisis has been relatively short-lived. Considering the long-term damage of the crisis in advanced economies, emerging countries must face new challenges. Even if, as stressed above, the European sovereign debt crisis may have systemic destabilizing effects, the main challenge is the dramatic rebound of net capital inflows to emerging economies. The most dynamic component of capital flows has been a portfolio of equity investment, while net credit flows from banks stay at a low level relative to that prior to the crisis. This rebound rests on push and pull factors.

Among the push factors, a key driver is the monetary policy easing in mature markets, that in real terms lead to low or negative policy rates. The interest rates differential between emerging and developed countries attracts capital flows into the former.

The main pull factor is the sizeable growth gap between emerging and developed countries. Primary commodity-producing countries benefit from the improved terms of trade.

The challenge for policymakers in emerging countries is twofold:

[5] Liabilities to nonresidents* / (Transferable deposits included in broad money* + Monetary base**); * Other depository corporation survey; ** Central bank survey. IMF IFS line 26C/ (line 14 + line 24).

- On the one hand, past experience suggests that an increase in persistence of flows tends to be followed by flow reversals. In other words, emerging countries are especially prone to boom-bust cycles. From this perspective, the main challenge is to avoid a disorderly market adjustment concerning capital flows.

- On the other hand, massive capital flows into emerging countries raise many concerns for monetary policy. Indeed, the exchange rates tend to appreciate not only in nominal terms but also in real terms, because of inflationary pressures due to the increasing of official reserves. This challenge is particularly important in the current context, insofar as policymakers face a dilemma. On the one hand, they must increase interest rates, in order to mitigate inflationary pressures. But such a reaction may increase capital inflows. On the other hand, lower interest rates are necessary, in order to discourage capital inflows. But such an expansionary monetary policy may increase the inflation rates in a context where the growth rate is high.

Few tools are available to face this dilemma. As a result, the main perspective is a more extensive use of capital controls to contain massive capital inflows. Brazil and South Korea, among others, have already introduced controls for capital inflows. The IMF does not exclude such a strategy, in its advice on economic policy dedicated to emerging countries.

References

Aizenman, J., Y. Jinjarak, M. Lee and D. Park 2012, "Developing Countries' Financial Vulnerability to the Euro Crisis: An Event Study of Equity and Bond Markets", *NBER Working Paper,* 18028.

Allegret, J.P., E. Becker-Pucar and K. Josifidis 2013, "Adjustment Mechanisms and Exchange Rate Regimes in New 2004 EU Members during the Financial Crisis", *Post-Communist Economies* 25-1, p. 1-17.

Balakrishnan, R., S. Danninger, S. Elekdag and I. Tytell 2011, "The Transmission of Financial Stress from Advanced to Emerging Economies", *Emerging Markets Finance and Trade* 47-3S2, p. 40-68.

Cavallo, E. and A. Izquierdo 2009, "Policy Responses to Sudden Stops: A Comparative Analysis", in Cavallo, E. and A. Izquierdo (eds), *Dealing with an International Credit Crunch, Policy Responses to Sudden Stops in Latin America,* Washington, D.C.: Inter-American Development Bank, p. 1-22.

Cerra, V. and S.C. Saxena 2008, "Growth Dynamics: The Myth of Economic Recovery", *The American Economic Review* 98-1, p. 439-457.

Coulibaly, B. 2012, "Monetary Policy in Emerging Markets Economies: What Lessons from the Global Financial Crisis?", *International Finance Discussion Papers,* 1042.

Dooley, M.P. and M.M. Hutchison 2009, "Transmission of the US Subprime Crisis to Emerging Markets: Evidence on the Decoupling-Recoupling Hypothesis", *Journal of International Money and Finance* 28-8, p. 1331-1349.

Furceri, D. and A. Zdzienicka 2011, "The Real Effect of Financial Crises in the European Transition Economies", *Economics of Transition* 19-1, p. 1-25.

Gallego, S., S. Gardó, R. Martin, L. Molina and J.M. Serena 2010, "The Impact of the Global Economic and Financial Crisis on Central Eastern and Southeastern Europe (CESEE) and Latin America", *Bank of Spain, Working Paper,* 1002.

IMF 2012, *Global Financial Stability Report, The Quest for Lasting Stability*, April.

—. 2010, *Global Financial Stability Report*, *Sovereigns, Funding, and Systemic Liquidity,* October.

—. 2010, "How Did Emerging Markets Cope in the Crisis?", *Strategy, Policy, and Review Department,* June.

—. 2009, *World Economic Outlook Update,* July.

Izquierdo, A. and E. Talvi 2009, "Policy Trade-offs for Unprecedented Times: Confronting the Global Crisis in Latin America and Caribbean", *Monograph,* Inter-American Development Bank.

OFCE 2011, "La très Grande Récession", *OFCE Les Notes*, 8-16, December.

Takáts, E. 2012, "Countercyclical Policies in Emerging Markets", *BIS Quarterly Review* June, p. 25-31

Yeyati, E.L., F. Sturzenegger and I. Reggio 2010, "On the Endogeneity of Exchange Rate Regimes", *European Economic Review* 54, p. 659-677.

CHAPTER FOUR

THE TRANSMISSION OF FINANCIAL CRISES FROM ADVANCED TO EMERGING ECONOMIES: THE TURKISH CASE

ALI ARI
KIRKLARELI UNIVERSITY
AND RAIF CERGIBOZAN
KIRKLARELI UNIVERSITY

1. Introduction

The recent global financial crisis is considered the most severe financial crisis and the most synchronised recession since the Great Depression. This crisis has affected financial systems across the world and economic activity in nearly all countries.

As is well-known, the crisis started as a subprime crisis in late 2007 in the highly leveraged US financial sector. The crisis then turned global, after the collapse of Lehman Brothers in late 2008. Several bail-out efforts, implemented by developed countries' public authorities in order to save financial institutions in trouble, have dramatically deteriorated their public finance situations. This applies especially in the Euro area, where sovereign debt crisis have struck Greece, Ireland, Portugal, Spain and Italy (PIIGS). These countries' non-resolved sovereign debt problems have thus led to serious doubts concerning the viability of the Eurozone.

Turkey, like other emerging markets, was deeply affected by this global crisis context, particularly after the bankruptcy of Lehman Brothers. The Istanbul Stock Exchange Index (ISE) fell by more than 50%, in the last quarter of 2008, the Turkish lira declined more than 25% against the US dollar in October 2008, the economy experienced a severe recession of nearly 5% of GDP from the fourth quarter of 2008 to the first quarter of

2010, and unemployment rates rose sharply to 14% in 2009 before falling back to around 9% in 2012.

Turkey is not unfamiliar with financial crises, as the 1977-80, 1994 and 2000-2001 crises confirmed. However, policy reforms implemented in the aftermath of the 2001 crisis, backed by the IMF stand-by credits within the framework of the stabilisation programme (namely Transition to the Strong Economy), restored relative economic stability, in terms of inflation (from over 50% in 2002 to 8% in 2012), budget deficit (from 12% of GDP in 2001 to 3.5% in 2012) and economic growth (on average 5.5% of GDP from 2002 to 2012).

Tight fiscal policies, accompanied by an independent central bank focusing only on price stability, were key issues behind the successful inflation targeting regime which has been implemented since mid-2002. High steady growth rates were also achieved by ensuring fiscal discipline with high primary budget surpluses (4% of GDP in the period from 2002 to 2008). The restructuring of the banking sector and large capital inflows also played an important role, as the banks' claims on the private sector doubled after 2002. Moreover, political stability has also been a key determinant of economic stability since the AKP came into single-party-government in November 2002.

However, these achievements cannot hide the vulnerabilities that the economy encounters. Sharp increases in current account deficits (more than 6% of GDP from 2002-2012), very high unemployment rates, a highly indebted private sector, and difficulties in attracting direct investments from abroad are the most highly notable of these vulnerabilities. Indeed, the economic growth strategy, which is closely related to export earnings and short-term capital inflows, seems to be the main reason behind the country's vulnerability to external shocks, as the May 2004, May 2006, and October 2008 episodes illustrated.[1]

It may be argued that Turkey is affected by the global crisis mainly through trade and financial channels. Sharp reversals in capital inflows to developing countries (sudden stop) accompanied by a significant slowdown of economic activity and a parallel collapse in export demand in developed countries clearly explain the emergence of the 2008 crisis and Turkish economic contraction which followed.

In this paper, we aim to empirically show the transmission effect of external shocks on the Turkish economy. As far as we know, there is not one single empirical paper which focuses on the transmission of shocks to the Turkish economy, except cross-country analyses that include Turkey in

[1] For more information on the Turkish economy, see Ari (2012) and Ari and Yilmaz (2013).

their samples of countries. This study aims to fill this gap, by estimating a logit model over the period January 2002-June 2011, in which contagion variables are included showing the effects of trade and financial linkages and global or common shocks in the occurrence of the Turkish crises.

The remainder of the paper is organised as follows: Section 2 proposes some definitions of contagion, and discusses empirical papers dealing with contagion issues. Section 3 presents the data and the econometric model used to analyse contagion effects on the Turkish economy. Section 4 examines and discusses estimation results. Finally, Section 5 concludes the analysis by offering a summary and some notes for further research.

2. Contagion: Theory and empirical evidence

In the literature, contagion is basically defined as the transmission of economic and financial shocks from one country to another. Edwards (2000) asserts that contagion reflects a situation whereby the effect of an external shock is larger than that predicted by experts and analysts. For Dornbusch et al. (2000), contagion is defined as a significant increase in cross-market linkages following a shock to an individual country (or group of countries). A broad definition of contagion for the World Bank, similar to Dornbusch et al. (2000), defines it as a cross-country transmission of shocks or general cross-country spillover effects. Fratzscher (2002) defines contagion as the transmission of a crisis to other countries.

For present purposes, the important question concerns the channels through which shocks are transmitted from one country to another. For Dornbusch et al. (2000), the causes of contagion can be conceptually divided into two categories: spillovers that result from the "normal" interdependence among economies, which means that global or local shocks can be transmitted across countries because of their real and financial linkages, and spillovers that are related to the behaviour of investors or other financial agents. The first type of crisis propagation is generally called "fundamentals-based contagion" (Calvo and Reinhart, 1996), while the second type is often termed "pure contagion" (Masson, 1998), and is said to be caused by "irrational" phenomena, such as financial panic, herd behaviour, loss of confidence, and increased risk aversion.

The first factor that explains the so-called fundamentals-based contagion is a common or global shock, also called a "monsoonal effect" by Masson (1998), which can trigger market adjustments on an international level. A common global cause, such as major economic shifts in industrial countries, changing oil prices, changes in US interest rates and/or the occurrence of a crisis in an 'important' country, can trigger crises in other countries.

A crisis in one country can be transmitted to other countries via trade links. A major trading partner of a country in which a financial crisis occurs could also experience a crisis following speculative attacks, as investors anticipate a decline in exports to the crisis country, and hence a deterioration in the trade balance. Speculative attacks and capital outflows then lead to currency devaluation (Dornbusch et al., 2000).

Competitive devaluations can also explain the transmission of local shocks. Devaluation in a country reduces the trade competitiveness of the countries with which it competes in third markets, hence putting pressure on its competitors' currencies (Gerlach and Smets, 1995). It should be noted that the risk of competitive devaluations is higher if competing countries export similar substitute goods to third markets.

The last factor that explains the so-called fundamentals-based contagion is financial links. In this sense, a financial crisis in one country can lead to direct financial effects on other countries, in terms of credits and capital flows. A crisis in one country may induce investors to readjust their portfolios for risk management or liquidity reasons, and to reduce their now-increased risk exposure by selling off securities whose returns are positively correlated with those assets in the crisis country (Caramazza et al., 2004). This problem of selling off assets becomes more serious if there is a "common creditor" country (a term coined by Kaminsky and Reinhart, 2000). Suppose that there is a single common creditor country with a heavy regional exposure, such as Japan in East Asia. When financial institutions from this common creditor country suffer an important deterioration in the quality of their loans to a particular country, they may in turn sell off more assets related to other countries in order to restore capital asset ratios or rebalance risk exposures, thereby generating spillovers to other countries (Van Rijckeghem and Weder, 2001).

The second category of contagion is linked to investors' behaviour in the financially integrated world economy. Therefore, the spread of a crisis depends to a large extent on a country's degree of integration within international financial markets. As emphasized by Dornbusch et al. (2000), "the higher the degree of integration, the more extensive could be the contagious effects of a common shock or a real shock to another country". Of course, the actions of investors may be individually or collectively rationally related to fundamental causes, but this does not change the fact that their behaviour, rational or irrational, leads to the transmission of shocks to other countries. However, the literature differs on the scope of rational versus irrational investor behaviour, both individually and collectively.

Following Dornbusch et al. (2000), we distinguish three categories of contagion due to investors' behaviour. First, investors take actions that are individually rational but that lead to excessive co-movements which cannot be explained by economic fundamentals. This type of contagion results from problems of liquidity and incentives, as explained through the aforementioned common creditor argument.

The informational asymmetry and market coordination failures may also lead investors to make rational decisions. Let us suppose that investors are imperfectly informed about the fundamentals of an economy. In this context, it is easier and less costly to follow other investors considered well-informed about a country's economic conditions (Calvo and Mendoza, 2000). This herd behaviour of less-informed investors may also be explained by the existence of a large investor of the Soros type. Even if these outcomes are considered individually rational behaviour, they can nevertheless cause financial volatility or crises.

Contagion is also considered a consequence of a sudden shift in investors' expectations and confidence. Such shifts, normally related to economic and financial fundamentals, may play a role in provoking crises and their transmission to other countries (Caramazza et al., 2004). As stated by Goldstein (1998), a crisis in one country can serve as a "wake-up call", leading financial markets to reassess other countries' fundamentals. Note that countries with weak fundamentals are more prone to contagion effects resulting from a shift in investors' behaviour.

Empirical papers focusing on crisis transmission mechanisms have concentrated on the Mexican crisis of 1994, the Asian crisis of 1997-98 (in the early stages), and on the recent 2008 global financial crisis. What is concluded on the basis of empirical evidence concerning the relative importance of different shocks, transmission mechanisms and vulnerabilities? As stated by Chui et al. (2004), results are mixed, "varying with the way propagation channels are quantified and the measure of spillovers adopted"; they also vary according to the selected sample period and countries. However, some general conclusions can be drawn.

Eichengreen et al. (1996), Glick and Rose (1999), Fratzscher (2000), Hernandez and Valdes (2001) and Rigobon (2001) find that currency crises are generally transmitted by trade links. However, Kaminsky and Reinhart (2000) and Caramazza et al. (2004) state that financial links are more important than trade links in crisis transmission. For Hernandez and Valdes (2001), Van Rijckeghem and Weder (2001) and Caramazza et al. (2004), common creditor indicators are significantly associated with a higher contagion probability. Kaminsky and Reinhart (2000) also argue that financial linkages explain spillovers in emerging market crises quite well, while trade links are relatively weak. However, they note that "it is difficult empirically to differentiate between the impact of financial and trade linkages". This statement is also confirmed by the results of De Gregorio and Valdes (2000). Moreover, Rigobon (2001) indicates that common shocks like US interest rates also explain crisis propagation.

Furthermore, Glick and Rose (1999), De Gregorio and Valdes (2000), Kaminsky and Reinhart (2000) and Froot et al. (2001) find that contagion is primarily a regional phenomenon, particularly in emerging market economies. In other words, a crisis in a specific region, say Latin America, tends to affect more the countries of the region than other countries in the world.

Most of the aforementioned papers find that macroeconomic weaknesses provoke contagion, as countries with weak fundamentals become vulnerable to a crisis. In this sense, similarities in macroeconomic weaknesses across countries can lead to contagious currency crises because these signals may induce a shift in investors' expectations (Ahlumawia, 2000).

Recently, some empirical studies have been conducted, investigating the transmission channels of the global financial crisis. Dooley and Hutchinson (2009) evaluate how financial markets in emerging economies reacted to the 2007-08 US financial turmoil via an OLS model. In a sample of 14 emerging countries—including Turkey—covering the period from January 2007 to January 2009, they focused on 5-year CDS spreads on sovereign bonds and equity prices. They find that all 14 countries, with different economic and political characteristics, reacted quite similarly, as their CDS spreads rose and their stock markets collapsed after the bankruptcy announcement of Lehman Brothers. This study also shows that currencies in the sample countries recorded an appreciation against the US dollar after the subprime crisis in 2007, but experienced a sharp depreciation after the Lehman failure in September 2008. These results indicate the importance of financial linkages in the transmission of volatility from an advanced economy (the US) to emerging markets.

Balakrishnan et al. (2009) assess the respective roles of common and country-specific factors in the transmission of financial stress from advanced to emerging economies. To this end, they use a large sample, comprising 17 advanced economies and 18 emerging markets—Turkey included—in a sample period between 1997 and 2009. They run three different econometric analyses: an estimation of a common co-movement of financial stress across emerging markets and advanced economies, a two stage econometric analysis of monthly financial stress co-movement using a country-by-country approach, and an annual panel data analysis of determinants of financial stress. They find that stress in advanced economies plays an important role in determining stress in emerging economies. Moreover, the transmission of stress is quite fast, as it takes only one to two months to reach emerging economies. However, the strength of co-movement varies substantially across countries, depending on emerging countries' economic vulnerabilities (current account and fiscal deficits, foreign reserves) and on their trade and financial openness. Furthermore, they also find that financial linkages are more important than trade linkages in stress transmission, and that global factors like falling interest rates and commodity prices have a small mitigating effect on crisis transmission.

Morales and Andreosso-O'Callaghan (2010) propose an analysis of contagion effects in a worldwide framework (a total of 58 countries—Turkey included—aggregated under regional classification patterns). They focus on correlation and contagion effects, where the US stock markets are considered as the source of contagion. They use the GARCH models to test for contagion over the period from January 2003 to May 2009. Their results find no strong evidence supporting contagion effects derived from the US stock markets, but suggest that instead of contagion, markets suffered from spillover effects on a worldwide basis. They also show that emerging economies tend to be affected by contagion effects to a larger extent than the developed countries.

Aloui et al. (2011) examine the extreme co-movement of stock markets, for a sample composed of four emerging markets (Brazil, Russia, India and China; BRIC) and the US market during the 2004-2009 period. According to the results of GARCH and Value at Risk (VaR) models, financial dependency on the US is higher for Brazil and Russia—countries which are highly dependent on commodity prices—than for China and India, whose economic growth depends largely on exports of manufactured products. In other words, economic structure (here, the trade patterns) explains the extremity and extent of cross-market interdependences.

Baldacci et al. (2011) assess the determinants of sovereign risk in emerging markets by focusing in particular on spillover effects across emerging economies. They use spatial econometrics techniques to explore spillovers in the sovereign bond market for 24 emerging economies—Turkey included—during the period 1995-2010. They find that common or global factors, i.e., global risk aversion and liquidity, explain the spread dynamics in emerging markets. In addition to global factors, they find that spillovers from advanced economies to emerging markets (and also across emerging markets) have been developed in recent years via trade and financial linkages. Finally, they affirm that geographical proximity is important for the spatial transmission of shocks.

3. Model

In this section, we investigate empirically the role of macroeconomic fundamentals and the importance of contagion effects on the occurrence of the Turkish crises. We use the multivariate logit approach, since it directly evaluates the conditional probability of a crisis, given a set of indicators. It also summarises the probability of a crisis in one easily interpretable number (Abiad, 1999) and lends itself to standard statistical tests that evaluate the robustness of the estimation results. The estimated logit model takes the following form:

$$\text{Prob}\left(C_t \middle| X_{t-k}\beta\right) = F\left(X_{t-k}\beta\right) \qquad (4.1)$$

where the probability of a crisis $C_t = 1$ is estimated one or k step before the occurrence of a crisis, conditional on a given set of explanatory variables X_{t-k}. β is the vector of coefficients and F is a cumulative distribution function. The right-hand side of the equation is constrained to 0 or 1, and is compared to the observed value of the binary crisis variable C_t.

3.1 Identifying crises

Since the crisis is a discrete event, a latent crisis variable is constructed in order to identify crisis episodes. Some empirical papers describe currency crises as large depreciation or devaluation episodes (Frankel and Rose, 1996, inter alia), while others define currency crises as cases in which a currency comes under severe speculative pressure (Eichengreen et al., 1994, 1996, inter alia). The crisis index ISP, which is naturally the dependent variable of our model, is composed of monthly real exchange rate changes and international reserves changes, weighted by the inverse of their respective standard deviations.

$$ISP_t = \frac{1}{\sigma_{RER}}\left(\frac{RER_t - RER_{t-1}}{RER_{t-1}}\right) - \frac{1}{\sigma_{RES}}\left(\frac{RES_t - RES_{t-1}}{RES_{t-1}}\right) \qquad (4.2)$$

where $RER = \left(NER \times P^{*} \right) / P$,

RER = Real exchange rate,[2]

NER = Nominal exchange rate (TL/US$),

P^{*} = Consumer prices index US,

P = Consumer prices index Turkey,

RES = International reserves – Gold (in US$),

σ_{RER} , σ_{RES} = Standard deviations of the index components.

Any month is classified as a crisis episode if the index value exceeds a specified threshold equal to the index mean μ_{ISP} plus two standard deviations of the index $2\sigma_{ISP}$.[3] The crisis index then becomes a binary crisis variable, which takes the value of 1 if a crisis occurs and 0 otherwise.

$$C_t = \begin{cases} 1 \text{ if } ISP_t > 2\sigma_{ISP} + \mu_{ISP} \\ 0 \text{ otherwise} \end{cases} \tag{4.3}$$

[2] The real rather than the nominal exchange rate changes are used, in order to differentiate a currency crisis episode from a significant nominal depreciation due to a high inflation rate.

[3] Many modelers (Eichengreen et al., 1996, inter alia) use a crisis-window (or exclusion window) of a duration period of between 3-36 months. This means they discard a second (or subsequent) crisis observation identified by the crisis index which occurs within a given proximity to the first crisis. In other words, they define as a crisis not only the crisis month, but also the whole period of the crisis-window. Bussière and Fratzscher (2002) justify this approach by pointing out the difficulty of predicting the exact timing of a crisis, rather than predicting whether a crisis will occur within a specific time horizon.

Figure 4-1 The crisis index (ISP) and crises identified by the ISP at the threshold of 2 standard deviations[4]

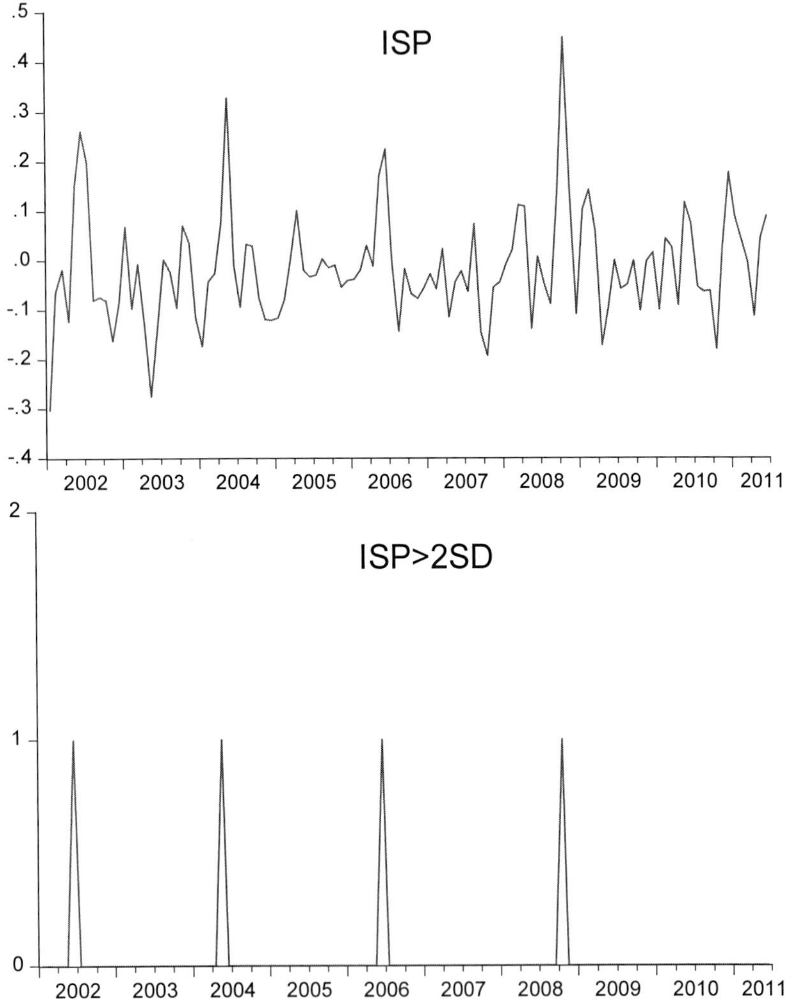

[4] Some may argue that the Turkish economy did not have four crisis episodes in this period, as indicated by the ISP index at the threshold of 2 standard deviations. We could correct this "problem" by determining the threshold level above two standard deviations, but this approach would result in losing these high pressure episodes.

3.2 Data

We use different macroeconomic and financial variables accompanied by contagion indicators. Most of the data are gathered from the Central Bank of Turkey, and completed with data from the IMF International Financial Statistics (IFS). The model is estimated by using monthly data for the period 2002:01-2011:06.

The selected explanatory variables, which are based on what prior theoretical and empirical analyses in the literature have suggested might be important, are presented in Table 4-1. Budget deficits have generally been considered as a source of vulnerability since the canonical model of Krugman (1979). In this sense, high budget deficits are expected to raise crisis probability, since they reduce available national savings and may lead to high inflation and interest rates.

An overvaluation of the national currency is also believed to raise crisis probability, since it leads to decreasing international competitiveness of a country as compared with its commercial competitors.[5]

Debt ratios and the maturity of debt are considered as one of the most important causes of recent financial crises (Chang and Velasco, 1999; Krugman, 1999). Therefore, the high ratio short-term foreign debt to international reserves increases vulnerability to liquidity problems, and hence raises crisis probability.

Financial vulnerabilities have also played an important role in the occurrence of recent financial crises. In the literature, different indicators representing financial fragility are used.[6] However, in the present study we construct an aggregated indicator that enables us to measure the impact of financial fragility on the outcome of the Turkish crises. This aggregated IFF indicator also allows us to lower probable co-linearity problems between different individual financial fragility indicators (Ari, 2012). The IFF is constructed as a weighted average of monthly changes in banking sector non-performing loans, in banking sector foreign exchange deposits, and in the money market rate. This index increases with a sharp growth in bank non-performing loans (measuring credit risk), a rise in bank foreign exchange deposits (measuring currency risk) and a significant rise in interest rates (measuring interest rate risk).

---

[5] Note that as an increase in the RER-hpRER indicator means a depreciation of the domestic currency, the expected sign is minus.

[6] See Ari (2010, 2012) for further information on financial fragility indicators.

$$IFF = \frac{1}{\sigma_{NPL}}\left(\frac{NPL_t - NPL_{t-1}}{NPL_{t-1}}\right) + \frac{1}{\sigma_{NIR}}\left(NIR_t - NIR_{t-1}\right)$$

$$+\frac{1}{\sigma_{RES}}\left(\frac{FXDepo_t - FXDepo_{t-1}}{FXDepo_{t-1}}\right) \quad (4.4)$$

where NPL = Bank non-performing loans,
NIR = Money market rate,
$FXDepo$ = Bank foreign exchange deposits,
σ_{NPL}, σ_{NIR}, σ_{FXDepo} = Standard deviations of the components of the index.

We take into account common or global shocks, trade links and financial linkages as contagion indicators. Changes in US interest rates are considered as a common shock that can trigger market adjustments on an international level. In this sense, the probability of a crisis increases in parallel to a rise in US interest rates, since investors would prefer to re-allocate their portfolios in favour of more stable placements. The domestic country may then record capital outflows and/or undergo a rise in external debt repayment costs.

Trade and financial spillover effects are represented by various indicators, as previous empirical studies have shown that the results are highly sensitive to how propagation mechanisms are specified and how crisis contagion is measured. In this sense, following Balakrishnan et al. (2009), in different logit estimations we use $Export$, $Export / GDP$, $Export + \mathrm{Im}port$ and $Trade$ variables for trade linkages, while we utilise $Liab$, $Liab / GDP$, $Liab + Asset$ and $Portfolio$ variables for financial linkages (see Table 4-1). The higher the degree of trade and financial openness of a country, the greater the crisis probability.

Table 4-1 Variables: definitions and sources

Variable	Definition	Source
ISP	Index of Speculative Pressure	Authors' calculations
Budget/GDP	General Budget Balance / GDP	CBT
RER-hpRER	Deviation of the Real Exchange Rate from Trend	CBT
SDebt/Reserves	Short-Term Foreign Debt / International Reserves	CBT
ISE	Istanbul Stock Exchange	CBT
IFF	Index of Financial Fragility	Authors' calculations
IUS	Nominal US Interest Rate	IFS
Export	Exports of Goods and Services	CBT
Export/GDP	Exports of Goods and Services / GDP	CBT
Liab	Portfolio Investments Liabilities	CBT
Liab/GDP	Portfolio Investments Liabilities / GDP	CBT
Export+Import	Exports of Goods and Services + Imports of Goods and Services	CBT
Liab+Asset	Portfolio Investments Liabilities + Portfolio Investments Assets	CBT
Trade	(Exports of Goods and Services + Imports of Goods and Services) / GDP	CBT
Portfolio	(Portfolio Investments Liabilities + Portfolio Investments Assets) / GDP	CBT

3.3 Model specification

The explanatory variables enter into the econometric analysis with a one-month lag (forecast horizon). The choice of a one-month forecast horizon may be inappropriate from the perspective of policymakers who favour a relatively long forecast horizon (from 12-24 months) in order to have enough time to take preventive policy measures. The sudden and brutal nature of currency crises nonetheless forces the researcher to opt for one-month lagged indicators.

Moreover, it should be noted that the forecast performance of the model is tested at 50%, 25% and 20% threshold levels. In fact, the forecast performance of an early warning system (EWS) model is measured through its ability to correctly predict actual crisis episodes. In order to evaluate the performance of an EWS, one compares the predicted probability of a crisis, typically produced by the EWS, with the actual crisis probability. As the predicted probability is a continuous factor, a necessary step consists in specifying a probability level (cut-off threshold) above which the predicted probability sends a signal, implying that the model expects an upcoming crisis at some point along the forecast horizon (Bussière and Fratzscher, 2002).

What then is the "optimal" threshold level? Choosing a lower threshold value would raise the number of correctly predicted crises, but only at the expense of increasing the number of false alarms (Type II errors). In contrast, choosing a higher threshold value would reduce the number of false alarms, but only at the expense of increasing the number of missed crises (Type I errors). The modeler solves this trade-off problem by defining a threshold probability according to the relative importance given to Type I versus Type II errors. As stated in Chui (2002), the modeler may naturally choose a cut-off threshold of 50%. However, as underlined in Esquivel and Larrain (2000), the sample is relatively unbalanced in favour of non-crisis periods. Therefore, choosing a threshold value of 50% would underestimate the predictive power of the model. This is why 50%, 25% and 20% threshold levels are used in order to evaluate the forecast performance of our model.

4. Estimation results

Our chosen methodology requires us to start with the study of the time series properties. As a consequence, we begin by performing unit root tests for explanatory variables, using the standard ADF and Phillip-Perron tests. The results of both tests confirm that all variables are stationary at level or in first differences. Other standard tests (descriptive statistics and correlation matrix) are also realised.[7]

Once these basic tests are conducted and the properties of the time series are clearly identified, we proceed by implementing the econometric analysis.

[7] In order not to extend the paper, these tests are not presented within its framework, but can be provided upon request.

As shown above, we use different sets of macroeconomic, financial and contagion variables. We estimate four different models that include different trade and financial contagion variables, along with the same macroeconomic and financial variables.

Table 4-2 Logit maximum likelihood estimations

Variables	Model 1	Model 2	Model 3	Model 4
DBudget/GDP$_{t-1}$	-13.7049	-23.2444	-14.0620	-15.3793
	(22.7854)	*(26.5502)*	*(22.6163)*	*(24.2781)*
RER-hpRER$_{t-1}$	-15.1623	-18.9447	-19.9189	-19.6641
	(10.8303)	*(12.8696*	*(13.0158)*	*(13.7350)*
DSDebt/Reserves$_{t-1}$	12.6476	17.3395	8.5134	20.0520
	(18.8957	*(18.9313*	*(16.6874)*	*(20.5575)*
DISE$_{t-1}$	-0.00010	-0.0011	-0.0009	-0.0010
	(0.0006)	*(0.0007)*	*(0.0005)*	*(0.0007)*
IFF$_{t-1}$	-6.6410	-10.3828	-9.3446	-7.1225
	(8.3242	*(9.9028)*	*(8.6661)*	*(10.2522)*
DIUS$_{t-1}$	9.3030*	13.0393*	10.8876*	11.0765*
	(5.5209	*(7.0957)*	*(6.5060)*	*(6.5401)*
Export$_{t-1}$	0.0001			
	(0.0004)			
Liab$_{t-1}$	-0.0007*			
	(0.0004)			
DExport+Import$_{t-1}$		-0.0001		
		(0.0003)		
Liab+Asset$_{t-1}$		-0.0011*		
		(0.0006)		
Export/GDP$_{t-1}$			42.2388	
			(121,7376)	
Liab/GDP$_{t-1}$			-176.2206**	
			(84.6236)	
DTrade$_{t-1}$				-19.5857
				(52.3868)
Portfolio$_{t-1}$				-214.49**
				(104.396)
Constant	-4.6364*	-7.1002**	-8.7551	-7.0597**
	(2.4772)	*(2.8506)*	*(7.6929)*	*(2.8565)*
Pseudo R^2	0.36	0.42	0.42	0.46
LR Stat	12.49	14.54*	14.51*	16.00**
Akaike Info	0.36	0.34	0.34	0.33

Notes: D before a variable indicates its first difference.
*Statistical significance at the 10% level.
**Statistical significance at the 5% level.
***Statistical significance at the 1% level

As illustrated in Table 4-2, none of the macroeconomic and financial variables are statistically significant in all four models. The variables $Budget/GDP$, $RER - hpRER$, $SDebt/\mathrm{Re}serves$ and ISE are correctly signed, but statistically insignificant. However, the IFF is neither correctly signed nor statistically significant.

These results are in fact quite surprising, but explicable. Tight fiscal policies implemented within the framework of the 2001 stabilisation programme achieved a relative fiscal discipline with high primary budget surpluses: budget deficits fell from 12% of GDP in 2001 to 3.5% in 2012. In this sense, budget deficits did not play a role in the occurrence of the Turkish currency crises over the analysis period.

Turkey also managed to reduce its public debt burden and to extend its maturity, in parallel with reducing inflation rates, increasing economic growth and lowering budget deficits, while the CBT's foreign exchange reserves quadrupled from 25 billion US dollars in 2001 to 110 billion in 2012. This is why the ratio of short-term debt to reserves cannot explain the Turkish crises that occurred over this period.

After the severe 2001 financial crisis, the Turkish authorities implemented key structural reform measures for the very vulnerable and fragile banking sector. "Bad" private banks were taken over by the Savings Deposit Insurance Fund (SDIF) and left out of the banking system. After that, they were recapitalised, merged and sold, mainly to foreign banking groups. Moreover, state owned banks were also recapitalised, and their governance structure was dramatically improved. Lastly, the regulatory and supervisory framework was radically improved by the establishment of a politically independent Banking Regulation and Supervision Agency (BRSA). In this sense, the restructuring of the Turkish banking sector has led to a strengthened and solid financial sector. Therefore, the Turkish crises were not caused by financial fragility during this period.

For contagion variables, US interest rates representing global shocks are correctly signed and statistically significant in all four models, like all variables representing financial linkages. Nevertheless, all variables representing trade linkages are correctly signed but are not statistically significant. In this sense, we can affirm that the transmission of shocks to the Turkish economy is generally realised through the financial channel, and global or common shocks have a significant impact on the occurrence of the Turkish crises.

Moreover, the logit models are quite robust, as the McFadden R^2 is above 40% and the LR statistical probability is below the 5% level.

Besides, the models perform quite well in predicting the Turkish crises in-sample, at 25% cut-off level (Table 4-3).

Table 4-3 Forecast performance of logit models

Cut-off level	Model 1	Model 2	Model 3	Model 4
C = 0.5				
% and number of Cor. predicted non crises	100% (108/108)	100% (108/108)	100% (108/108)	99.07% (107/108)
% and number of Cor. predicted crises	0% (0/4)	25% (1/4)	25% (1/4)	50% (2/4)
C = 0.25				
% and number of Cor. predicted non crises	98.15% (106/108)	96.3% (104/108)	95.37% (103/108)	97.22% (105/108)
% and number of Cor. predicted crises	50% (2/4)	75% (3/4)	50% (2/4)	50% (2/4)
C = 0.2				
% and number of Cor. predicted non crises	97.22% (105/108)	96.3% (104/108)	95.37% (103/108)	96.3% (104/108)
% and number of Cor. predicted crises	50% (2/4)	75% (3/4)	50% (2/4)	50% (2/4)

5. Conclusion

This paper has aimed to illustrate the role of contagion effects in the occurrence of the Turkish crises, during the period 2002-2011. The models show the importance of financial linkages in the transmission of shocks to the Turkish economy. Global shocks represented by US interest rates also play an important role in the occurrence of the Turkish crises.

The models show that even if the Turkish economy seems more stable in the post-2001 period, thanks to the large reform process implemented since the 2001 crisis, it still remains vulnerable to external shocks, as the May 2004, May 2006 and October 2008 events confirm. The economic growth strategy, which is heavily dependent on export earnings and short-term capital inflows, is the main reason behind these vulnerability problems. In this regard, reducing the dependence on foreign capital requires an increase in public and private savings, which might finance dynamic and sustainable economic growth. This transformation would also break the parallelism between economic growth and widening current account deficits, which are a source of vulnerability for the domestic economy.

Crisis risks for Turkey still exist, as the Euro area cannot find a way out of the sovereign debt crisis. The EU is currently Turkey's biggest trade partner (the EU represented about 40% of Turkey's total exports in 2012), and Turkey also has very close financial linkages with Europe. In this sense, the deepening of the debt crisis in Europe would surely affect the Turkish economy.

This case study complements the IMF's focus on surveillance of a country's vulnerabilities, through EWSs. However, there is still much we do not know about the spread of crises. As stated by Chui et al. (2004), further empirical research on the behaviour of international investors would help in assessing the likely future incidence of contagion.

References

Abiad, A.G. 2003, "Early Warning Systems: A Survey and a Regime-Switching Approach", *IMF Working Paper,* 03-32.

—. 1999, "Early Warning Systems for Currency Crises: A Markov-Switching Approach with Application to South Asia", *Mimeo,* University of Pennsylvania, Philadelphia.

Ahlumawia, P. 2000, "Discriminating Contagion: An Alternative Explanation of Contagious Currency Crises in Emerging Markets", *IMF Working Paper,* 00-14.

Aloui, R., M.S.B. Aïssa and D.K. Nguyen 2011, "Global Financial Crisis, Extreme Interdependences, and Contagion Effects: The Role of Economic Structure?", *Journal of Banking & Finance* 35, 130-141.

Ari, A. 2012, "Early Warning Systems for Currency Crises: The Turkish Case", *Economic Systems* 36-3, p. 391-410.

—. 2010, *Crises Financières Turques dans un Monde Globalisé: Développement d'un Système d'Indicateurs d'Alerte*, Saarbrücken: Editions Universitaire Européennes.

Balakrishnan, R., S. Danninger, S. Elekdag and I. Tytell 2009, "The Transmission of Financial Stress from Advanced to Emerging Economies", *IMF Working Paper,* 09-133.

Baldacci, E., S. Dell'Erba and T. Poghosyan 2011, "Spatial Spillovers in Emerging Market Spreads", *IMF Working Paper,* 11-221.

Berg, A., E. Borensztein and C. Pattillo 2005, "Assessing Early Warning Systems: How They Worked in Practice?", *IMF Staff Papers* 52, p. 462-502.

Bussière, M. 2007, "Balance of PaymentsCrises in Emerging Markets: How Early were the 'Early' Warning Signals?", *ECB Working Paper,* 713.

Bussière, M. and M. Fratzscher 2002, "Towards a New Early Warning System of Financial Crises", *ECB Working Paper,* 145.

Calvo, G.A. and E.G. Mendoza 2000, "Rational Contagion and the Globalization of Securities Markets," *Journal of International Economics* 51-1, p. 79-113.

Calvo, S., and C. Reinhart 1996, "Capital Flows to Latin America: Is There Evidence of Contagion Effect?", in Calvo, G.A., M. Goldstein and E. Hochreiter (eds), *Private Capital Flows to Emerging Markets after the Mexican Crisis,* Washington, D.C.: Institute for International Economics.

Candelon, B., E.I. Dumitrescu and C. Hurlin 2009, "How to Evaluate an Early Warning System?Towards a United Statistical Framework for Assessing Financial Crises Forecasting Methods", *Meteor Research Memoranda,* 10-046.

Caramazza, F., L. Ricci and R. Salgado 2004, "International Financial Contagion in Currency Crises", *Journal of International Money and Finance* 23, p. 51-70.

Chang, R. and A. Velasco 1998, "Financial Crises in Emerging Markets: A Canonical Model", *New York University Economic Research Reports,* 98-21.

Chui, M., S. Hall and A. Taylor 2004, "Crisis Spillovers in Emerging Market Economies: Interlinkages, Vulnerabilities and Investor Behaviour", *Bank of England Working Paper,* 212.

De Gregorio, J., S. Edwards and R.O. Valdes 2000, "Controls on Capital Inflows: Do They Work?,"*Journal of Development Economics* 63-1, p. 59-83.

Demirguc-Kunt, A. and E. Detragiache 1998, "The Determinants of Banking Crises: Evidence from Developing and Developed Countries", *IMF Staff Papers* 45, p. 81-109.

Dooley, M. and M. Hutchinson 2009, "Transmission of the U.S. Subprime Crisis to Emerging Markets: Evidence on the Decoupling-Recoupling Hypothesis", *NBER Working Paper,* 15120.

Dornbusch, R., Y.C. Park and S. Claessens 2000, "Contagion: Understanding How it Spreads", *The World Bank Research Observer* 15-2, p. 177-97.

Edison, H.J. 2003, "Do Indicators of Financial Crises Work? An Evaluation of an Early Warning System", *International Journal of Finance & Economics* 8, p. 11-53.

Edwards, S. 2000, "Contagion", *The World Economy* 23-7, p. 873-900.

Eichengreen, B., A.K. Rose and C. Wyplosz 1996, "Contagious Currency Crises", *NBER Working Paper,* 5681.

Eichengreen, B., A.K. Rose and C. Wyplosz 1995, "Exchange Rate Mayhem: The Antecedents and aftermath of Speculative Attacks", *Economic Policy* 21, p. 249-312.

Eichengreen, B., A.K. Rose and C. Wyplosz 1994, "Speculative Attacks on Pegged Exchange Rates: An Empirical Exploration with Special Reference to the European Monetary System", *NBER Working Paper,* 4898.

Esquivel, G. and F. Larrain 2000, "Explaining Currency Crises", *El Trimestre Economico* 67, p. 191-237.

Frankel, J.A. and A.K. Rose 1996, "Currency Crashes in Emerging Markets: An Empirical Treatment", *Journal of International Economics* 41, p. 351-366.

Fratzscher, M. 2003, "On Currency Crises and Contagion", *International Journal of Finance and Economics* 8, p. 109-129.

Froot, K., P. O'Connell and M. Seasholes 2001, "The Portfolio Flows of International Investors", *Journal of Financial Economics* 59, p. 151-193.

Gerlach, S., and F. Smets. 1995, "Contagious Speculative Attack", *European Journal of Political Economy* 11, p. 5-63.

Glick, R. and A. Rose 1999, "Contagion and Trade. Why are Currency Crises Regional?", *Journal of International Money and Finance* 18, p. 603-618.

Goldstein, M. 1998, "The Asian Financial Crisis: Causes, Cures, and Systemic Implications", *Institute for International Economics Policy Analyses in International Economics,* 55.

Hernandez, L. and R. Valdes 2001, "What Drives Contagion: Trade, Neighbourhood, or Financial Links?", *IMF Working Paper,* 01-29.
Kaminsky, G.L. and C.M. Reinhart 2000, "On Crises, Contagion, and Confusion" *Journal of International Economics* 51-1, p. 145-168.
Kaminsky, G.L. and C.M. Reinhart 1999, "The Twin Crises: The Causes of Banking and Balance-of-Payments Problems" *The American Economic Review* 89, p. 473-500.
Kaminsky, G.L., S. Lizondo and C.M. Reinhart 1998, "Leading Indicators of Currency Crises", *IMF Staff Papers* 5, p. 1-48.
Krugman, P. 1999, "Balance Sheets, the Transfer Problem, and Financial Crises", *International Tax and Public Finance* 6, p. 459-472.
—. 1979, "A Model of Balance of Payments Crises", *Journal of Money, Credit and Banking* 11, p. 311-325.
Lestano, L. and J. Jacobs 2007, "Dating Currency Crisis with ad hoc and Extreme Value-based Thresholds: East Asia 1970-2002", *International Journal of Finance and Economics* 12, p. 371-388.
Masson, P. 1998, "Contagion: Monsoonal Effects, Spillovers, and Jumps between Multiple Equilibria", *IMF Working Paper,* 98-142.
Morales, L. and B. *Andreosso-O'Callaghan 2010, The Global Financial Crisis: World Market or Regional Contagion Effects?,* MFA (Midwest Finance Association) Annual Meeting, February 24th-27th February, 2010, Las Vegas, Nevada.
Peduzzi, P. J. Concato, E. Kemper, T.R. Holford and A.R. Feinstein 1996, "A Simulation Study of the Mumber of Events per Variable in Logistic Regression Analysis", *Journal of Clinical Epidemiology* 49, p. 1373-1379.
Rigobon, R. 2002, Contagion: How to Measure It?, in Edwards, S. and J.A. Frankel (eds) *Preventing Currency Crises in Emerging Markets,* Chicago: The University of Chicago Press, p. 269-334.
Rijckeghem, C.V. and B. Weder 2001, "Sources of Contagion: Is it Finance or Trade?", *Journal of International Economics* 54, p. 293-308.
Rodrik, D. 2012, "The Turkish Economy after the Crisis", *Ekonomi-tek* 1, p. 41-61.
Saqip, O.F. 2002, "Interpreting Currency Crises – A Review of Theory, Evidence, and Issues", *German Institute for Economic Research Discussion Paper,* 303.

CHAPTER FIVE

EUROPEAN AUTOMOTIVE INDUSTRY: BEFORE AND AFTER THE GLOBAL FINANCIAL CRISIS

ADEM BALTACI
KIRKLARELI UNIVERSITY
AND HUSEYIN BURGAZOGLU
KIRKLARELI UNIVERSITY

1. Introduction

The 2008 global crisis, which started in the US housing market, and then spread to financial sector and the real sector, was considered to be "the crisis of the century" by the United Nations, and "the most dangerous financial shock the world economy has encountered since 1930s" by the IMF. The crisis has had a deep and severe impact over recent years. As the economic and financial interdependencies between countries through globalisation increased in recent years, the crisis rapidly spread to other economies, leading to negative consequences in many parts of the world. Europe experienced its share of these consequences, and such negative influences on both macro and micro indicators resulted in the triggering of the European debt crisis. This crisis, which touched economic, social and political life in Europe deeply, had a negative effect on all sectors of the economy, and on manufacturing sectors in particular.

For both developed and developing countries, the automotive sector holds a strategically distinctive importance as compared to many other sectors, in terms of added value and employment, and because of its close relationship with other sectors of the economy. A boom or depression in the automotive sector affects all other economic indicators in a country. From this point of view, revealing how the automotive sector (which constitutes one of the most important dynamics in the European economies) was affected by the crisis can offer a particular perspective upon an assessment of the impact of the crisis in the real sector.

To analyse the impacts of the crisis on the automotive sector, we take into account export level, the manufacture level of motor vehicles, automobile sales, the level of employment within the sector, and sector competitiveness. The sample countries are Germany, France, the UK, Italy, Portugal and Spain.

The paper is organised as follows. In the second section, we present a brief review of the emergence of the global crisis and the European debt crisis. In the third section, we examine how the European automotive sector has been affected by the crisis. Finally in the fourth section, we conclude by giving some remarks.

2. The 2008 global financial crisis

Financial crisis is not a new phenomenon. The severe crisis in 1929, also named the Great Depression, is the most striking example seen until today (Earle, 2009). After a period of relative stability in the post-World War II period, the world economy again became familiar with recurrent crisis episodes, following the collapse of the Bretton Woods system in 1971, which deeply affected many economies.

The recent global crisis, influencing not only a few countries but the economic and social structure of the whole world, has put the issue of "crisis" at the top of the agenda in academic studies. Actually, we need a profound analysis of crisis, because the crisis deeply affected not only countries' economic and social structures, but also the life of many people (Brandtner and D'Ecclesia, 2012). However, we should point out that in spite of many past studies, the nature of crises, and the reasons behind their outcomes, have still not been fully understood.

However, we can draw a rough framework for economic crises. At first, uncertainty begins to dominate the economy, which leads to a decrease in the demand for goods. Because of this decrease, investors' desire to invest diminishes. At the same time as the credit transfer from the financial markets to the private sector reduces, investment expenditures decrease further, leading to increasing unemployment rates. This context worsens demand conditions (Petrakis, 2012), resulting in economic recession.

Financial crises became more frequent following the collapse of the Bretton Woods system in 1971, in particular in emerging markets. Almost all of the developing countries experienced at least two financial crises in the period following the 1980s. Despite the relative decrease in the number of crises occurring in developed countries over this period, these countries still underwent several crises as well, at different times. For example; from 1850 to 2011, there were 10 crises in the UK, 11 in France, 7 in Germany, 12 in Italy, 12 in the US and 7 in Sweden (Lessig, 2012). In addition to these crises, the 2007-2008 economic crisis was considered to be the worst shock after the Great Depression, causing serious damage to the global financial system.

The first symptoms of the 2008 global financial crisis were seen from the atmosphere of panic that set in on the international markets, due to delays in repayments of mortgage credits in 2007. Following the case of Lehman Brothers, one of the most important actors in the mortgage-based investment market which went bankrupt in September 2008 (Lane, 2012), and the AIG, the biggest insurance company of complex financial products which was saved through state involvement, there was a great decline across the world financial markets (Yurtsever, 2011). The giant companies in the banking and investment sectors were heavily affected by the decrease in repayments, either directly or indirectly, and this led investors to question the shares of these companies. This provoked a chain reaction which caused these companies and their investors to suffer great financial losses (Petrakis, 2012). Hence, mortgage-based investments lost their value quickly, and this caused the collapse of financial system not just in the US but throughout the whole world (Yurtsever, 2011).

Thus, the crisis touched the real sector, as production structures both in the US and in the rest of the world were negatively affected. In order to rescue financially troubled institutions in the financial sector and to promote economic growth, central banks reduced interest rates and injected considerable amounts of cash into the markets (Comiskey and Madhogarhia, 2009). Although there was a serious monetary expansion, and interest rates were at very low level, there was no significant improvement in production levels, because of the negative expectations of manufacturing companies and the confidence problem. As a result, economic growth was seriously dampened, especially in developed countries (Grigorev and Salikhov, 2009). The GDP growth rate fell from 2.7% in 2007 to -3.2% in 2009 (Yurtsever, 2011). This economic recession led to a significant rise in unemployment rates during this period (Quiggin, 2009).

The global financial crisis, which started with the collapse of the mortgage market in late 2007, then turned into a serious economic and political crisis which threatened the European countries, particularly those in the Eurozone (Wyplosz, 2011). This crisis, emerging in early 2010, has threatened the euro, which is considered the second most important foreign exchange reserve in the world.

Structural deficiencies in the Eurozone can be seen as one of the most important factors in the occurrence of the crisis (Hopkin, 2012). With the foundation of the EMU and the transition to a common currency in 1999, the credit ratings of the EU members became stable. For example, Ireland's and Spain's credit rating rose to triple-A in 2001 and 2004 respectively. With the transition to a common currency, these countries' borrowing possibilities at low interest rates increased considerably. However, a strong euro penalised these countries, as their imports increased while their export revenues decreased substantially. Therefore, these countries recorded serious external and budget deficits. The theoretical and technical structure of the EMU did not authorise currency devaluation, which in the past had allowed countries like Portugal, Italy, Ireland, Greece and Spain (PIIGS) to maintain their competitiveness (Lane, 2012), which prevented them from correcting their imbalances. In this context, the borrowing strategy in the pre-crisis period became the only choice for the aforementioned countries, in terms of seriously increasing their debt ratios.

On its tenth anniversary in 2009, the euro was deemed a success, despite some existing problems within the Eurozone. However, the viability of the euro has now been called in question, as the debt problems of the aforementioned countries has greatly increased because of the bailing out of troubled financial institutions by monetary and fiscal authorities. Saving and nationalisation policies implemented by governments to decrease the impact of the financial crisis on financial institutions, and in particular on banks, have led to a sharp increase in public debt. This has caused a sovereign debt crisis in the Eurozone (Prinz and Beck, 2012).

In addition to bail-out efforts, almost all European countries implemented various incentive programmes in response to liquidity problems existing in international capital markets. These expansionary policies augmented more fiscal and debt problems for many European countries, particularly in PIIGS. Of course, debt problems for PIIGS are not solely related to their bail-out efforts, but also to their budget deficits (Jablecki, 2012). The European countries most affected by the 2008 financial crisis are the countries whose public debt to GDP ratios were already high.

The turning point, when the European debt crisis became a serious problem, was due to an increase in interest rates because of investors' confidence problems regarding debt repayments (Dietrich et al., 2011;

Overbeek, 2012) particularly for PIIGS, where interest rates were 4-8% points higher as compared with Germany and Holland. When the financial markets began to worry about repayment of existing debt stock, interest rates rose dramatically, which in turn worsened public debt dynamics (Schularick, 2012).

The unwillingness of some countries, such as Germany, to help countries experiencing serious debt problems deepened the crisis in the Eurozone further (Schularick, 2012). The German public authorities in particular (Ocal and Eren, 2012) emphasize that PIIGS countries should implement severe restrictions, such as important deductions in welfare expenditure and a decrease in wages, and also advocated more privatisation in education, health and retirement systems as a mean of exiting the crisis. These precautions are seen as an obligation not only for PIIGS countries, but also for other European countries like France, which has a significant debt burden (Yurtsever, 2011).

Furthermore, there is also an approach that advocates the necessity of dividing the Eurozone into different zones (Mundell, 2011). In that sense, reconstruction of the Eurozone seems a solution to the on-going debt crisis. However, this strategy should be seriously considered prior to being pursued, as it may signal the end of the EU.

3. The impact of the crises on the automotive sector in the EU

In the EU, the biggest motor vehicle manufacturer of the world, the automotive sector has a vital importance for growth, export revenues and employment. With an annual turnover of about 850 billion euros, a tax income of 378 billion euros, and an export volume of 77 billion euros, this sector is among the primary sectors in the European economies (Isac, 2009).

Companies in the automotive sector provide employment to about 2.3 million people around Europe. Moreover, it is estimated that the automotive sector provides employment to more than 12 million workers through relevant sub-sectors. This sector makes up 6.5% of total employment in the EU's production sector. Even though it represents a low percentage rate in terms of the number of firms (roughly 0.8%), more than 11% of the total production value is realised by the automotive sector. Figure 5-1 presents the relationship between the GDP of the EU countries and the manufacturing output of the automotive sector over the years. The close relationship between these two indicators is important, as it indicates the positioning of the automotive sector in the economy.

The automotive sector is closely related to many other sectors because of its nature. In terms of supply, related sectors include the following: electricity, electronics, information technology, steel, chemicals, and plastic. More than 20% of the steel and 30% of the aluminium produced are used in the production of motor vehicles (Anonymous, 2009). This correlated structure of the automotive sector with other sectors confirms its increasing importance in the EU countries' economies.

Figure 5-1 The relationship between GDP and the automotive sector (EU-25)

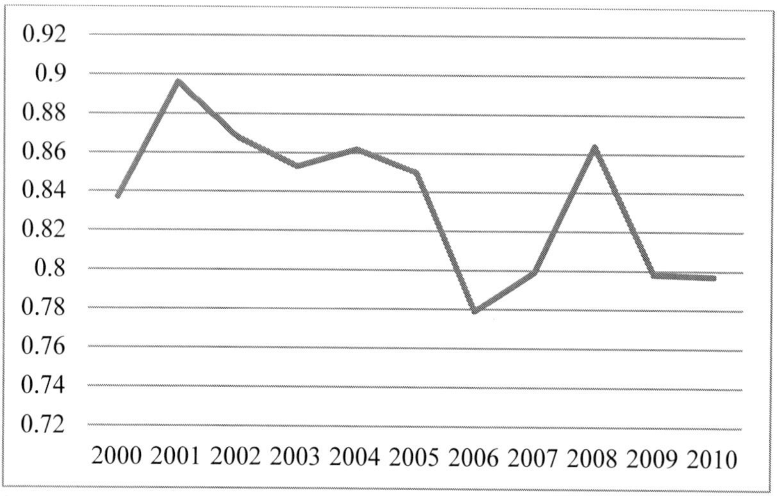

Source: Compiled using data gathered from Eurostat

We will examine Germany, France, Spain, Italy, Portugal and the UK, in order to see the impact of the crisis on the automotive sector. We will review export figures, manufacturing levels, car sales and the competitiveness of the aforementioned countries. The data is obtained from, the Eurostat, the United Nations Commodity Trade Statistics Database, the Organisation Internationale des Constructeurs d'Automobiles, and the European Automobile Manufacturers' Association.* The study covers the period from 2004 to 2011.

*As indicators of some countries such as Germany and Portugal are much higher or lower respectively, this distorts the interpretation of the figures. These countries are therefore shown in separate graphs.

3.1 Export

As a result of the economic crisis which started in late 2008, an important decline was observed in the market. The economic recession in the US, China and the UK, which are the most important export partners of the Eurozone countries, caused considerable stagnation in export levels (Hodson, 2012). However, as seen in the figures below, there was a considerable recovery in terms of export revenues in 2010 and 2011. It should be noted that Germany, the UK and Portugal were able to return to their pre-crisis levels.

Figure 5-2 Germany's car export revenues (in millions US$)

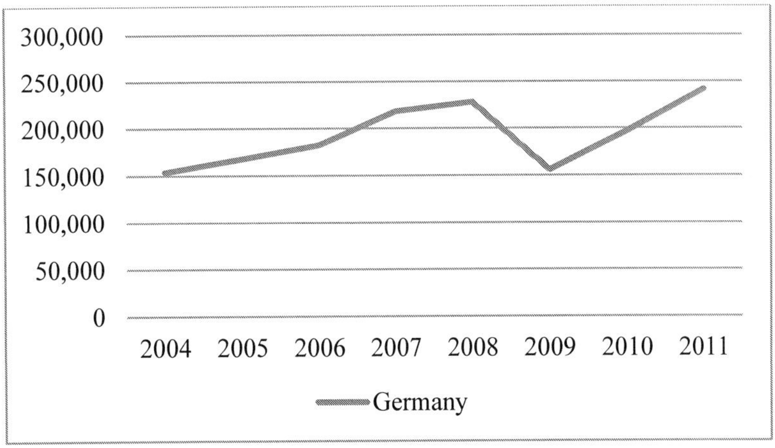

Germany, the leading country in the export of motor vehicles in the EU, experienced a severe decline in export revenues of over 30% in 2009, regressing to its 2004 levels. Yet, thanks to the implemented expansionary policies, it showed a quick recovery in 2010 and 2011 (Hodson, 2012), exceeding pre-crisis levels to reach 240 billion US dollars.

For other countries, the financial crisis had a similar impact: in terms of motor vehicle export figures in the UK and France, we observe a dramatic fall of over 30%; while the automotive sectors in Spain and Portugal seem to be less affected by the crisis, with a falling rate of about 25%. As in Germany, the sector recovered quickly in 2010, but only the UK automotive sector reached its pre-crisis levels, with export revenues of about 44 billion US$. For Portugal, a country with lower export revenues in the automotive sector relative to other countries, a similar process occurred: an increase up to 2008, a significant decline in 2009, and a quick recovery in 2011.

Figure 5-3 Car export revenues: France, Italy, Spain, the UK (in millions US$)

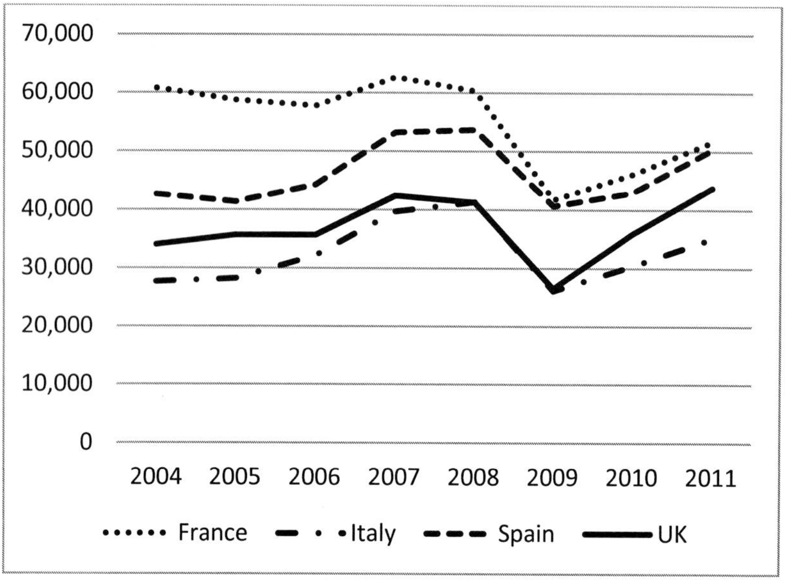

Figure 5-4 Portugal's car export revenues (in millions US$)

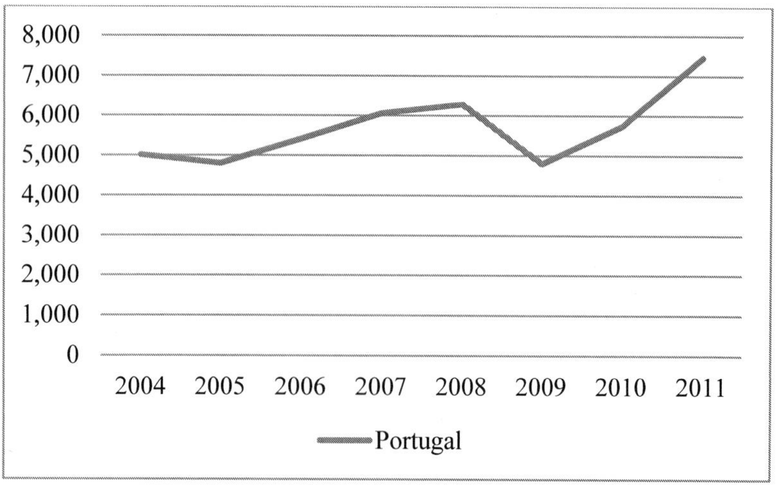

3.2. Production

Production in the automotive sector in the EU countries was also negatively influenced by the global crisis, as seen in the figures below. In Germany, production started to fall in late 2007, and reached its lowest level in 2009, with a decline of 17%. With a recovery in 2010 and 2011, the level of manufacturing rose to 6.3 million vehicles, bringing it back to pre-crisis levels.

The experience in motor vehicle manufacturing was not a heart-warming story for other countries, as it was for Germany. For example, in France and Spain, the deterioration started in 2004 and was accelerated by the impact of the crisis. Even if there was a slight increase in 2010 and 2011, production levels are lower than the 2004 figures. Moreover, the situation is similar for the UK and Italy. For the UK, production level seems to be more volatile, and for Italy, there has as yet been no recovery.

Portugal has also had a regression in its production levels since 2006. With the effect of the crisis, the level of production regressed to its lowest levels in recent years, but began to rise after 2009. Despite this notable increase, production has still not reached the level attained prior to the fall of 2006.

Figure 5-5 Germany's car production

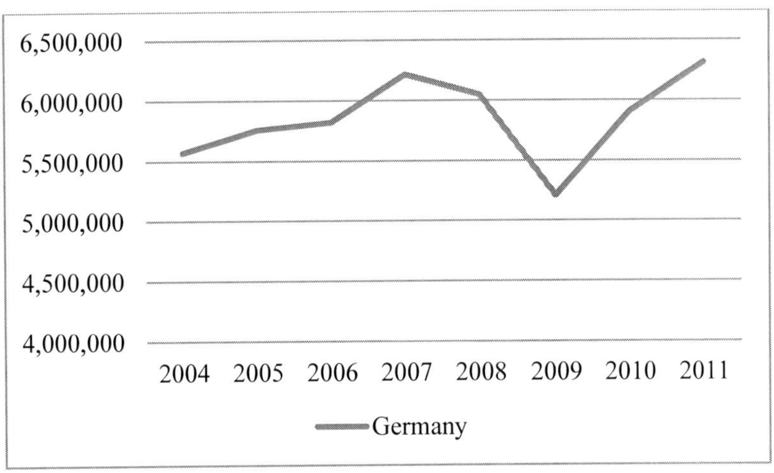

Figure 5-6 Car production in France, Italy, Spain, the UK

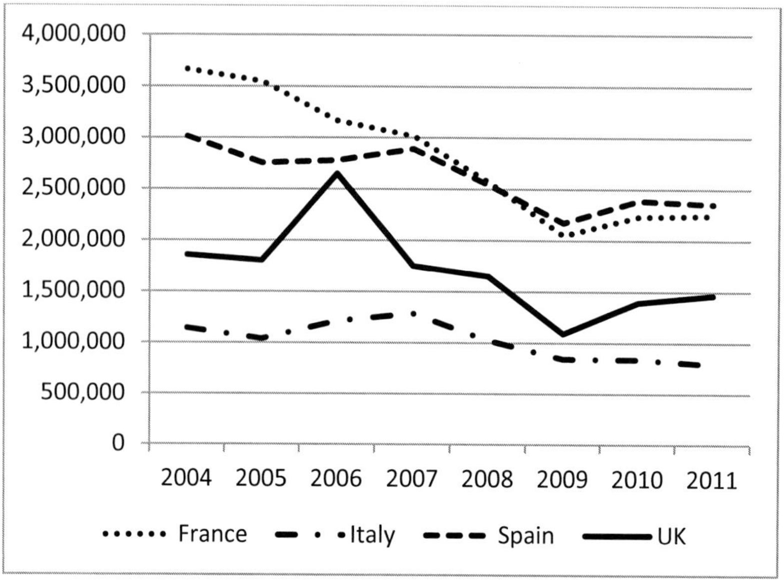

Figure 5-7 Portugal's car production

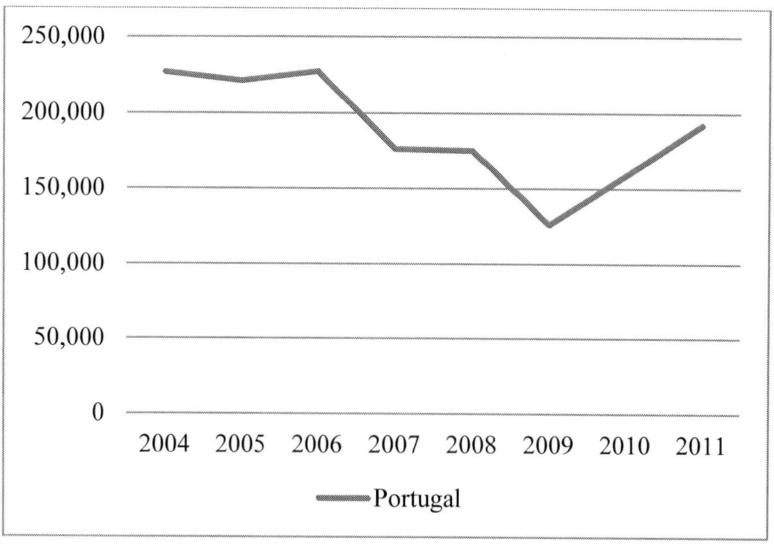

3.3. Car sales

Following the 2008 economic crisis, the sales of both commercial vehicles and passenger cars fell dramatically. In particular, with rising economic uncertainty and increasing unemployment rates, contractions in the domestic market led to an important decrease in car sales (Haugh et al., 2010; Lee-Makiyama, 2012).

The first of the countries significantly affected by the crisis was Spain, where car sales have been decreasing since 2007. By the end of 2011, car sales had regressed to 930.000, a fall of of more than 50% as compared with 2007. Similarly, Italy experienced a significant reduction in car sales (of 30%), falling down below 2 million in 2011. The increase in the cost of raw materials is one of the most important reasons for the fall in car sales in countries such as Italy and Spain, which are specialised in small and medium cars with a low profit margin (Lee-Makiyama, 2012).

France also felt the deep impact of the crisis in 2009 in terms of car sales. However, contrary to Italy and Spain, we can observe a recovery in 2010 and 2011. By the end of 2011, an increase of 25% was observed in car sales as compared to 2009 levels. On the other hand, unlike other countries, Germany experienced a significant increase in its car sales in 2009, due to some temporary precautions. Nevertheless, as seen in Figure 5-8, these precautions were short-lived, since we observe a significant decline (of about 22%) in 2010 (Grigolon et al., 2012). With an increase in 2011, figures began to return back to pre-crisis levels.

The UK had also been experiencing a decline in car sales figures since 2004. Besides a saturated market, difficulties in getting loans after the crisis worsened the situation (Haugh et al., 2010). In addition to the difficulty of obtaining loans under suitable conditions, other related costs led consumers to postpone their transactions.

In 2009, Portugal also had a notable fall of over 25% in sales figures because of the crisis. However, it recovered in 2010 and reached previous sales levels again. But this recovery was short-lived, as car sales fell back again, to below 2009 levels.

It should be noted that even if there was a decrease in car sales in Europe during the crisis period, the decline in American and Japanese brands was higher than those of the European brands. While sales of European car brands decreased at a rate of 7% between 2008-2010, American and Japanese car brands recorded a decline of 17% and 23.5% respectively (Lee-Makiyama, 2012). Moreover, even though there was a notable decline in demand for vehicles across Europe, especially in Spain, Italy, and the UK, increases were recorded in some countries, such as Finland, Belgium and Luxemburg (Isac, 2009).

Figure 5-8 Car sales in France, Germany, Italy, Spain, the UK

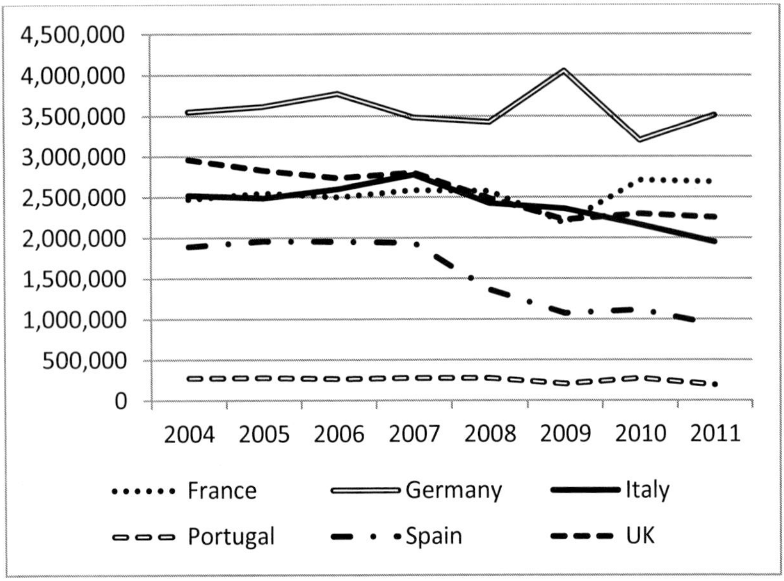

Figure 5-9 Car sales in Portugal

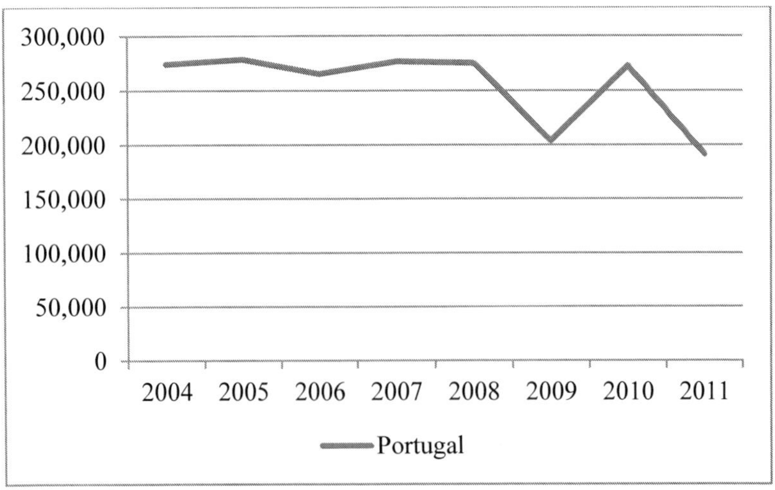

3.4. Employment

One of the most significant negative effects of the economic crisis was on employment in the automotive sector. In Germany, where the automotive sector is an important source of employment, there was a significant decline between 2007 and 2010. Employment in 2010 decreased by 12% as compared to 2007, reducing from 843.000 to 750.000. In 2011, we observe an increase of 5%, due to flexible wage policies implemented particularly after 2010 (Hodson, 2012).

In Spain, the decreasing trend in employment in the automotive sector since 2004 created a difference of 14%: employment levels fell from 163,000 to 140,000. The situation is similar in the French automotive sector, as the level of employment fell to 225,000, a decline of about 20%. However, the country most deeply affected was the UK, where the level of employment fell to 130,000, which represents a decrease of about 40%.

On the other hand, Italy and Portugal were the only countries which did not experience a decline in employment between 2004 and 2010. Despite a significant fall in car production, Italy preserved its existing level of employment in the sector, quite surprisingly, while Portugal recorded an increase of about 4% in 2008 and 2009. Policies followed by the Portuguese government to prevent unemployment rates rising are the main reason of this growth (Gorjao, 2012).

Figure 5-10 Employment in automotive sector in Germany

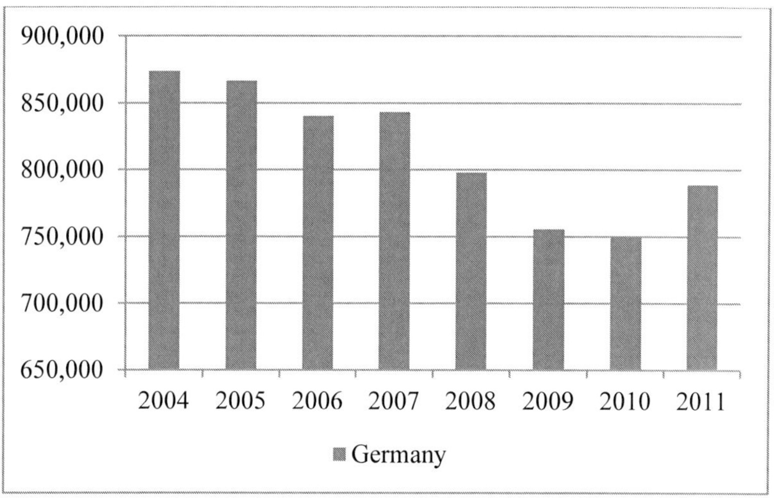

Figure 5-11 Employment in automotive sector in France, Italy, Spain, the UK

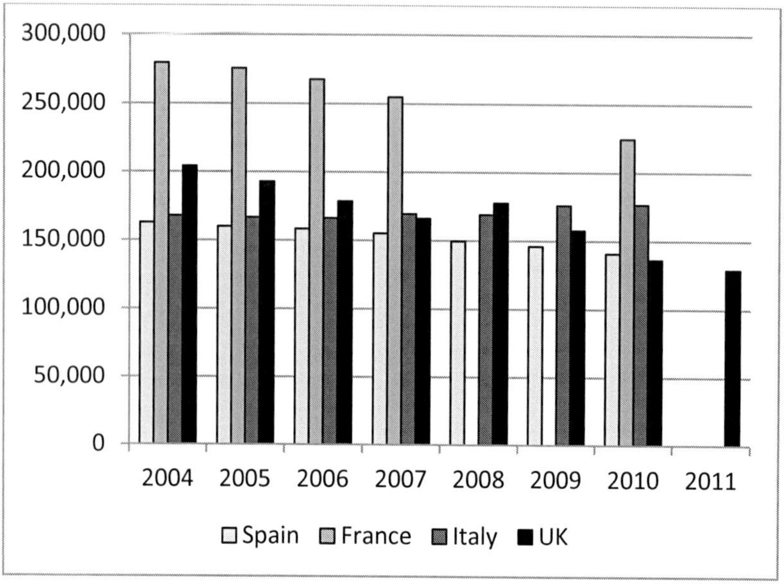

Figure 5-12 Employment in automotive sector in Portugal

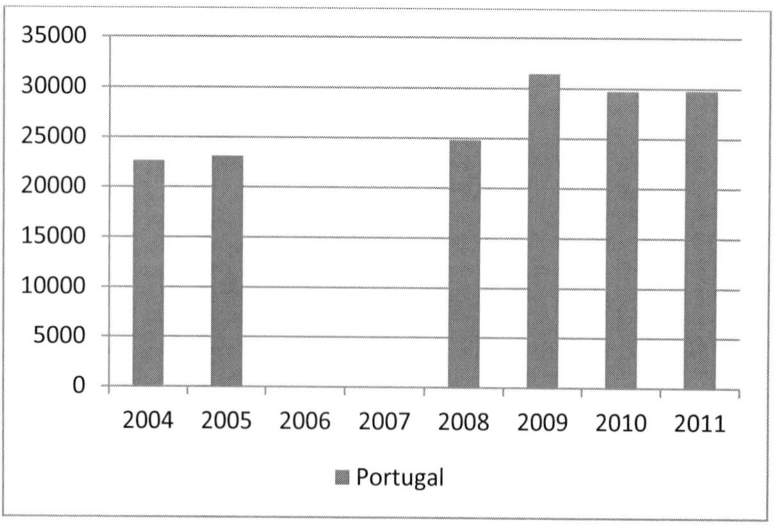

3.5. Competitiveness

The last field to be reviewed in relation to the automotive sector is the level of competitiveness. The competitiveness of sectors was determined using Balassa's RCA approach (Addison-Smyth, 2005). Balassa stated that the comparative superiority of a country in terms of a certain good or industry can be measured using an index that presents the proportion of the share of this good or industry in world trade in terms of its share of the country's total exports (Lee, 2003). Accordingly, the index is calculated as follows:

$$RCA_i = (X_i/X)/(X_{iw}/X_w) \qquad (5.1)$$

where RCA_i : Revealed Comparative Advantage for sector i

X_i : Country's export revenues from sector i

X : Country's total exports

X_{iw} : World export revenues from sector i

X_w : Total world exports

If $RCA_i > 1$, the country has a comparative advantage in sector i.

If $RCA_i < 1$, the country does not have a comparative advantage in sector i.

As seen in Figure 5-13, the crisis did not, in general, affect the competitiveness level of countries. In fact, during the crisis period some countries' competitiveness (Germany, Spain and Portugal) increased in the automotive sector. This surprising result is related to these countries' decreasing total export revenues: in fact, total exports in these countries fell more compared to exports in the automotive sector, which enabled the competitiveness index of the automotive sector to remain stable.

As indicated in Figure 5-13, Spain has the highest rate of competitiveness (of about 2.5). Its RCA index reached its highest point in 2009, before falling in 2010 and 2011. Germany also has a high and rising rate of competitiveness in the automotive sector. This result may be explained by large state investments in the automotive sector during the crisis period (Grigolon et al., 2012). For this reason, in spite of the severe global crisis, Spain and Germany recorded high RCA indexes in the period 2009-2012.

France is the one of the countries whose competitiveness in the automotive sector regressed during this period. The RCA index shows a permanent decline after 2004, falling from 1.58 to 1.17. Italy is the only country whose RCA index remained below the unity. This demonstrates that Italy does not have any advantage of competitiveness in the automotive sector. Even if the index recorded an increase before the crisis period, it fell back to 0.89 in 2011.

Figure 5-13 RCA index (France, Germany, Italy, Portugal, Spain, the UK)

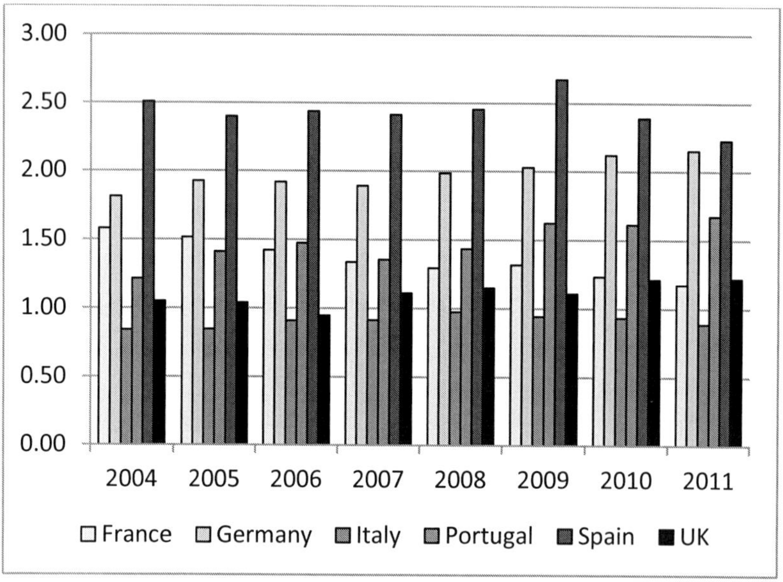

5. Conclusion

The global financial crisis that started in late 2007 in the US, and then spread to the whole world, is one of the most serious crises ever seen: it deeply affected not only the financial sector but also the real economy, particularly the manufacturing sectors; thus, unemployment rates increased dramatically

The automotive sector, being one of the sectors most highly influenced by the crisis, deserves a profound examination because of its central position in the economies of many countries. In the present study, we analysed the changes in the automotive sector via important sectorial indicators. According to our analysis, the global crisis seriously hit the automotive sector in Europe, as production and export levels fell radically during the crisis period. Even if some countries such as Germany experienced a quick recovery in terms of production levels in 2010-2011, France, the UK, Italy and Spain were unable to return to their pre-crisis levels.

The negative impact of the crisis was also observed in terms of sales of new cars. The reduction in car sales was higher in Spain, Italy and Portugal, as these countries were the most affected by the global crisis in terms of growth and employment. State aids and other implemented expansionary policies only induced a small and short-lived relief period.

However, the level of employment provided by the automotive sector was most affected in Germany, France and the UK, which are considered to have been less affected by the crisis, while there were few losses in terms of employment in Spain, Italy and Portugal. This difference is actually explained by the fact that these countries supported their production sectors by raising public debt ratios.

Surprisingly, the crisis did not have a deep impact upon the competitiveness of the automotive sectors in different countries, except in France, which recorded a very major decline (of 36%) in its RCA index.

In the period 2010-2012, we observe positive signs of recovery in all six countries' automotive sector, thanks to applied governmental policies. However, very small improvements in terms of economic growth, employment and private consumption threaten the EU's future. In this sense, the resolution of the debt crisis in Europe has taken on great importance.

References

Addison-Smyth, D. 2005, "Ireland's Revealed Comparative Advantage", *Quarterly Bulletin Articles*, February, p. 101-114.

Anonymous 2009, "Europe's Automotive Sector: Working toward Economic Recovery", *Foreign Policy* 174, p. 2-3.

Brandtner, M. and R.L. D'Ecclesia 2012, "Special Topic: Financial Crisis", *Review of Managerial Science* 6, p. 203-205.

Comiskey, M. and P. Madhogarhia 2009, "Unrevealing the Financial Crisis of 2008", *Political Science and Politics* 42-2, p. 271-275.

Dietrich, D., T. Knedlik and A. Lindner 2011, "Central and Eastern European Countries in the Global Financial Crisis: A Typical Twin Crisis?", *Post-Communist Economies* 23-4, p. 415-432.

Earle, T.C. 2009, "Trust, Confidence, and the 2008 Global Financial Crisis", *Risk Analysis* 29-6, p. 785-792.

Gorjao, P. 2012, "Portugal and Straitjacket of the European Financial Crisis", *Italian Journal of International Affairs* 47-4, p. 64-68.
Grigolon, L., N. Leheyda and F. Verboven 2012, "Public Support for the European Car Industry: An Integrated Analysis", *Centre for European Economics Research Discussion Paper*, 12-077.
Grigorev, L. and M. Salikhov 2009, "Financial Crisis 2008", *Problems of Economic Transition*, 51-10, p. 35-62.
Haugh, D., A. Mourougane and D. Chatal 2010, "The Automobile Industry in and beyond the Crisis", *OECD Economics Department Working Papers*, 745.
Hodson, D. 2012, "The Eurozone in 2011", *Journal of Common Market Studies* 50, p. 178-194.
Hopkin, J. 2012, "A Slow Fuse: Italy and EU Debt Crisis", *Italian Journal of International Affairs* 47-4, p. 35-48.
Isac, N. 2009, "Competitiveness and Strategy for Automobile Industry in Europe", *Annals of the University of Petrosani - Economics* 9-2, p. 51-56.
Jablecki, J. 2012, "The European Sovereign-Debt Crisis: Failure of Regulation?", *Critical Review: A Journal of Politics and Society* 24-1, p. 1-35.
Lane, P.R. 2012, "The European Sovereign Debt Crisis", *The Journal of Economic Perspectives* 26-3, p. 49-67.
Lee, S. 2003, "Patterns of Canada's Revealed Comparative Advantage in the United States", *University of Regina Discussion Paper*, 104.
Lee-Makiyama, H. 2012, "FTAs and the Crisis in the European Car Industry", *European Centre for International Political Economy Policy Briefs*, 02-2012.
Lessig, J.J. 2012, "What Do We Need to Bring about a Financial Crisis? A Long-Term Look at the Development of Banking Systems, Money Supply and Crisis 1850-2010", *European Review of History* 19-6, p. 899-923.
Mundell, R. 2011, "The European Fiscal Reform and the Plight of the Euro", *Poznan University of Economics Review* 11-1, p. 7-22.
Ocal, F.M. and M.V. Eren 2012, "European Debt Crisis and its Analysis", *International Research Journal of Finance and Economics* 97, p. 115-126.
Overbeek, H. 2012, "Sovereign Debt Crisis in Euroland: Root Causes and Implications for European Integration", *Italian Journal of International Affairs*, 47-1, p. 30-48.
Petrakis, P. 2012, *The Greek Economy and the Crisis Challenges and Responses*, Berlin, Heidelberg: Springer.

Prinz, A. andH. Beck 2012, "Fighting Debt Explosion in the European Sovereign Debt Crisis", *Intereconomics* 47-3, p. 185-189.
Quiggin, J. 2009, "Unemployment: The Coming Crisis", *Impact*, Winter, p. 8-9.
Schularick, M. 2012, "Public Debt and Financial Crises in the Twentieth Century", *European Review of History* 19-6, p. 881-897.
Wyplosz, C. 2011, "European Debt Crisis: What is the Way Out", *CASE Network E-Briefs* 4, p. 1-3.
Yurtsever, S. 2011, "Investigating the Recovery Strategies of EU from the Global Financial Crisis", *Procedia Social and Behavioral Sciences* 24, p. 687-695.

PART III:

MEASURES

CHAPTER SIX

EFFICIENCY OF THE FED'S MONETARY POLICY DURING THE GLOBAL FINANCIAL CRISIS

CEMIL ERARSLAN
KIRKLARELI UNIVERSITY
AND YUKSEL BAYRAKTAR
ISTANBUL UNIVERSITY

1. Introduction

Before the global crisis, market participants all over the world had a common opinion that financial crises were peculiar to the developing countries, due to their structural problems and implemented macroeconomic policies. With the exception of the European Exchange Rate Mechanism (ERM) crisis which occurred in 1992, there had been no serious crisis in the developed countries for 15 years. This case led to an increased confidence among investors in the economies of the advanced countries, especially in the US.[1] Due to its reputation as the most advanced economy in the world, among investors the US was considered as insurance against economic crises, and as a safe haven. Thus, in the first half of the 2000s, the US economy attracted intensive foreign capital from all over the world, particularly from China, Japan and the Gulf countries. These foreign capital inflows increased funds for financial institutions that

---

[1] Today Alan Greenspan, who was the chairman of FED between 1988 and 2006, is seen as the major figure responsible of the current financial crisis in the US, even if he was a legend among investors before the crisis. Investors hold the opinion that the US would not experience a crisis, or that economic problems which the US might suffer would be short-lived and temporary, as long as Greenspan was at the head of FED (Basti, 2008).

were redirected to mortgages on the one hand, and on the other caused inflationary trends in the economy, by increasing aggregate demand due to credit growth (Basti, 2009).

However, repayment on high-risk subprime mortgages remained well below expectations, and banks reported significant losses after rapid declines in housing prices. Eventually, all of these issues led to the occurrence of the August 2007 financial crisis. The crisis, which was triggered by declarations of bank losses, caused an increase in credit risk and then a banking liquidity crunch. Naturally, a panic in the financial markets affected the real economy in a short time, by causing a crisis of confidence (Reinhart and Rogoff, 2008). This panicked situation caused a bank run when depositors started to withdraw their funds from banks (Buiter, 2008), as monetary policies were not adapted to the crisis context.

Consequently, the US fell into a deep economic crisis in which real output and employment rates declined. Because of the central role of the US in the world economy, this economic crisis quickly turned into a global one (Reinhart and Rogoff, 2008).

The main reasons behind the global financial crisis are as the following (Buiter, 2008):

- Securitisation of mortgage funds by the financial institutions in an uncontrolled way.
- Incorrect assessments of rating agencies related to investment funds.
- Excessive increases in the debt levels of banks.
- Losses of private banks due to the inefficient financial intermediation activities.
- Regulation in loanable funds market and lack of supervision.
- Limits on the possibilities of finding funds due to the decline in liquidity levels of financial institutions.
- Persistent raising of the short-term interest rates by the FED and its insufficient funding of the interbank market.

Although there are many reasons for this economic crisis, inconsistent FED monetary policies played a dominant role. As a result of the monetary policy aiming at increasing interest rates over the period 2004-2008, a liquidity crunch occurred, due to inadequately funded financial markets. To face the crisis, the FED made a change to its monetary policy strategy by implementing a policy to reduce interest rates. However, despite such measures, due to the huge loss of confidence in the markets, the FED could not prevent the negative downturn in the financial markets that affected the real economy. The FED's inconsistent monetary policies deepened the crisis instead of preventing it. As a result, this led to an increased scepticism towards a loose monetary policy in times of crises which failed to exert enough impact to solve the crisis of confidence. Therefore, this FED experience gave rise to a new debate about the features that an active monetary policy should have.

The aim of the study is to discuss the effectiveness of monetary policies pursued by the FED in fighting the global financial crisis. To this purpose, Section 2 analyses those FED pre-crisis monetary policies that contributed to the occurrence of the financial crisis.[2] Section 3 addresses the components and the effectiveness of the FED monetary policy in fighting the financial crisis. Finally, Section 4 concludes by giving some indications about the features of an active monetary policy which could combat financial crises.

2. The pre-crisis situation: High interest rate policy and securitisation of mortgage funds

By raising policy interest rates in 2005,[3] the FED lost one of its main functions, i.e., funding financial institutions that have short-term liquidity problems. Furthermore, increases in interest rates pushed up borrowing costs in the interbank market, causing a failure in short-term cash obligations for financial institutions. Thus, the financial crisis occurred in August 2007 because of the liquidity crunch on the US financial markets. In this sense, the FED's high interest rate policy (Figure 6-1) may be seen as one of the main reasons behind the US economic crisis.

The economic recession between March and November 2001 in the US economy caused a sharp decline in asset prices. The terrorist attack on September 11, 2001, the failure of some of the biggest companies in 2002, and the invasion of Iraq in 2003 are considered signs of dark clouds hanging over the US economy at the beginning of the past decade. The Federal Open Market Committee (FOMC), in response to the recession in 2001, decreased interest rates from 6.5% in late 2000 to 1.75% in December 2001, and then to 1% in June 2003, as shown in Figure 6-1. Here, the FED aimed to increase bank loans to the private sector that

---

[2] See Tari et al. (2011) for detailed information on the causes of the global crisis.

[3] FED increased its policy rates which were 1.35% by the end of 2004 to 3.22% in 2005, 4.97% in 2006, and 5.25% in 2007.

would lead to increases in real output (Bernanke, 2010). This policy resulted in increases in economic growth, but created pressures on general prices. Consequently, until 2007, prices (particularly on the housing market) inflated in the US, causing a boom in the financial markets. According to Bernanke (2010), the expansionary monetary policy implemented by the FED to fight the recession in 2001 was a major cause of the bubble in the housing markets.[4] In order to prevent the boom becoming more significant, the FOMC raised interest rates again in June 2004, after the elimination of stagnation tendencies in the US economy. As a result, the FED's lending rates reached 5.25% in June 2006 (Bernanke, 2010). Although the FED's strategy of re-raising interest rates in mid-2004 is an important reason for the liquidity crunch, it is not the only reason.

Figure 6-1 The FED's target rate (1988-2011)

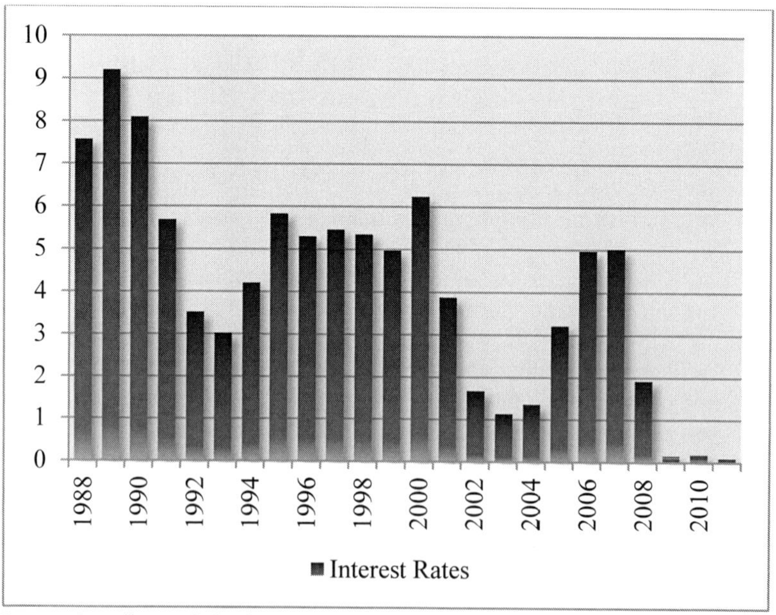

Source: http://www.federalreserve.gov/

---

[4] The most popular mortgage application at the US financial markets during 2003 and 2004 was the "Adjustable Rate Mortgage" (ARM). One-third of mortgage funds that banks sold to their customers in that period consisted of these ARMs.

Another important cause of the liquidity crunch in financial institutions is the excessive securitisation of mortgage loans in the context of inefficient supervision. In this sense, the rapid decline in housing prices in the US in late 2006 led financial institutions that purchased troubled funds to suffer huge losses. This negative period led to bank losses, increasing risks on credit contracts, and a liquidity crunch. An emerging panic and a loss of confidence in the financial markets affected the real economy in a very short time, in terms of real output, national income and employment rates. Therefore, both the level of mortgage securitisation and subprime mortgages stand out as important factors triggering the financial crisis (Reinhart and Rogoff, 2008).

Once the process is analysed, it is clear that the FED's inconsistent monetary policies in the 2000s played a major role in the emergence and spread of the financial crisis. Two main errors made by the FED stand out. The first is that the FED continuously increased policy interest rates during the period 2004-2007, in spite of the risk of a liquidity crunch for financial institutions. As a consequence, it became increasingly difficult to find cash and credit on the financial markets. The second critical mistake was that the FED allowed financial institutions to massively lend mortgage loans without taking into account equity and deposit structures. This policy caused an "excessive securitisation" phenomenon, increasing risky investments in the US financial markets. As the rate of return on granted credits (non-performing loans) was lower than expected, as in August 2007, financial institutions could not rollover their mortgage-based debts, and a financial crisis broke out. This led to a panic, which caused a crisis of confidence: depositors started to withdraw their deposits from banks, and there was a great fall in stock market indexes.

3. The FED's monetary policy to fight the financial crisis

When the crisis broke out, the FED first tried to act in accordance with Taylor Rule and inflation targets. However, it had to implement an active expansionary monetary policy after the panic, which was caused by lack of liquidity in financial markets. In doing so, the liquidity crunch was significantly compensated for by an increase in money supply (Selge et al., 2010). In this context, policy interest rates were reduced from 5.25% in late 2007 to 2% in 2008. Through the expansionary monetary policy, the FED aimed to provide liquidity to the financial sector and to increase aggregate demand. On the other hand, the FED improved bank lending standards, in order to avoid problems related to non-performing loans in the financial markets (Hampel et al., 2009). However, in spite of low interest rates, confidence problems in the markets massively increased the risk of debt instruments after September 2007, as the risk premium of corporate bonds increased to approximately 200 basis points. Therefore, the abnormal increases in risk premiums compensated for the decline in interest rates. Furthermore, an increased risk rate on the markets led to banks and other financial intermediaries tightening their lending conditions (Mishkin, 2009).

Figure 6-2 shows the interest, unemployment and inflation rates in the US between 1988 and 2011. As seen in Figure 6-2, the FED mainly used interest rates to overcome the recession episodes by reducing targeted interest rates in 1991, 2001 and 2008. By doing so, the FED aimed to stop increases in unemployment rates by stimulating real growth. Declines in interest rates led to decreases in unemployment rates during the 1991 and 2001 recessions, but not during the financial crisis of 2007-2009. For instance, in 2007, interest rates and unemployment rates were in the 4-6% bracket, while in 2009 interest rates were set to zero, unemployment rates reached the level of 10%, and inflation rates were below 0% (Rudebuch, 2009). In this sense, we can claim that a loose monetary policy might not reduce unemployment by increasing real production.

During the global financial crisis, which led to a major economic collapse, the FOMC found that the FED's policy rate of 0% was insufficient, and proposed to mobilise all monetary policy instruments to help the economy to recover. In addition to the changes in traditional monetary policy instruments, it made changes in the structure and size of its balance sheets by purchasing troubled financial assets, which created a moral hazard problem in the markets. Moreover, the FED developed its relationship with the markets by creating a more transparent communication strategy. These moves comforted firms and households, and oriented their expectations towards the monetary policy objectives (Rudebuch, 2009).

Expansionary monetary policy implemented by the FED to fight the financial crisis moderately decreased both credit and macroeconomic risk by lowering interest rates. If the FED had applied a tight monetary policy during the financial crisis, consumption and investment spending would have decreased, causing a more severe contraction in economic activity. Moreover, increases in interest rates would have made the estimation of the real asset value more difficult, and both valuation and macroeconomic risk would have increased, resulting in a greater economic contraction. In this sense, monetary policies followed by the FED during the financial crisis were appropriate, and helped to reduce the negative effects of the financial crisis (Mishkin, 2009).

Figure 6-2 Unemployment rates, inflation rates and target Federal fund rate in the US (1988-2011)

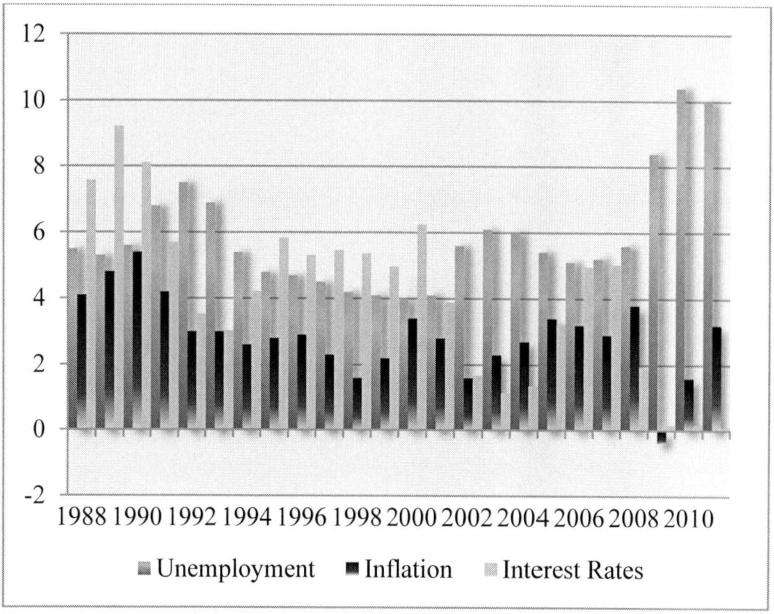

Source: http://www.federalreserve.gov/

During the global crisis, the FED made a transition to a monetary policy strategy based on balance sheet size with changes in compositional structure, as the global financial crisis led the central banks to face problems other than those in the standard areas of monetary policy theory. In general, the most operational monetary policy instrument used to influence the markets is short-term interest rates. However, as lowering interest rates proved totally insufficient for providing financial stability, the FED's attention turned to other monetary policy instruments. During the period of widespread instability, the FED provided liquidity to the markets by increasing demand for financial assets. In this context, it can be stated that the FED's expansionary credit policy (purchasing mortgage-based troubled assets) was relatively efficient in helping to ensure a relative financial stability. In this sense, to reduce economic stagnation, the FED used direct purchase and repurchase transactions through open market operations, and these expanded the FED's obligations to a great extent (Curdia and Woodford, 2010).

With the deepening of the economic crisis, the FED developed new funding tools such as TAF (Term Auction Facility), PDCF (Primary Dealer Credit Facility) and TSLF (Term Securities Lending Facility), in addition to more traditional monetary policy tools. TAF provided an early debt payment opportunity for commercial banks, and thus gave them a chance to win back an early payment discount. In this way, TAF opened up an opportunity to eliminate the problematic funds. As for PDCF, it led to a decrease in banks' liquid funds congestion, after the FED purchased commercial bank debt from investment banks. Finally, with TSLF, it became easier for investment banks to purchase treasury bonds and mortgage-based securities on the secondary market. With this attempt, the FED helped the government to borrow more easily from the financial markets and boosted demand in the second hand mortgage market. In fact, by facilitating these new funds, the FED formally accepted securitised mortgage-based funds and declared that it would match these funds with treasury bills. The credit programmes implemented by the FED to reduce the impact of the economic crisis are the following (Cecchetti, 2008):

- 100 billion US$ for TAF.
- 100 billion US$ for 28-day repurchase agreements for mortgage-based assets.
- 200 billion US$ for TSLF.
- 36 billion US$ for foreign exchange swaps.
- 30 billion US$ for PDCF.
- 29 billion US$ for supporting the sale of Bear Stearns.

The FED injected the largest amount of credit in October 2008, when 300 billion dollars of credit was released through the CPFF (Commercial Paper of Financial and non-Financial Corporation) programme. With the CPFF programme, the FED aimed to facilitate the purchasing of securities. Another radical measure taken by the FED was to give financial support to rescue operations of the Treasury in November 2008 and January 2009 for Citigroup and Bank of America. In this way, for the first time in its history, the FED participated in a rescue operation directly. While the Treasury Department was opening up 15 billion dollars of long-term credit to Citigroup and Bank of America, the FED made a commitment to purchase the unsold troubled assets which had been put on the market by banks. Therefore, we can say that the FED used its monetary policy in combating the economic crisis by increasing the credit supply and expanding liquidity provisions (Kuttner, 2009).

The FED's expansionary monetary policy practices, implemented during the 2008 crisis (reducing interest rates[5] and purchasing financial assets through open market operations), increased its total reserves (800 billion USD). This reflects the significant amount of asset acquisitions in the financial markets. However, a large part of these financial assets were composed of "toxic assets" that led to the expansion of FED's debt to the markets (Kuttner, 2009).

Figure 6-3 Interest rates and the FED's total reserves

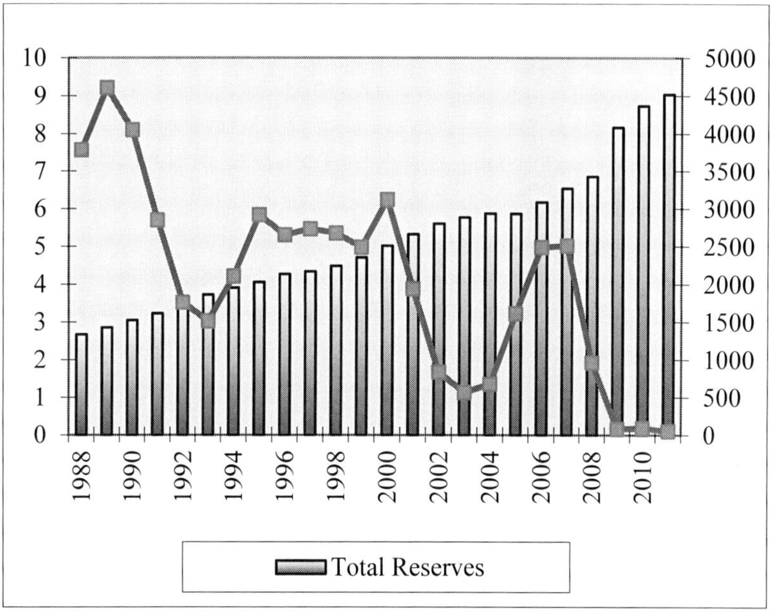

Source: http://www.federalreserve.gov/

When buying troubled assets from financial markets, the FED utilised two major programmes, TARP (Troubled Asset Relief Programme) and TALF (Term Asset-Backed Securities Loan Facility). Using the TARP programme introduced on 3 October 2008, the FED purchased troubled financial assets valued at 700 billion US$ and, under the TALF programme announced on 17 March 2009, it purchased consumer bank loans valued at 200 billion US$ (Tarr, 2009).

[5] The FED reduced its policy rates from 5.02% in 2007 to 1.92% in 2008, 0.16% in 2009, and 0.18% in 2010.

As shown in Table 6-1, the FED's total reserve assets increased from 880.4 billion US$ to 2058.4 billion US$, in the period 2007-2009. This rise is a result of the loose monetary policy followed by the FED in order to increase the liquidity level in the financial markets, by pulling foreign exchange and gold from the market with open market operations and by increasing the supply of loanable funds. This expansion led to a rise in the FED's gold and foreign exchange reserves, from 59.3 billion US$ in 2007 to 1026.1 billion US$ in 2009. During the same period, direct loans (primary credits) went up to 66.5 billion US$, term auction credit rose to 371.3 billion US$, and Primary Dealer Credits increased to 33.4 billion US$. Therefore, as previously highlighted, the FED attempted to expand the aggregated demand in order to solve the crisis by taking steps to increase the volume of liquidity in the economy. However, the dimensions of the economic crisis that spilled over outside US borders required some additional measures, as well as those measures taken within the country. The FED therefore chose to make a number of agreements with the central banks of the other countries.

The FED made swap extension agreements with the ECB and the Bank of Sweden to fight the global crisis. The purpose of these agreements was to establish a link between the financial system and the central bank balance sheets through the aforementioned measures. The FED identified two key objectives, related to the management of assets and liabilities on central banks' balance sheets: the first was to control the balance sheets of financial institutions; the second was to keep the financial institutions' asset composition under control. In connection with these objectives, the FED kept foreign exchange reserves, short-term debt, public papers and gold reserves of financial institutions under supervision over a certain period of time (Cecchetti, 2008).

However, in spite of all these measures, the problems of some banks could not be fully solved. The popular term "zombie banks" has recently been used to describe such banks. This situation also raises the following question: if the FED had implemented a different monetary policy, would the current economic situation be better? The answer is definitely "no", because the size of the liquidity shortage in the economy made it necessary for the FED to inject liquidity into financial markets by purchasing assets. Nevertheless, when the particular problems of a number of financial institutions are put aside, it can be seen that injecting liquidity into financial markets through the FED funding policy managed to reduce market fever and prevented the financial crisis from deepening further (Kling, 2010).

Table 6-1 FED's total reserve assets (in billionUS$, 2007-2009)

	July 4, 2007	Jan. 2, 2008	March 19, 2008	Oct. 24, 2008	Jan. 14, 2009
Securities					
Held Outright	790.6	740.6	660.5	486.6	505.3
Re-Purchase Agreements	30.3	56.3	62	86	40
Loans					
Primary Credits	0.2	4.9	0.12	39.3	66.5
Term Auction Credit		40	80	262.3	371.3
Primary Dealer Credit			28.8	105.7	33.4
Asset-backed Commercial Paper (ABCP)				72.7	16.1
Other Credit Extension Agreements				44.6	0
Other Assets and Reserves (including Foreign Reserves and Gold Reserves)	59.3	84	49.3	116.7	1026.1
Total Reserves	880.4	925.7	890.7	1213.9	2058.4

Source: Furceri and Mourougane (2009)

Although this new FED strategy to fight the economic crisis revitalised the functions of the financial system, purchasing unsold financial institution securities imposed large costs on taxpayers. In fact, the FED financed banks in lack of liquidity, due to inappropriate investment decisions. As the FED's sources are based on taxes paid by American citizens, it can be seen that large sections of US society actually carried the burden and the cost of the crisis. However, depositors and taxpayers did not display a negative reaction to the transfer of public resources to financial institutions, given the extraordinary terms of the crisis. On the contrary, financial rescue operations carried out by the FED and the Treasury were rather welcomed, in the hope of re-normalising the economy (Kling, 2010).

4. Conclusion

In 2001, the expansionary monetary policy implemented by the FED to overcome the recession led to mortgage funds becoming attractive, and this later became a major cause of the housing bubble. However, in the subsequent period (2004-2007), this expansionary monetary policy was followed by a contrary and restrictive policy, where deposit structures created an "over-securitisation" phenomenon. These policy inconsistencies led to the outbreak of the financial crisis.

To exit the financial crisis, the first step taken by the FED was to give up the tight monetary policy in favour of an expansionary one, in order to provide liquidity to the financial sector and to expand aggregate demand. However, the crisis of confidence that emerged after the financial crisis increased the size of risk premiums, and absorbed the positive results of the expansionary monetary policy. In order to resolve the crisis of confidence, the FED purchased the assets of troubled financial institutions. Moreover, the FED also used other unconventional methods, like the direct transfer of funds, bankruptcy protection and expropriation, in order to eliminate the crisis of confidence. Indeed, the FED gave financial support to the rescue operations of Citigroup and Bank of America; it transferred resources to Bear Stearns, Freddy Mac and Fannie Mae; it mediated bankruptcy protection of Lehman Brothers and expropriation of the insurance company AIG. All the measures taken by the FED in the context of the economic crisis aimed to eliminate the atmosphere of panic in the financial markets, by positively changing economic agents' expectations.

As a result, one can affirm that the FED prevented a further deepening of the crisis in the US financial system, with the help of these traditional and unconventional policies, after 2008. However, these policies have led to an increase in troubled assets and liabilities for the FED.

With reference to the FED experience, the necessary requirements for monetary policies in crisis resolution, management and prevention are as follows:

- Keeping short-term policy rates at low levels to provide liquidity.
- Increasing the deposit insurance and lowering re-discount rates.

- Effective monitoring of the financial system.
- Re-regulating the financial system.
- Introducing restrictions for securitisation.
- Putting financial institutions' re-purchase agreements under control.
- Preventing excessive borrowing by closely monitoring bank balance sheets.
- Purchases of troubled assets by central banks.
- An international coordination of monetary policies with other central banks.

References

Basti, E. 2009, "2008 Global Financial Crisis and the Turkish Financial System", *Ç.Ü. Sosyal Bilimler Enstitüsü Dergisi* 18-2, p. 89-103.

Bernanke, B.S. 2010, "Monetary Policy and the Housing Bubble", *Speech at the Annual Meeting of the American Economic Association*, Atlanta, January 3.

Buiter, W. 2008, "Lessons from North Atlantic Financial Crisis", in Felton, A. and C. Reinhart (eds), *The First Global Financial Crisis of the 21st Century,* London: VoxEU and Centre for Economic Policy Research, p. 129-131.

Cecchetti, S.G. 2008,"Federal Reserve Policy Responses to the Crisis of 2007–8: A Summary", in Felton, A. and C. Reinhart (eds), *The First Global Financial Crisis of the 21st Century,* London: VoxEU and Centre for Economic Policy Research, p.113-115.

Curdia, V. and M. Woodford 2010, "The Central-Bank Balance Sheet as an Instrument of Monetary Policy", *NBER Working Paper,* 16208.

Furceri D. and A. Mourougane 2009, "Financial Crises: Past Lessons and Policy Implications", *OECD Economics Department Working Paper,* 668.

Hampel, B., M. Schenk and S. Rick 2009, "The U.S. Mortgage Crisis Causes, Effects and Outlook Including Suggested Credit Union Responses", *Credit Union National Association,* January.

Kling, A. 2010, "The Case for Auditing the FED is Obvious", *CATO Institute Briefing Paper,* 118.

Kuttner, K.N. 2009, "The Fed's Response to the Financial Crisis: Pages from the BOJ Playbook, or a Whole New Ball Game?", *Columbia University Center on Japanese Economy and Business Working Paper,* 282.

Mishkin, F.S. 2009, "Is Monetary Policy Effective during Financial Crises?",*NBER Working Paper,* 14678.

Reinhart, C.M. and K.S. Rogoff 2008, "Is the 2007 U.S. Sub-Prime Financial Crisis So Different? An International Historical Comparison", *NBER Working Paper,* 13761.

Rudebuch, G.D. 2009, "The Fed's Monetary Policy Response to the Current Crisis", *FRBSF Economic Letter,* 2009-17.

Selgin, G., W.D. Lastrapes and L.H. White 2010, "Has the FED Been a Failure", *CATO Institute Working Paper,* 2.

Tari, R., C. Eraslan and Y. Bayraktar 2011, "Küresel Ekonomik Kriz ve Belirleyicileri Üzerine Bir Değerlendirme", in Çetinkaya, M. (ed), *Küresel Ekonomik ve Finansal Kriz,* Ankara: Nobel Kitabevi, p. 7-27.

Tarr, D.G. 2009, "Bailouts and Deficits or Haircuts: How to Restore U.S. Financial Market Stability", http://ssrn.com/abstract=1401555.

CHAPTER SEVEN

A NOTE ON THE NEW MONETARY POLICY OF THE CENTRAL BANK OF TURKEY

FATIH OZATAY
TOBB UNIVERSITY OF ECONOMICS AND TECHNOLOGY AND TEPAV

1. Introduction

Starting from the 1980s up to the global crisis, an important number of central banks primarily focused on price stability. In the aftermath of the collapse of Lehman Brothers and the financial turmoil that followed, this policy framework has been criticised for ignoring financial stability and for failing to react to asset price bubbles. It is now widely admitted that in addition to price stability, monetary policy should also focus on financial stability. If so, the following questions arise: How can a new monetary policy framework be designed with these two final aims? What should the policy tools be? What should the new institutional setup be?

Consequently, a new literature that aims to answer these questions has emerged. Most of these studies take inflation targeting as their starting point, and seek to extending this regime to incorporate financial stability as well (see, among others, Bailliu et al., 2012; Glocker and Towbin 2012; Woodford, 2012). While some of these studies analyse how the policy reaction function of an inflation targeting central bank changes when a catch-all variable reflecting financial stability to an otherwise standard Neo-Keynesian model is added (e.g., Woodford, 2012), some others, using a similar setup, search for other policy tools in addition to short-term policy rates of the central bank to achieve both financial and price stability (e.g., Bailliu et al., 2012). A positive finding is that using additional tools may lower the value of the loss function of the central bank, depending upon the circumstances.

The policy response of various important central banks to the global crisis led to a surge in short-term capital inflows to most of the emerging economies, thus leading to an appreciation of domestic currencies and a sharp rise in domestic credit volume. For example, as of April 2011, the IMF reports a significant pickup in real credit growth in real per capita terms: in Brazil, Colombia, India, and Indonesia this is in the range of 10-20%, and in Turkey it exceeds 20% (WEO, IMF, April 2011). Evidence for appreciation pressures in emerging economies is also abandoned.

The CBT is among the leading central banks to have given a policy response to the likely financial instability that may cause rapid credit growth, domestic currency appreciation, and the associated deterioration in current account deficit. The CBT started to use a new monetary policy in November 2010 and, as time evolves, the framework has been revised in line with new developments. The following paragraph is taken from an important document of the CBT (CBT, 2011):

> In the period from the adoption of the new policy framework in November 2010 to intensifying uncertainties in the European economy in August 2011, the Central Bank aimed at limiting short-term capital flows and preventing excessive appreciation of the Turkish lira on the one hand, and ensuring more controlled growth in domestic credit and domestic demand on the other. Due to the strong risk appetite and the surge in short-term capital flows in this period, the Central Bank widened the interest rate corridor by reducing the overnight borrowing rate. Thus, interest rates in overnight markets were let to be lower than policy rates, which gave rise to an increase in the downward volatility of overnight market rates and a decline in very short-term capital flows. Meanwhile required reserve ratios were raised significantly in the same period to avert excessive credit growth and contain domestic demand...

In this paper, we aim to evaluate this new "multi aim—multi tool" monetary policy of the CBT, by focusing on the October 2010-August 2011 period. In the second section, we discuss tools used to mitigate rapid credit growth. Our main point is that under certain conditions (rather short deposit maturity, continuing credit demand, and inflation targeting) increasing the required reserve ratios would be counter-productive, unless macroprudential tools such as the capital adequacy ratio are used. This brings us to the necessary institutional setup. In the third section, we briefly discuss alternatives, and juxtapose the Turkish case with these alternatives. The fourth section briefly investigates the effects of another new policy of the CBT: depreciating the lira in order to bring down current account deficits to more manageable levels, which causes some ambiguity in curbing short-term capital inflows. The final section concludes our study.

2. Required reserve ratio as an additional policy tool in inflation targeting

The CBT is one of the leading inflation targeting central banks that has actively used required reserve ratios as an additional policy tool. The second half of 2010 witnessed a surge in short-term capital inflows, an appreciation pressure on the lira, a widening of current account deficit, and a rapid credit expansion. Seeing these developments as a threat to financial stability, one of the responses of the CBT was to gradually raise required reserve ratios. This move was principally aimed at curbing rapid credit expansion. The first reserve ratio increase was rather mild (0.5%), becoming effective in the first half of October 2010, and unwinding the measures taken during the wake of the crisis. The reserve ratio increases which followed were much more significant, and primarily targeted at mitigating rapid credit growth. A final reserve ratio increase was made in April 2011. With this final arrangement, the required reserve ratio increased by almost 8%, more than the initial level during this period.

Two important points should be emphasized; first, an inflation targeting central bank should supply the amount of liquidity demanded by the banking sector, in order to keep short-term interest rates in the interbank money market close to its policy rate. Otherwise, the policy rate will become meaningless and will jeopardise the functioning of the inflation targeting framework. Put differently, if the interest rate is fixed, then the money supply should accommodate fluctuations in money demand. Second, in Turkey at the start of the new monetary policy, the average maturity of deposits was about 45 days, whereas the banking sector could borrow from the central bank with a 7-day maturity period. This means that for the banking sector, the alternative to raising funds from the public was to raise funds from the CBT. Of course, there has always been an upper bound limit to borrowing from the CBT, determined by the value of eligible collaterals. However, this upper limit was far from binding during the implementation of this new policy.

Through the end of 2010, the economy was growing well above the potential growth rate, and demand for credit was increasing, as a result. The banking sector was more than eager to meet this demand. Given that short-term borrowing through open market operations from the CBT was a close substitute for the deposits lost to the CBT as a result of required reserve ratios, the banking sector increased its borrowing from the CBT.

Consequently, required reserves held at the CBT and the short-term borrowing from the CBT moved upwards in tandem (Figure 7-1). As expected, there was no change in the rate of increase of credit growth during the same period, relative to the first nine months of 2010. Indeed, the credit growth rate increased slightly in the first half of 2011 (Table 7-1).

Figure 7-1 Required reserves (RR) held at the CBT and the short-term borrowing of the banking sector from the CBT (OMO, September 3, 2010-July 1, 2011 (billion lira, weekly data)

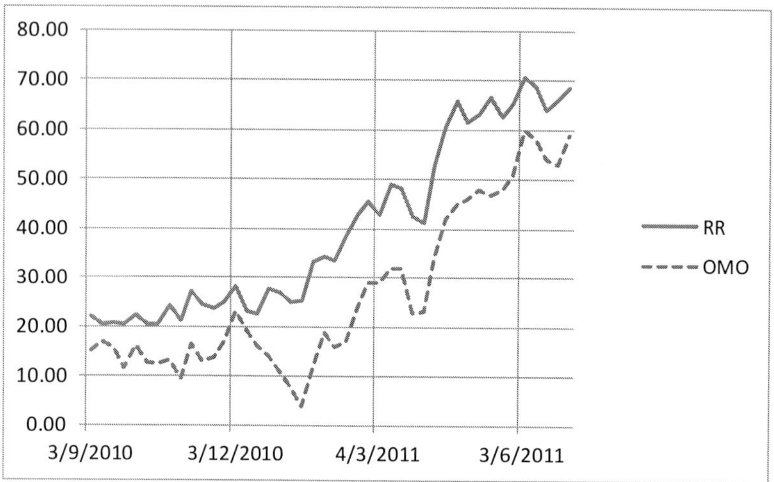

Source: Central Bank of Turkey

In the second half of June 2011, the BRSA entered the picture, and increased the capital adequacy ratio for certain types of credit, in order to curb rapid credit expansion. As of August 2011, the economic situation in Europe started to deteriorate, causing a significant reduction in global risk appetite. Consequently, the last quarter of 2011 witnessed a rather sharp reduction in credit growth rate. While it is rather difficult (if not impossible) to conduct a counter-factual study in order to pinpoint which factor (the BRSA decision or the intensifying uncertainties due to the situation in Europe) was the main driving force, we can assume that the BRSA decision was one—if not the main—factor. We should note that after the relative calming of conditions in Europe, credit growth continued to remain at significantly low levels in 2012, supporting our argument (Table 7-1).

This brings us to the discussion of which tools should be under monetary policy control, if financial stability is to be one of its main aims in addition to price stability. Furthermore, what alternative institutional setups can there be?

Table 7-1 Average domestic currency credit growth (%)

	Domestic currency credit growth (%)
2010	
First 9 months	29.7
Last quarter	32.2
2011	
First 6 months	34.8
First quarter	30.1
Second quarter	39.1
Third quarter	31.0
Fourth quarter	18,8
2012	
First quarter	15.2
Second quarter	25.4
Third quarter	20.6

Note: Average annualised percentage changes with respect to the previous period of 13-week average credit volumes.
Source: Banking Regulation and Supervision Agency.

3. A short glance at possible institutional setups and the situation in Turkey

The coordination between monetary policy and micro and macroprudential polices has been an active area of discussion in recent times. One prominent report in this context is BIS (2011) which analyses four alternative institutional setups.

In the first option, macroprudential policy responsibility is given to more than one institution. To establish coordination between these institutions, the pros and cons of establishing a financial stability coordination committee are discussed. Such a setup needs at least some clear identification of the responsibilities and powers of this committee. An important question to raise in this context concerns what the relationship between an independent central bank and such a committee would be.

The second option is to have separate microprudential, macroprudential and monetary policy authorities. Once more, a coordination issue arises. On the third option, a monetary policy authority conducts macroprudential policy while there is a separate microprudential authority. The final option is to have an authority responsible from monetary policy and macro and microprudential policy. Whichever option is chosen, it is essential to pinpoint such macroprudential tools and which institutions can make use of these tools.

On June 8, 2011, the "Financial Stability Committee" was established in Turkey. The head of the committee is the Treasury minister, and its members are the governor of the CBT, the Undersecretary of the Treasury, the presidents of the BRSA, the Capital Markets Board of Turkey, and the Deposit Insurance Fund. A noteworthy detail is that this committee was not established by new law, but by an amendment to a Council of Ministers degree for a new ministry setup (which is not connected to the committee).

An important shortcoming is the absence of a detailed description of responsibilities and powers of this committee. We do not know whether the committee is more of an advisory board, or whether it has the power to enforce the decisions it makes upon its members. For example, if the committee is an advisory one, and one of the member institutions disagrees with a decision that other members ask to be taken, who will have the final word? Will the public be informed about the proposals of others, and the reason why that particular institution abstained from taking the decision? If the committee is not an advisory one, will the independence of its independent members not be jeopardised? Similar questions can be formulated. However, the important point is that these matters had not been publicly discussed before the amendment; and moreover, the CBT has not yet informed the public about its decision.

4. Depreciation policy and inflation

The paragraph taken from the CBT, presented in the introduction of this study, clearly indicates how the CBT aimed at depreciating the lira, in order to halt the widening of the current account deficit and to place its mode of finance on a more sustainable path. To achieve this aim, it widened the interest rate corridor by significantly reducing the overnight borrowing rate. Consequently, the CBT deliberately let interest rates determined by overnight markets diverge from its policy rate. This policy was put into force to create ambiguity regarding daily short-term market rates, by increasing the downward volatility of overnight market rates. The

CBT also reduced its policy rate, in two successive moves, to 6.25% from 7% (Figure 7-2).

Figure 7-2 Short-term interest rates of the CBT and the short-term rate determined in the overnight market (market rate, October 1, 2010-December 31, 2011, %)

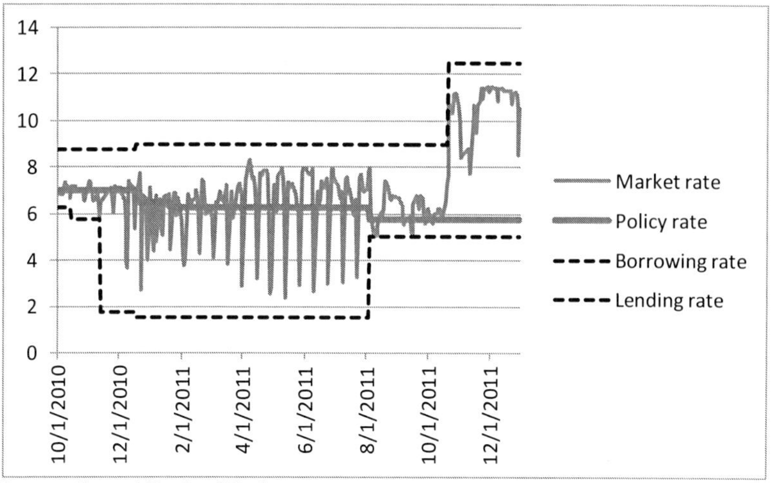

Source: Central Bank of Turkey

Starting in August, global risk appetite followed a downward trend, due to the worsening economic conditions in Europe. This in turn began to increase the depreciation pressure on the lira, already depreciating due to the policy of the CBT. A few weeks later, the intensification of uncertainties started to sharply depreciate the lira, and the CBT initiated the implementation of a policy contrary to that which had been implemented in the first seven months of 2011. Following a greatly questioned mild rate cut in early August, it increased its lending rate and let the market rate fluctuate upwards and diverge from its policy rate in an upward direction (Figure 7-2, the erratic line is the market rate).

Notice that the short-term market rate diverged wildly from the policy rate. This is not something to be expected from an inflation targeting central bank. After all, in order for the policy rate to function (that is, in order for the transmission mechanism to work properly), the policy rate and the short-term market rate should go hand in hand. An inflation targeting central bank is able to keep two rates as close as possible, via open market operations. But, interestingly enough, in the period analysed, open market operation seem to have been used to allow the two rates diverge from each other.

There is no doubt that inflation targeting is not a policy framework that can be used under all conditions. Indeed, based on the lessons drawn from the global financial crisis, the framework has, increasingly, been criticised. Nonetheless, the main point here is not that inflation targeting is a monetary policy framework that must be applied, but rather, that inflation targeting and its main tool—macroprudential policy and some of its other tools—can undermine each other's effectiveness. This point should be taken into consideration when choosing appropriate tools for implementing macroprudential policies.

Figure 7-3 Consumer inflation rates: January 2009-October 2012 (annual % rates)

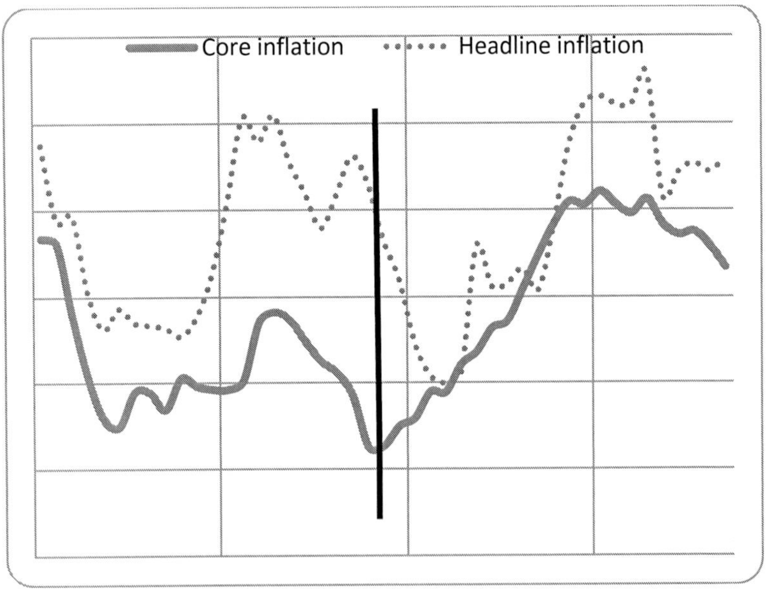

Source: Turkish Statistics Institute

As a first response to the CBT's new policy, due to the decline in global risk appetite, the lira depreciated considerably. The value of an equally weighted euro and dollar currency basket increased with respect to the lira by 25% in the October 2010-December 2011 period. Consequently, both headline and core consumer inflation increased significantly (Figure 7-3). Moreover, Turkey's inflation rate remained well above the inflation rates of its competitors (Table 7-2).

Table 7-2 Year-end inflation rates (%)

	2010	2011	2012
Czech Republic	2.3	2.4	3.1
Colombia	3.2	3.7	2.7
Indonesia	7	3.8	5
Mexico	4.4	3.8	4
Hungary	4.7	4.1	5.4
South Korea	3	4.2	2.2
Chile	3	4.4	2.5
Poland	3.1	4.6	3.2
South Africa	3.5	6.1	5.3
Brazil	5.9	6.5	5
Turkey	6.4	10.4	7.4

Note: 2012 figures are the estimates of the IMF.
Countries are listed in ascending order according to the 2011 inflation rates.
Source: IMF

5. Conclusion

The global financial crisis showed the importance of financial stability once more. We have a well-developed theory and a rich accumulation of practices by various central banks to ensure price stability. This is not true of a monetary policy that bears both a price stability and a financial stability objective. New literature in this area has been emerging, but for the time it remains in its infancy.

In this note, we have discussed the new monetary policy framework of the CBT in the October 2010-December 2011 period. Starting from October 2010, the CBT declared that it would both aim at price and financial stability. Consequently, it tried to increase its number of policy tools. We documented various shortcomings of this policy. The important point is that on inflation targeting (and its main tool, macroprudential policy) and some of its other tools can undermine each other's effectiveness. This point should be taken into consideration when choosing appropriate tools for the purposes of implementing macroprudential policies.

References

Bailliu, J., C. Meh and Y. Zhang 2012, "Macroprudential Rules and Monetary Policy when Financial Frictions Matter", *Bank of Canada Working Paper,* 2012-6.

BIS 2011, "Central Bank Governance and Financial Stability", *Study Group Report,* May.

CBT 2011, "Monetary and Exchange Rate Policy for 2012", December.

Glocker, C. and P. Towbin 2012, "Reserve Requirements for Price and Financial Stability: When are They Effective?", *International Journal of Central Banking* 8-1,p. 65-113.

IMF 2011, *World Economic Outlook*, April.

Woodford, M. 2012, "Inflation Targeting and Financial Stability", *NBER Working Paper,* 17967.

CHAPTER EIGHT

CENTRAL BANKING SINCE THE EIGHTIES

PHILIPPE GILLES
UNIVERSITE DU SUD, TOULON-VAR
AND CECILE BASTIDON GILLES
UNIVERSITE DU SUD, TOULON-VAR

1. Introduction

When academic studies addressed the problem of central banking in the 1980s, the issue of the reputation and credibility of monetary authorities became central. Though reputation and credibility are often used as interchangeable concepts, we think that they should be distinguished (Gilles, 1992).

- The notion of "Credibility" is evaluated according to the difference between the results and official announcements of monetary policy, with the following two variants:
  * "*Average Credibility*" is the measure of the expected difference between the announcements and the realisation of monetary policy, and of the related behaviour of economic agents. The smaller the difference, the greater the credibility.
  * "*Marginal Credibility*" measures the ability of monetary policy announcements to influence economic agents' expectations.

- "Reputation" is used in another context. It can be defined in a restrictive sense, following Weber (1991): Reputation is the probability of coherence and consistency of the continuation of monetary policy, according to economic agents.

The relationship between economic agents and the monetary authority is a strategic game. The authority plays first, by defining the rules and the targets of monetary and financial policies, and making them public knowledge. Economic agents then adjust their expectations concerning the realisation of these policies. Finally, the authority chooses the monetary policy that will actually be conducted. Therefore, information is asymmetric, and the authority has more information than the public. Moreover, they act after having observed the actual value of random variables, which is another information advantage over economic agents. Indeed, they do not know with certainty whether the monetary authority will attain its goals or not.

The whole game is, therefore, a probabilistic framework in which the public evaluates the likelihood that the central bank behaves rigorously: it is rigorous if the announced rule is implemented whatever happens, and if the authority never switches to a discretionary policy. This probability is known as the *reputation of the central bank.* In each period, the public compares the results with policy announcements, evaluates the credibility of the central bank and possibly revises its assessment, according to a Bayesian rule.

In the academic literature, the evaluation of the possible difference between the announcement and the realisation of monetary policy may cover different areas. To mention just *a few examples*:

- General monetary policy guidelines (Christensen and Blackburn, 1989).
- Control of the money supply (Cukierman and Meltzer, 1986);
- Interest rates setting (Artus, 1989).
- Inflation control systems (Fellner, 1982; Backus and Driffill, 1985).
- Demand-side policies (Koromzay, 1982).
- The inflation-unemployment dilemma (Barro, 1986).
- Effects of devaluation on the trade balance and competitiveness (Andersen and Risager, 1991).

Because of the importance of the expectations of economic agents, post-Keynesian economists like Tobin and Kaldor say that the present most commonly accepted need for a close correlation between the announcement and the realisation of monetary policy raises the question of the principle of announcement effects themselves. In their opinion, the public announcement of the monetary target by the central bank has many *adverse effects* (Tobin, 1983). For this reason, a "fine tuning" discretionary policy is preferable. Priority should be given to market stabilisation and defence against short-term speculative attacks (Dornbusch, 1980). Notice that this position is remarkably relevant in the present context of the "subprime crisis", followed by "the global financial crisis" and "the European sovereign debt crisis".

Let us go *back to the 1980s*, and the concern for competitive disinflation in the period of the strong rise of neoliberalism. In this context, the definition of the reputation and credibility of the central banker is reduced to two main criteria: an economic dimension, with a focus on inflation targeting; and an institutional dimension, with a focus on the independence of the central bank. The reputation and credibility of a central bank are strong when inflation control is effective and there is a high degree of independence from the government.

Let us examine these two points in detail. First, *inflation targeting:* it is interesting to notice that the definition of inflation by European central banks is a quantitativist definition. This was true for the Bundesbank, of course, but is also true for the other central banks of the European Monetary System (EMS). It remains true for the ECB, in accordance with Article 105 of the European Community Treaty. This definition of inflation is based on the generalised Fisher equation, in which for a given level of interest rates, there is a direct relationship between money supply and prices in the long-term. Thus, the ECB uses a wide range of indicators, including M3 and its components and counterparts, notably credit.

The *ECB's reference value* for monetary growth, namely an annual growth rate of 4.5% for the broad aggregate M3, was announced on 13 October, 1998. During its meeting on December 5, 2002, the ECB Governing Council confirmed this reference value. At its meeting on May 8, 2003, the Council decided that it would no longer conduct a review of this reference value on an annual basis, though it would continue to assess the underlying conditions and assumptions. Jean Claude Trichet confirmed this medium-term orientation of the monetary policy when he became the second president of the ECB on November 1, 2003. This monetarist view of central banking is in accordance with the early canonical models of reputation and credibility: for instance, Barro and Gordon (1983) or Cukierman (1986). This is a quite different view from the twin goals of price stability and full employment contained in the Federal Reserve Act (Owen-Glass Act).

Secondly, the *independence of the central bank* (Woehrling, 1990): this can be measured by the type of appointment procedures for board members, by the length of the members' terms to office, or by the correlation of the appointments or replacements with electoral cycles. Central bank independence indicators, in a narrow sense, can be completed by various parameters, which include the quality of the current administration (Alesina and Tabellini, 1988; Schelling, 1982), the proposals of the candidates during election campaigns and the election results (Bowen, 1943), and the "climate of elections" in general (Rogoff and Sibert, 1988; Alesina et al., 1991).

Indeed, following Alesina and Cukierman (1990), in the eventuality of a *trade-off* between a policy that maximises its chances of being re-elected and another that maximises global aggregate welfare, policymakers most often choose vagueness and ambiguity. This can cause a sudden worsening of the reputation and credibility of the central bank, if it is dependent on executive power. For Rogoff (1985), Cohen (1988), and Cohen and Michel (1988), credibility requires that the central bank governor is both independent of the government and conservative.

Finally, the *broader political debates* (Mistral, 1991): government decisions are constantly evaluated by markets, and their assessment of the sustainability of economic—especially fiscal—policies determines the decisions of economic agents. In this case, central bank independence may correct excesses. Eventually, notice that the reputation and credibility of monetary authorities may increase: firstly, with intermediation because of an improved control of the money supply; secondly, with fiscal policy coordination in an integrated economic area (Oudiz and Sachs, 1984); thirdly, with an institutional coordination at the national level. In this last case, for instance, in the early 1980s the French government created a Liaison Committee between the Central bank, the Treasury, the Paris clearing house, and the French regulatory authorities (Butsch, 1988).

In fact, the theoretical evaluation of the reputation and credibility of central banks shows only minor changes since the academic literature of the 1980s.

The other aspect of the qualitative assessment of central banking is the ability of central banks to manage and prevent economic, monetary and financial crises. This assessment essentially depends on the choice of an economic *paradigm*. If one believes that the hypothesis of market efficiency is validated, then this assessment is positively connected with minimal public authority intervention. In this case, public involvement is restricted to information transparency and market discipline measures. On the opposite side, if one believes in the natural instability of financial markets, which is our hypothesis, then central banking in particular and public intervention in general are both legitimate and necessary. Indeed, the stability of monetary, banking and financial systems is a "public good" since each economic agent benefits from this stability. However, they do not properly take into account the aggregated costs of financial instability, hence the need for strong public intervention.

Furthermore, if financial stability can be considered as a "public good", it is *not a "common good"*. Some economic agents do not have an interest in financial stability, because their benefits derive strictly from financial market volatility. Finally, in the context of economic globalisation, "market failures" are sometimes associated with "state failures" (Stiglitz, 2000). International financial stability is a "global public good" (Kindleberger, 1986) or a "regional public good", for instance at the European level. Thus, it is necessary to design public policies, and central banks policies in particular, at the international or, at least, the regional level. Otherwise, the production of these goods by each government tends to be suboptimal, since all the other states benefit from this production. In this case, the evolution of banking regulation is quite exemplary: central bankers have realised since the 1980s that domestic regulation is deficient in a context of international portfolio diversification and interdependent national systems, hence the Basel banking supervision accords. This analysis in terms of "public goods" also helps to explain one of the causes of the present Euro area crisis: in 2010, Greece, a small domestic economy, could have been saved at little cost by European solidarity. Today, Portugal, Spain and Italy are also affected by contagion and in need of a bail-out.

With the advent of globalisation, meaning both instability of domestic financial systems and an extensive use of market finance, a short-term capital account constraint replaces the medium-term economic development constraint. Countries become more vulnerable to external shocks, particularly to liquidity shocks. Moreover, this submission of state sovereignty to the individual interests of a part of market operators increased market risks.

In this context, national frameworks of political, economic, financial and monetary regulations are *ineffective*. International capital markets become the main source of balance of payments financing, both for financing requirements and exchange rate adjustments. In this context, financial crises, possibly combined with currency crises in the case of twin crises, made the history of the last three decades. Thus, the evolution of central banking has to be framed in the proper perspective of the historical nature of these crises.

The paper is organised as follows: Section 2 proposes a short review of crisis models and the occurrence of the 2008 global crisis. Section 3 discusses some orthodox monetary policies, through domestic and international last-resort lending. Section 4 examines unconventional monetary policies, particularly used to tackle the global crisis. Finally,

Section 5 concludes the analysis with some remarks on unconventional monetary policies.

2. Crisis models and the global crisis

Dornbusch (2001) has distinguished between "*old-style crises*", caused by real exchange rates distortions and external imbalances and "*new-style balance sheet crises*" resulting from banking fragility. The Eichengreen et al. (1995) typology of crises consists of first, second and third generation crises. Each type of crisis is theoretically explained by a specific model (Bastidon, 2002).

First generation models (Agenor et al., 1992) are based on a "fundamentalist" scheme. Crises are triggered by inconsistent economic policies, in the sense of Kydland and Prescott (1977). In the canonical first generation crisis models, there is a persistent money-financed budget deficit, and the government uses a limited stock of reserves to peg its exchange rate. This policy is, ultimately, unsustainable. In a broad sense, first generation crises triggers also include other types of degradation of macroeconomic fundamentals: for instance, sovereign debt crises like the 1980s developing countries debt crisis, or the 1980s and 1990s European Monetary System crises (Krugman, 1996). The onset of the crisis should not take economic agents by surprise, since it can be fully anticipated. However, note that if the country has moral hazard behaviour (Aglietta and de Boissieu, 1999) first generation crises become more complex and less predictable, because the actual macroeconomic fundamentals targets are not public knowledge.

In *second generation models* (Eichengreen, 1996), the crisis results from a shift in private expectations, related to the same macroeconomic fundamentals as in the first generation models. Second generation crises occur either in the case of a predicted—and not actual—future deterioration, or in the case of purely self-fulfilling expectations. In both cases, the crisis is a liquidity crisis, and extends from the capital account to the current account: if economic agents expect a liquidity shortage, there will inevitably be a crisis, though this liquidity shortage and jump from the "good" to the "bad" equilibrium is in fact the result of their own decisions.

With the emerging markets crises of the 1990s and the early 2000s in Mexico (1994), South-east Asia (1997), Russia (1998), Argentina (1999-2000), and Turkey (2000-2001), theoretical crises analysis (see for instance Dooley, 1997; Aglietta and de Boissieu, 1999) turns to the fragility of domestic financial systems, including banking systems. In a context of multiple equilibria, third generation crises are then defined as "first generation crises, with underlying deteriorated fundamentals [...], resulting from private microeconomic decisions" (Aglietta and de Boissieu, 1999). Those microeconomic decisions are conditioned both by a speculative logic asset (including equities and currencies), price expectations, and mimetic polarizations. This relationship between the microeconomic and macroeconomic levels can potentially cause a systemic risk dynamic with contagion mechanisms.

The scenario of the current crisis, which is once again a banking system crisis, is remarkable for three reasons. In fact, it could even be called a fourth generation crisis:

- Firstly, this crisis originated in the failure of securitisation. This failure led to a contagious contraction of liquidity in money and capital markets.

- Secondly, systemic contagion is not primarily linked with aggregated insolvency, but with the illiquidity of financial intermediaries. Normally, deposit banks should enable customer payments in conformity with bank loans, and investment banks should provide market intermediation liquidity, that is to say, contribute to a proper amount of securities trading and thus reduce trading fees and foster market price convergence to their fundamental values. If some of these banks are illiquid, the smooth operating of these systems is disrupted.

- Finally, public policies that were conducted to manage this illiquidity crisis have significantly deepened government deficits and debt, and have in turn created the conditions of the present sovereign debts crisis.

This *central role of liquidity* is visible in the consequent increase in risk premiums just before bank failures, or today government defaults. This illustrates the fact that this crisis results from a liquidity shortage in credit markets much more than from deteriorated fundamentals. Consequently, both the regulation of bank capital and fiscal policy rules regarding deficit and debt ceilings are inadequate.

The genesis of the current crisis is threefold: innovation, deregulation and liquidity (Mistral, 2009):

- At the beginning of the story is a typical pattern of financial crises, based on an initial business euphoria phase. In the context of easy borrowing, economic agents use maximum leverage effects to increase their return on assets.

- Next is an unprecedented technicality of financial innovation, especially in securitised products and derivatives instruments. The outstanding total of bonds, shares and other assets held by commercial banks is now four times bigger than the world GDP. The outstanding total of derivatives instruments is almost twelve times bigger (Lubochinsky, 2009)! Credit risk is relocated outside of the regulated banking system and opacity is increased, resulting in the quasi-impossibility of tracking securitised (ABS) and repackaged instruments (CDO). Therefore, the volatility of capital markets has significantly increased, and contagion mechanisms are strengthened.

A fourth generation crisis would then be a third generation crisis resulting in a sovereign debt crisis, in the peculiar context of asymmetric information generated by technicality of financial innovations, controlled or even developed by the banks themselves. This is a *historical benchmark* with respect to central banking: in the case of the first three generations of crises, the role of central banking is limited to conventional lending of a last resort with minor variants. Conversely, in the current crisis, unconventional monetary policies are definitely necessary.

3. Theory and modus operandi of the lender of last resort

Before we discuss the legitimacy of lending of last resort in each of the first three generations of crises, we will return to the *historical origin* of the theory and modus operandi of the lender of last resort. This is an extremely old problem, dating back to Baring (1797) and Thornton (1802) in particular. In the case of banking crises caused by credit booms, which are likely to become liquidity crises if contagious defiance generalises, they show that restoring domestic financial system's stability and market confidence requires the central bank to be endowed with a public rationality. This public rationality will result in the use of last-resort lending in the form of bail-outs and open market policies (Cartapanis and Gilles, 2003). This action is then the insurance of continuity in payments, in response to both domestic causes of crises (the "internal drain", resulting from a loss of confidence and excessive hoarding) and external causes (the "external drain" resulting from convertibility crises, unfavourable exchange rates and gold outflows).

This analysis is supplemented by Bagehot (1873) with the distinction made between illiquid banking institutions (which the lender of last resort can bail out), and insolvent institutions (where there should be no disruption of the logic of the market). This distinction, with the addition of the unpredictability of interventions principle, is the *guideline* of lending of last resort, in order to both ensure the effectiveness of bail-outs and to control moral hazard behaviours.

When we return to the *present time,* the first three generations of crises all legitimate, in various degrees, last-resort lending (Aglietta and de Boissieu, 1999). In the case of first generation crises, this action is perhaps less important. The adoption of consistent public policies primarily requires an increase in foreign exchange reserves, in order to avoid a currency crisis and an excessive cost of structural adjustment. Hence, these crises may be managed with the support of the international community. If there is multilateral intervention, the central bank will not have to act alone, since part of the loan will be made by (for example) the IMF.

Conversely, the prevention or management of second generation crises requires last-resort intervention to correct market coordination failures. In this case, the lender of last resort is fully legitimated, because of the social cost of these market failures. The fear of a liquidity shortage triggers a bank run, followed by a liquidity dry-up. Then, the first expectation is self-validated. Lending of last resort has to coordinate private expectations and decisions concerning the "good equilibrium". Central banks, for instance, may conduct concerted actions, like the Bundesbank and Banque de France in the fall of 1992, or the FED and Bank of Japan in June 1998. This is not a context of asymmetric information, so at the very beginning last-resort lending has no moral hazard externality, unlike the usual. But this is only temporary, and the central bank has to involve "market maker" private agents, as well as public authorities.

In third generation crises, which refer to financial intermediation failures, the lender of last resort intervention is required to reduce self-fulfilling liquidity outflows and to stem contagion processes. In this case, we (Bastidon et al., 2007, 2008a, 2008b) have shown that last-resort lending should be used to manage and prevent crises if and only if the international lender of last resort (which could be the IMF, for instance) and the central bank are informed on the subject of domestic markets and banking systems. Therefore, they will act at a macroeconomic level, as an usual lender of last resort, but also at a microeconomic level, since there will be selective lending to commercial banks according to a *broad-sense Bagehot rule with three types of banks*

- The first group of banks is liquid and solvent. It can face the run without advance liquidation of assets, but has to be bailed out in the logic of a catalytic effect in order to avoid domestic deposit withdrawals caused by widespread contagious risk aversion.

- The second group of banks is illiquid but solvent. It can face the run by liquidating all or part of its long-term assets, but the liquidation costs it bears requires a bail-out in a recapitalisation logic.

- The third group of banks is insolvent and should not be bailed out.

In this framework, the efficiency of last-resort lending requires two levels of selective bail-out: first, the eligibility of crises countries; secondly, the possible eligibility of banks from those recipient countries. Therefore, in the context of contagious liquidity crises and globalised markets, if there is systemic risk, there is a need for international cooperation. This mechanism is not taken into account in generational crises models, but has to be considered in order to define the current practice of last-resort lending. In particular, the issue of an international lender of last resort with a true international monetary authority and the ability to "bail in" the private sector has to be addressed (Gilles, 2002).

The *transposition* of domestic last-resort lending to international last-resort lending by multilateral institutions is not straightforward (Meltzer, 2000). For instance, should there be a single international lender of last resort, or would collaboration between central banks be preferable (Kindleberger, 1978)? Will it be possible to achieve the optimal degree of coordination of prudential regulations, banking supervision and last-resort lending (Goodhart, 1988)? Should the intervention of the international lender of last resort be predictable, for example with an ex ante conditionality mechanism (Bastidon, 2003), or should it, on the contrary, be characterised by a form of "constructive ambiguity" (Goodhart and Huang, 2000)?

The national or international lender of last resort has to face the same two crucial problems: moral hazard and predictability, or not, of its approach and intervention.

There is "moral hazard" where the protection against a given risk, for example last-resort lending (which is a form of collective insurance), makes the risk realisation more likely. Indeed, capital markets are not perfect markets: lenders and borrowers do not have the same information and both commonly have positive risk aversion and limited liability. Thus, it is generally impossible to achieve optimal results. In the case of international last-resort lending for example, if a sovereign borrower knows that there may be a bail-out, there is an incentive to take advantage of information asymmetries and make excessively risky policy choices. The government, of course, is better informed of the existing public deficits and debt, reform implementations, and economic forecasts.

With systemically important banking institutions or countries, moral hazard is exacerbated because they are almost certain they will be bailed out since they are "too big to fail". We have shown that information asymmetry between the IMF, for example, and this type of sovereign borrower may become voluntary, in the sense that the IMF does in fact know much more about the country's macroeconomic fundamentals than is pretended. In this case, the primary objective of the IMF, namely to prevent a global systemic crisis resulting from the single default of one country, outweighs the usually binding conditionality principle (Bastidon and Gilles, 2001). The 1998 Russian crisis is a perfect example: the IMF was forced to be a lender of last resort in a highly peculiar game where the Russian authorities pretended to observe IMF conditions including tax reforms, and the IMF pretended that these conditions were being observed. In other words, if the IMF had refused to pay, there might have been a global systemic crisis; but multilateral intervention led to a delay in the necessary adjustments.

The second challenge of last-resort lending is the usual central banking dilemma between *"rules" and "discretion"*. Should the lender of last resort, whether international or national, be transparent and make the intervention rule public knowledge? Or is "constructive ambiguity" preferable? Once again, the transposition of the domestic last resort-lending scheme to the international level is not straightforward. Indeed, "constructive ambiguity" seems to be more appropriate for national last-resort lending, since the central bank has both the monopoly on money issuance and an informational advantage as regards its own domestic financing system. However, this is not true for an international lender of last resort. In this case, there can be a practical position on the basic principles of international last-resort lending (Aglietta and de Boissieu, 1999): not to reveal very strict rules and, at the same time, not to overuse discretionary "surprise effects".

4. Unconventional monetary policies

The magnitude and length of the current crisis pushed these traditional central banking problems, which are still relevant, into the background. Central banks were forced to adopt exceptionally accommodating monetary policies, the so-called "*unconventional monetary policies*". These unconventional monetary policies are threefold: large official interest rate cuts, with a commitment to keep them at extremely low levels; new credit facilities; and large asset purchases. These measures have radically and in all likelihood definitively modified the issue of central banking.

Here is a *short chronology* of unconventional monetary policies. After the collapse of Lehman Brothers in 2008, market strains significantly intensified. Financial intermediaries built up larger stocks of liquid assets, reduced their balance sheets, and credit market conditions tightened. Total lending for the private sector contracted, and confidence indicators deteriorated dramatically. In this context, advanced economies' central banks decided to act together. On October 8 2008, a coordinated action by the FED, Bank of Canada, BoE, ECB, Swiss National Bank and Bank of Sweden reduced official interest rates by 50 basic points. Although the ECB had raised its main refinancing rate by 25 base points to 4.25% only three months earlier, the Council decided to turn back and reduce it to 3.75%. The ECB kept lowering its official rates until 7 May 2009. The main refinancing rate was reduced to 1%, its lowest level since the creation of the EMU. The deposit facility rate was set at 0.25%, and the marginal lending rate at 1.75%. Since then, rates have not been modified, except for a short 8-month period between April and December 2011. Meanwhile, the ECB has conducted long-term refinancing operations. The first 12-month operation (in June 2009) consisted of a 442 billion euros liquidity injection, which is an unprecedented amount in a single operation. The following 12-month operation was conducted 3 months later (in September 2009) and the demand for loans remained high at 75 billion euros. Finally, during the December 2009 12-month operation, the demand for loans was 96 billion euros. Of course, these three operations had a significant impact on the size of the ECB balance sheet.

At the end of 2009, *easing strains* on financial markets led the ECB to begin a gradual exit from unconventional measures, in order to avoid a market dependency on central bank liquidity provision. Foreign currency liquidity injections and variable rates tender procedures in the regular three-month longer-term refinancing operations were stopped (until March 2010). Nevertheless, during this period, the ECB was pragmatic and accepted, in April 2010, to delay the decision to return to the initial collateral rule of long-term refinancing operations. The reduced rating thresholds were maintained.

This practical approach allowed Greece to be rescued when Greek debt (and also Spanish and Portuguese debts) was downgraded by S&P. This is the context of the 110 billion euros Greek rescue package decided by the Euro area countries, with the support of the IMF. Furthermore, the ECB decided to suspend the rating threshold collateral rule of long-term refinancing operations in the case of Greek debt. In spite of these measures, contagious risk increased, threatening the stability of the whole Euro area. Therefore, in May 2010, the Euro area countries decided, with the assistance of the IMF, to create a 750 billion euros fund to bail-out Greece and help other struggling governments like Portugal, Spain and Ireland. Since then the *ECB involvement* has remained at high level. On May 10th 2010, the ECB Executive Board decided on the following:

- Firstly, the ECB would conduct private and also public bond buyouts.

- Secondly, the exit strategy from unconventional measures would be temporarily interrupted, and the ECB would conduct 6-month fixed rate refinancing operations.

- Thirdly, the dollar swap lines with the US Federal Reserve System would be reactivated, in order to provide dollar liquidity to the Euro area.

Note that these measures were taken in accordance with the mandate of the ECB. The primary objective of the ECB is, as we have seen, to maintain price stability. But *Article 105* of the European Community Treaty mentions that the ECB should also promote the smooth operation of payment systems. This is why the ECB Executive Board stressed that the decision to buy back private and public debts would not affect the orientation of monetary policy.

We see that the ECB and the FED both took unprecedented measures in order to limit the extent of the global financial crisis and its impact on the real economy. They both lowered official interest rates to the lowest levels ever, and used unconventional monetary policies to provide markets and financial institutions with liquidity. Of course, the exact measures of the ECB and FED differ because of *differences in their statutory mandates and governance*, and because of specific economic and financial backgrounds. The statutory mandate of the FED includes maximum employment, stable prices, and moderate long-term interest rates. In this context, the magnitude of the subprime mortgage and housing crises in the US justifies the decision to conduct massive bond buyouts since late 2008. Conversely, since the financing of the European economic activity is less dependent on financial markets than in the US, the action of the ECB has been more oriented towards banks.

Let us now look at the academic literature on the peculiar mechanisms of this crisis. Global financial crises trigger specific large amplification effects that increase the expected financial acceleration (Adrian and Shin, 2009). Those amplification effects allow shocks to a single market to propagate through the whole financial system, leading to both fast and heavy drops in the value of financial assets and large increases in the costs of external finance to economic agents (Blanchard, 2009). In this context, the crisis occurs in two steps. In the first step, the *initial shock is transmitted to the interbank market*. Generalised financial crisis follows. This crisis timeline with a key role of the interbank market is described, for instance, by Bordo (2008) or Freixas and Jorge (2008).

From the moment that amplification effects exist, conventional monetary policy instruments are not sufficient to contain the crisis (Karadi and Gertler, 2011). Official interest rates are lowered as long as the minimum level ("the zero lower bound" as stated by Bernanke and Reinhart, 2004) is not reached. When this level is reached, central banks still have two instruments: (1) massive use of last-resort lending, in addition to the usual refinancing operations; and (2) asset purchases, in order to affect their prices and returns (Caruana, 2010; Korinek, 2011). These three elements (rapid and large cuts in official interest rates, massive use of last-resort lending and asset purchases by the central bank) are constitutive of unconventional monetary policies. In the case of banking crises ("bank runs"), combined with market liquidity crises ("twin runs"), unconventional monetary policies are then conducted in accordance with a similar argument to last-resort lending: the aim is to restore market functioning while substituting for it, in order to limit financial instability.

There are many academic assessments of unconventional monetary policies, through focusing on the FED's action. Some of these demonstrate that it was effective, and eased financial market strains (Fahr et al., 2011; Sarkar and Shrader, 2010). Generally speaking, DSGE models with a financial acceleration effect show a positive impact of central bank policies (Cúrdia and Woodford, 2009). For instance, Gertler and Karadi (2011) go further, with a model of an optimal unconventional response to financial intermediation disruption. However, in their model, the central bank issues risk-free debt securities and finances economic activity: public finance constraints are not included. Yet, the possibility of another systemic crisis, with an impossibility to use the official interest rates instrument and strong public finances constraints cannot be excluded, hence the importance of modelling central banks' response in the context of *public debt markets strains*.

Theoretical models are necessary to avoid a worsening in the credibility of central bankers, possibly resulting from the implementation of unconventional monetary policies considered as discretionary measures. The former agreement about the macroeconomic goals of central banking is in part questioned and another, including theoretical analysis of financial stability, would be substituted (Goodhart and Tsomocos, 2007; Buiter and Sibert, 2008; Fahr et al., 2011). Our current work (Bastidon et al., 2012) is intended to contribute specifically to this search for a new consensus. In the model the additional supply of government bonds, required to finance the banking sector rescue programs and recovery policies, deteriorates market evaluation on public debts: even if there exist "flight to quality" effects concerning government bonds, the central bank may have to purchase part of the issuances to maintain the desired level of liquidity.

In our model, a "modern" central bank quantifies the amount of asset purchases in public and private bonds markets, taking into account the additional issuance of government bonds resulting from the financial crisis. These asset purchases are a response to private liquidity shortages in these markets. On this basis, we show that the *amount of bond buyouts* depends on three key factors:

- Firstly, for a given additional supply of public bonds, resulting from financial crises management fiscal policies, the amount of public debt buyouts depends on the initial situation of public finances. If the public deficit is structurally high, the central bank will have to run large bond buyouts in order to achieve its public debt market liquidity target. Otherwise, the central bank's involvement is lower and thus its independence is strengthened.

- Secondly, the amounts of private and public bond buyouts depend on the initial level of official interest rates. If this level is relatively high, the central bank has an additional instrument. The higher the initial level of interest rates, the lower the amount of bond buyouts for the same results.

- The third key element is the relationship between the interbank market and other markets. If there is a direct connection, the amplification of the initial shock, which in the first phase was limited to the interbank market, will cause widespread liquidity shortages. In this case, the central bank will have to run large bond buyouts.

Finally, we show that from the moment financial amplification effects exist: (1) fiscal policies should preferably be cautious and coordinated; (2) crisis management monetary policies should be strictly limited in time; (3) central banks should conduct a particularly careful monitoring of market liquidity indicators, which are the most correlated to the interbank market. The aim of this on-going work on the crisis and recent monetary policies practice episodes is to model the underlying rule of this practice and in particular of bond buyouts, in order to enhance private anticipations coordination.

5. Conclusion

If the central banks' monetary policy response to the current crisis has led to numerous innovations in the operational framework, the principle of unconventional measures existed before the crisis, as evidenced by the 2004 typology by Bernanke et al. (2004). According to the latter, unconventional monetary policy measures can be classified into three categories:

- A first type of measure intended to guide private sector interest rate expectations.
- A second type of measure intended to increase the size of the central bank balance sheet and the monetary base.
- And finally a third type of measure intended to change the structure of the central bank assets.

This typology is obviously still accurate. Finally, while some see unconventional monetary policy measures as dangerous, as Ben Bernanke points out in an interview with the Financial Times on January 5 2009, the danger might lie in sticking too rigidly to conventional practice in the case of a major crisis. "One of my conclusions from my study of the Great Depression is that people tend to think of orthodoxy as safe," he said. "But strategy should depend on the situation. In a severe crisis, orthodoxy can prove to be a very bad strategy."

References

Adrian, T. and H.S. Shin 2009, "Money, Liquidity, and Monetary Policy", *The American Economic Review* 99-2, p. 600-605.

Agenor, P., J. Bhandari and R. Flood 1992, "Speculative Attacks and Models of Balance of Payment Crises", *IMF Staff Papers* 39, p. 357-394.

Aglietta, M. and C. de Boissieu 1999, "Le Prêteur International en Dernier Ressort", in Varii Auctores, *Architecture Financière Internationale,* Rapport du CAE, 18, Paris: La Documentation Française, p. 97-127.

Alesina, A., G.D. Cohen and N. Roubini 1991, "Macroeconomic Policy and Elections in OECD Democracies", *NBER Working Paper,* 3830.

Alesina, A. and A. Cukierman 1990, "The Politics of Ambiguity", *TheQuarterly Journal of Economics* CV-4, p. 829-850.

Alesina, A. and G. Tabellini 1988, "Credibility and Politics", *European Economic Review* 32-2/3, p. 542-550.

Andersen, T. M. and O. Risager 1991, "The Role of Credibility for the Effects of a Change in the Exchange Rate Policy", *Oxford Economic Papers* 43-1, p. 85-98.

Artus, P. 1989, "Comportement des Banques Centrales et Structure des Taux d'Intérêt", *Revue Française d'Economie* IV-2, p. 89-107.

Backus, D. and J.Driffill 1985, "Inflation and Reputation", *The American Economic Review* 75-3, p. 530-538.

Bagehot, W. 1873, *Lombard Street*, London: Kegan Paul, 1878.

Baring, F. 1797, *Observations on the Establishment of the Bank of England, and on the Paper Circulation of the Country,in Selected Tracts 1694-1804*, London:Gregg International Publisher Ltd, Bank of England, 1968.

Barro, R.J. 1986, "Reputation in a Model of Monetary Policy with Incomplete Information", *Journal of Monetary Economics* 17-1, p. 3-20.

Barro, R.J. and D.B. Gordon 1983, "Rules, Discretion and Reputation in a Model of Monetary Policy", *Journal of Monetary Economics* 12-1, p. 101-121.

Bastidon, C. 2002, "Financement Extérieur des Pays en Développement: Une Revue de la Littérature des Modèles de Dette et de Crises Financières", *Région et Développement* 15, p. 147-165.

—. 2003, "Un modèle de Conditionnalité *ex ante* de l'Intervention Multilatérale", Presented at the *20th Symposium on Banking and Monetary Economics*, GDR, Birmingham, 5-6 June.

Bastidon, C. and P. Gilles 2001, "Prêteur en Dernier Ressort et Statut de *Too Big to Fail* d'un Emprunteur Souverain: Le 'Jeu de Faux Semblants'Appliqué à la Crise Financière Russe", *Economie Appliquée* LIV-2, p. 129-151.

Bastidon, C., P. Gilles and N. Huchet 2007, "Un Modèle de Prêt International en Dernier Ressort avec Sélectivité du Renflouement", *Région et Développement* 26, p. 113-129.

Bastidon, C., P. Gilles and N. Huchet 2008a, "A Selective Bail-out International Lending of Last Resort Model", *Annals of Economics and Finance* 9-1, p. 103-114.

Bastidon, C., P. Gilles and N. Huchet 2008b, "The International Lender-of-Last Resort and Selective Bail-out", *Emerging Markets Review* 9-2, p. 144-152.

Bastidon, C., P. Gilles and N. Huchet 2012, "Amplification Effects and Unconventional Monetary Policies, *Theoretical and Applied Economics* XIX-2, p. 13-30.

Bernanke, B.S. and V.R. Reinhart 2004, "Conducting Monetary Policy at very Low Short-Term Interest Rates", *The American Economic Review* 94-2, p. 85-90.

Bernanke, B.S., V.R. Reinhart and B.P. Sack 2004, "Monetary Policy Alternatives at the Zero Bound: An Empirical Assessment", *Brooking Papers on Economic Activity* 35-2, p. 1-78.

Blackburn, K. and M. Christensen 1989, "Monetary Policy and Policy Credibility: Theories and Evidence", *Journal of Economic Literature* XXVII-1, p. 1-45.

Blanchard, O.J. 2009, "The Crisis: Basic Mechanisms, and Appropriate Policies", *IMF Working Paper*, 09-80.

Bordo, M. 2008, "An Historical Perspective on the Crisis of 2007-2008", *NBER Working Paper,* 14569.

Bowen, H.R. 1943, "The Interpretation of Voting in the Allocation of Economic Resources", *The Quarterly Journal of Economics* LVIII-1, p. 27-48.

Buiter, W. and A. Sibert 2008, "The Central Bank as the Market-maker of Last Resort: From Lender of Last Resort to Market-maker of Last Resort", in Felton, A. and C. Reinhart (eds), *The First Global Financial Crisis of the 21st Century, London: VoxEU and Centre for Economic Policy Research,* p. 171-178.

Butsch, J.L. 1988, "Les Banques Face à l'Instabilité Financière. Le Rôle des Autorités de Contrôle des Etablissements de Crédit", *Revue d'Economie Politique* 98-5, p. 731-745.

Cartapanis, A. and P. Gilles 2003, "Prévention et Gestion des Crises Financières Internationales: Une Analyse Rétrospective de H. Thornton", *Cahiers d'Economie Politique* 45, p. 175-210.
Caruana, J. 2010, "Unconventional Monetary Policies in Times of Crisis", *SUERF Studies* 1, p. 113-123.
Cohen, D. 1988, "What Caused the Rise of Conservatism: A French View", *Economic Policy* 6, p. 196-219.
Cohen, D. and P. Michel 1988, "How Should Control Theory Be Used to Calculate a Time-Consistent Government Policy?",*The Review of Economic Studies* LV-2, p. 263-274.
Christiano, L.J., R. Motto and M. Rostagno 2010, "Financial Factors in Economic Fluctuations", *ECB Working Paper,* 1192.
Cukierman, A. 1986, "Measuring Inflationary Expectations: A Review Essay", *Journal of Monetary Economics* 17-2, p. 315-324.
Cukierman, A. and A.H. Meltzer 1986, "A Theory of Ambiguity, Credibility, and Inflation under Discretion and Asymmetric Information", *Econometrica* 54-5, p. 1099-1128.
Cúrdia, V. and M. Woodford 2009, "Conventional and Unconventional Monetary Policy", *Federal Reserve Bank of New-York Staff Reports,* 404.
Dooley, M. 1997, "A Model of Crises in Emerging Markets", *NBER Working Paper,* 6300.
Dornbusch, R. 2001, "A Primer on Emerging Market Crisis", *NBER Working Paper,* 8326.
—. 1980, "Exchange Rate Economics: Where Do We Stand?", *Brookings Papers on Economic Aactivity* 1, p. 143-185.
Eichengreen, B. 1996, "Speculative Attacks: Fundamentals and Self-Fulfilling Prophecies", *NBER Working Paper,* 5789.
Eichengreen, B., A. Rose and C. Wyplosz 1995, "Exchange Market Mayhem: The Antecedents and Aftermath of Speculative Attacks", *Economic Policy* 21, p. 249-312.
Fahr, S., R. Motto, M. Rostagno, F. Smets and O. Tristani 2011, "A Monetary Policy Strategy in Good and Bad Times. Lessons from the Recent Past", *ECB Working Paper,* 1336.
Fellner, W. 1982, "In Defense of the Credibility Hypothesis", *The American Economic Review* 72-2, p. 90-91.
Freixas, X. and J. Jorge 2008, "The Role of Interbank Markets in Monetary Policy: A Model with Rationing", *Journal of Money, Credit and Banking* 40-6, p. 1151-1176.
Gertler, M. and P. Karadi 2011, "A Model of Unconventional Monetary Policy", *Journal of Monetary Economics* 58-1, p. 17-34.

Giannone, D., M. Lenza, H. Pill and L. Reichlin 2011, "Non-Standard Monetary Policy Measures and Monetary Developments", *ECB Working Paper,* 1290.
Gilles, P. 1992, "Incertitude, Risque et Asymétrie d'Information sur les Marchés Financiers. Une Revue de la Littérature et une Analyse en Termes de Réputation et de Crédibilité", *Revue Française d'Economie* VII-2, p. 53-115.
Gilles, P. 2002, "La Finance Globale et les Marchés du Capital dans une Perspective de Régulation de la Nouvelle Architecture Financière Internationale", in Dockès, P. (ed), *Ordre et Désordres dans l'Economie Monde,* Paris: P.U.F., coll. 'Quadrige', p. 303-331.
Goodhart, C.A. and H. Huang 2000, "A Simple Model of an International Lender of Last Resort", *Economic Notes* 29-1, p. 1-11.
Goodhart, C.A. 1988, *The Evolution of Central Banks*, Cambridge: The MIT Press.
Goodhart, C.A. and D.P. Tsomocos 2007, "Analysis of Financial Fragility", *Mimeo,* London School of Economics.
Kashyap, A. and J. Stein 2000, "What Do a Million Observations on Banks Have to Say about the Transmission of Monetary Policy?", *The American Economic Review* 90-3, p. 407-428.
Kindleberger, C. P. 1986, "International Public Goods without International Government", *The American Economic Review* 76-1, p. 1-13.
Kindleberger, C.P. 1978, *Manias, Panics and Crashes, A History of Financial Crises*, London: Macmillan.
Korinek, A. 2011, "Systemic Risk-Taking, Amplification Effects, Externalities, and Regulatory Responses, *ECB Working Paper,* 1345.
Koromzay, V. 1982, "Credibility and Demand Restraint", *The American Economic Review* 72-2, p. 86-89.
Krugman, P. 1996, "Are Currency Crises Self-Fulfilling?", *NBER Macroeconomics Annual* 11, p. 345-407.
Kydland, F. and E. Prescott 1977, "Rules rather than Discretion: The Inconsistency of Optimal Plans", *Journal of Political Economy* 85-3, p. 473-492.
Lenza, M., H. Pill and L. Reichlin 2010, "Monetary Policy in Exceptional Times", *ECB Working Paper,* 1253.
Lubochinsky, C. (ed) 2009, *Les Marchés Financiers dans la Tourmente: Le Défi du Long Terme*, Paris: PUF, Descartes & Cie, Les cahiers 'Le Cercle des Economistes'.
Meltzer, A. (ed) 2000, *Report of the International Financial Advisory Commission*, Washington.

Mistral, J. 2009, “En Amérique, un Retour de l'Etat mais pas de Socialisme!”, in Lubochinsky, C. (ed), *Les Marchés Financiers dans la Tourmente: Le Défi du Long Terme*, Paris: PUF, Descartes & Cie, Les cahiers ‘Le Cercle des Economistes’, p. 87-91.

—. 1991, “Le retour des faux prophètes”, *Le Monde*, 15 October, 18.

Oudiz, G. and J. Sachs 1984, “Macroeconomic Policy Coordination among the Industrial Economies”, *Brooking Papers on Economic Activity* 1, p. 1-64.

Rogoff, K. 1985, “The Optimal Degree of Commitment to an Intermediate Target”, *The Quarterly Journal of Economics* C-4, p. 1169-1189.

Rogoff, K. and A. Sibert 1988, “Elections and Macroeconomic Policy Cycles”, *The Review of Economic Studies* LV-1, p. 1-16.

Sarkar, A. and J. Shrader 2010, “Financial Amplification Mechanisms and the Federal Reserve’s Supply of Liquidity during the Crisis”, *Federal Reserve Bank of New-York Staff Reports*, 431.

Schelling, T.C. 1982, “Establishing Credibility: Strategic Considerations”, *The American Economic Review* 72-2, p. 77-80.

Stiglitz, J. 2000, *Principes d'Economie Moderne,* Bruxelles, Paris: De Boeck.

Thornton, H. 1802, *An Enquiry into the Nature and Effects of the Paper Credit of Great Britain*, ed. by F.A. Hayek. Fairfield, Conn.:Augustus M. Kelley Publishers, 1978.

Tobin, J. 1983, “Monetary Policy: Rules, Targets, and Shocks”, *Journal of Money, Credit and Banking* XV-4, p. 506-518.

Weber, A.A. 1991, “Reputation and Credibility in the European Monetary System”, *Economic Policy* 12, p. 57-102.

Woehrling, F. 1990, “The Independent Central Bank, Democracy, and the Principles of Monetary Management”, *De pecunia* II-1, p.117-127.

PART IV:

REMEDIES

CHAPTER NINE

THE EUROPEAN CRISIS AND ITS REFLECTIONS ON TURKEY*

ALI ARI,
KIRKLARELI UNIVERSITY
MEHMET HONDUR
MINISTRY OF DEVELOPMENT OF TURKEY,
ECONOMIC MODELLING DEPARTMENT
MUHSIN KAR,
NECMETTIN ERBAKAN UNIVERSITY
KIVILCIM METIN OZCAN,
NECMETTIN ERBAKAN UNIVERSITY
GÜRAY VURAL,
DELEGATION OF THE EUROPEAN UNION TO TURKEY
AND DILEK YIGIT
TURKEY UNDERSECRETARIAT OF TREASURY,
DIRECTORATE GENERAL OF FOREIGN ECONOMIC RELATIONS

1. Introduction

The financial crisis that broke out in the second half of 2007 in the US real estate market, and then became global with the bankruptcy of Lehman Brothers in September 2008, caused a serious contraction in the economies of almost all countries around the world in 2009. The fiscal and monetary

* The first version of this paper was prepared as a report for the Institute of Strategic Thinking (SDE), Ankara. The authors thank the Institute for its financial support, Dr. Sidika Basci, Coordinator of Economic Programme of SDE and Ms. Merve Arabaci for their comments and contributions.

policies and other emergency measures implemented to support the financial sector aimed to re-establish confidence in the financial markets and to reduce the impact of the crisis on the non-financial sector. However, even if these policies were relatively successful, they were accompanied by serious social and economic problems. The nationalisation of the debts of some private banks led to a critical increase in public debt and a rise in concerns about the repayment of this debt. As a result, some countries like Greece, Ireland, Portugal, and Spain encountered serious debt problems. The decrease in the ratings of these countries by credit rating agencies (S&P, Moody's, or Fitch) and the unclear debate concerning who should bear the cost of the crisis have made it difficult for the EU to exit the crisis. This on-going crisis in Europe has also increased concerns about the future of the EU.

In this paper, we analyse in detail the occurence of the European debt crisis, its impact on other countries, in particular on Turkey, and discuss the effectiveness of the policy measures and probable exit strategies from the crisis. The rest of the paper is organised as follows. Section 2 investigates the foundation of the EU from a historical perspective. Section 3 assesses the causes of the European debt crisis. Section 4 examines the policy measures taken to fight the crisis and its repercussions on the financial market and real economy. Section 5 focuses on the impacts of this crisis on the Turkish economy, since Turkey has a long-standing relationship with the EU. Section 6 discusses some probable solutions and possible ways to exit this on-going crisis situation.

2. An overall assessment according to the Maastricht convergence criteria

Although the idea of forming a union dates back to olden times, the first concrete steps were taken in the aftermath of World War II. Politicians and bureaucrats like Robert Schuman and Jean Monnet believed in the necessity of French and German reconciliation in order to create a peaceful and stabilised Europe. In this sense, with the participation of six countries (France, Germany, Italy, the Netherlands, Luxemburg and Belgium) the European Coal and Steel Community (ECSC) was founded in Paris, in 1951.

In 1957, in order to solidify the peace between the traditional European rivals, the European Economic Community (EEC) was established by the Treaty of Rome, as a step towards a more closely unified Europe. Through this Treaty, the member states aimed towards cooperation in the economic arena under a supranational institution, and implemented a series of reforms beginning with the preliminary step of liberalising foreign trade and capital movements. The free circulation of the factors of production enabled the implementation of common policies essential to economic integration. Accordingly, the EEC became a full Customs Union in 1968, and a common agricultural policy (CAP) was launched.

In order to create a Single Market within the European Community (EC) by 1992, the "Single European Act" (SEA) was signed in 1986, removing all physical, technical and financial obstacles between member nations. The Maastricht Treaty (formally, the Treaty on European Union or TEU), signed on 7 February 1992, created the EU and led to the creation of a single European currency, the euro, and the EMU or the Eurozone. This process was completed on January 1, 2002 when the euro became the official currency of the Eurozone. The European integration process has recently acquired a higher dimension, with discussions on the European constitution and the signing of the Lisbon Treaty.

The benefits of the Union now became reasons for its vulnerability, as crises could no longer be easily contained within borders, and as members gave up substantial autonomy under the supranational institution they also stripped themselves of the ability to effectively mediate the effects of crises. Economic instability and uncertainty about the resolution of the present crisis has started to threaten the future of the euro and the EU.

In order to understand the background to this problem, it would be useful to evaluate member states in accordance with the Maastricht convergence criteria on budget deficits, government debt, inflation rates, and interest rates (Karluk, 1998; Savas, 1999).

2.1. Budget deficits

The Maastricht convergence criteria require that the ratio of the annual government budget deficit to GDP must not exceed 3% at the end of the preceding fiscal year. If not, it is at least required to reach a level close to 3%. Only exceptional and temporary excesses would be granted for exceptional cases. When the selected EU countries are analysed in terms of the budget deficit to GDP ratio, one can clearly observe that many of the Eurozone member countries had assured fiscal discipline just before the outbreak of the crisis in the US in 2007 (Table 9-1). Countries like Ireland and Spain, which have recently struggled with a debt crisis, had budget surpluses from 2003 and 2005, respectively, to 2007. The data indicates that a different dynamic played a role in the debt crises of the Southern member countries of the Eurozone.

2.2. Government debt

According to the Maastricht convergence criteria, the ratio of gross government debt to GDP must not exceed 60%. Even if the target cannot be achieved, due to specific conditions, the ratio must have sufficiently diminished and must be approaching the reference value at a satisfactory pace. As shown in Table 9-2, the government debt to GDP ratio of member states followed a slightly increasing trend from 2002 to 2008. However, the occurrence of the global crisis in late 2008 led to an important rise in the total debt stock of the EU member countries, from 62% in 2008 to 83% in 2011. Similarly, the Eurozone member countries' total debt burden over GDP grew from 70% to 87%. The most significant rise occurred in Ireland, Greece, and Portugal.

2.3. Inflation rates

According to the Maastricht convergence criteria, inflation rates in a member country cannot be more than 1.5 percentage points higher than the average of the three best performing (lowest inflation) member states of the EU. As shown in Table 9-3, the inflation rate was around 2% in the overall Union. This rate rose to 3.1% in 2011, due to expansionary economic policies. It thus seems that price stability was not a concern in the pre- and post-crisis periods, even in the indebted countries of today.

2.4. Interest rates

According to the Maastricht convergence criteria, a member state's nominal long-term interest rate must not be more than 2 percentage points higher than that of the three lowest inflation member states. As shown in Table 9-4, Greece, Ireland, and Portugal differ from other member states in terms of this criteria in the aftermath of the crisis.

After evaluating member states according to the Maastricht convergence criteria, it is difficult to say that the EU member countries had common factors in play leading up to the debt crisis. For instance, the fiscal deficits of all the member states except Greece were below the criteria in 2007. On the other hand, in 2008 the debt to GDP ratios of Ireland and Spain were 44% and 40% respectively. Even this limited information implies that the debt crisis in the Eurozone countries was due to different factors.

Table 9-1 General budget balance to GDP (%)

	2001	2002	2003	2004	2005	2006	2007	2008	2009	2010	2011
EU-27	-1.5	-2.6	-3.2	-2.9	-2.5	-1.5	-0.9	-2.4	-6.9	-6.5	-4.5
Belgium	0.4	-0.1	-0.1	-0.1	-2.5	0.4	-0.1	-1.0	-5.6	-3.8	-3.7
Germany	-3.1	-3.8	-4.2	-3.8	-3.3	-1.6	0.2	-0.1	-3.2	-4.3	-1.0
Ireland	0.9	-0.4	0.4	1.4	1.7	2.9	0.1	-7.3	-14.0	-31.2	-13.1
Greece	-4/5	-4.8	-5.6	-7.5	-5.2	-5.7	-6.5	-9.8	-15.6	-10.3	-9.1
Spain	-0.5	-0.2	-0.3	-0.1	1.3	2.4	1.9	-4.5	-11.2	-9.3	-8.5
France	-1.5	-3.1	-4.1	-3.6	-2.9	-2.3	-2.7	-3.3	-7.5	-7.1	-5.2
Italy	-3.1	-3.1	-3.6	-3.5	-4.4	-3.4	-1.6	-2.7	-5.4	-4.6	-3.9
Hungary	-4.1	-9.0	-7.3	-6.5	-7.9	-9.4	-5.1	-3.7	-4.6	-4.2	4.3
Holland	-0.2	-2.1	-3.1	-1.7	-0.3	0.5	0.2	0.5	-5.6	-5.1	-4.7
Austria	0.0	-0.7	-1.5	-4.4	-1.7	-1.5	-0.9	-0.9	-4.1	-4.5	-2.6
Poland	-5.3	-5.0	-6.2	-5.4	-4.1	-3.6	-1.9	-3.7	-7.4	-7.8	-5.1
Portugal	-4.8	-3.4	-3.7	-4.0	-6.5	-4.6	-3.1	-3.6	-10.2	-9.8	-4.2
Slovakia	-6.5	-8.2	-2.8	-2.4	-2.8	-3.2	-1.8	-2.1	-8.0	-7.7	-4.8
Finland	5.1	4.1	2.6	2.5	2.8	4.1	5.3	4.3	-2.5	-2.5	-0.5
Sweden	1.5	-1.3	-1.0	0.6	2.2	2.3	3.6	2.2	-0.7	0.3	0.3
UK	0.5	-2.1	-3.4	-3.5	-3.4	-2.7	-2.7	-5.0	-11.5	-10.2	-8.3

Source: Eurostat

Table 9-2 Government debt to GDP (%)

	2001	2002	2003	2004	2005	2006	2007	2008	2009	2010	2011
EU-27	61.0	60.4	61.9	62.3	62.9	61.6	59.0	62.5	74.8	80.0	82.5
Belgium	106.5	103.4	98.4	94.0	92.0	88.0	84.1	89.3	95.8	96.0	98.0
Denmark	49.6	49.5	47.2	45.1	37.8	32.1	27.1	33.4	40.6	42.9	46.5
Germany	59.1	60.7	64.4	66.3	68.6	68.1	65.2	66.7	74.4	83.0	81.2
Ireland	35.1	31.9	30.7	29.4	27.2	24.5	24.8	44.2	65.1	92.5	108.2
Greece	103.7	101.7	97.4	98.6	100.0	106.1	107.4	113.0	129.4	145.0	165.3
Spain	55.6	52.6	48.8	46.3	43.2	39.7	36.3	40.2	53.9	61.2	68.5
France	56.9	58.8	62.9	64.9	66.4	63.7	64.2	68.2	79.2	82.3	85.8
Italy	108.2	105.1	103.9	103.4	105.4	106.1	103.1	105.7	116.0	118.6	120.1
Hungary	52.7	55.9	58.6	59.5	61.7	65.9	67.1	73.0	79.8	81.4	80.6
Holland	50.7	50.5	52.0	52.4	51.8	47.4	45.3	58.5	60.8	62.9	65.2
Austria	66.8	66.2	65.3	64.7	64.2	62.3	60.2	63.8	69.5	71.9	72.2
Poland	37.6	42.2	47.1	45.7	47.1	47.7	45.0	47.1	50.9	54.8	56.3
Portugal	53.5	56.6	59.2	61.9	67.7	69.3	68.3	71.6	83.1	93.3	107.8
Finland	42.5	41.5	44.5	44.4	41.7	39.6	35.2	33.9	43.5	48.4	48.6
Sweden	54.7	52.5	51.7	50.3	50.4	45.0	40.2	38.8	42.6	39.4	38.4
UK	37.7	37.5	39.0	40.9	42.5	43.4	44.4	54.8	69.6	79.6	85.7

Source: Eurostat

Table 9-3 Inflation rates (%)

	2002	2003	2004	2005	2006	2007	2008	2009	2010	2011
EU-27	2.1	2	2	2.2	2.2	2.3	3.7	1	2.1	3.1
Eurozone-17	2.3	2.1	2.2	2.2	2.2	2.1	3.3	0.3	1.6	2.7
Germany	1.4	1	1.8	1.9	1.8	2.3	2.8	0.2	1.2	2.5
France	1.9	2.2	2.3	1.9	1.9	1.6	3.2	0.1	1.7	2.3
UK	1.3	1.4	1.3	2.1	2.3	2.3	3.6	2.2	3.3	4.5
Greece	3.9	3.4	3	3.5	3.3	3	4.2	1.3	4.7	3.1
Ireland	4.7	4	2.3	2.2	2.7	2.9	3.1	-1.7	-1.6	1.2
Italy	2.6	2.8	2.3	2.2	2.2	2	3.5	0.8	1.6	2.9
Portugal	3.7	3.3	2.5	2.1	3	2.4	2.7	-0.9	1.4	3.6
Spain	3.6	3.1	3.1	3.4	3.6	2.8	4.1	-0.2	2	3.1

Source: Eurostat

Table 9-4 Interest rates (%)

	2002	2003	2004	2005	2006	2007	2008	2009	2010	2011
EU-27	4.9	4.2	4.3	3.7	4.0	4.5	4.5	4.13	3.8	4.3
Eurozone-17	4.9	4.1	4.1	3.4	3.8	4.3	4.3	3.8	3.6	4.4
Germany	4.7	4.0	4.0	3.3	3.7	4.2	3.9	3.2	2.7	2.6
France	4.8	4.1	4.1	3.4	3.8	4.3	4.2	3.6	3.1	3.3
UK	4.9	4.5	4.9	4.4	4.3	5.0	4.5	3.3	3.3	3.0
Greece	5.1	4.2	4.2	3.5	4.0	4.5	4.8	5.1	9.0	15.7
Ireland	5.0	4.1	4.0	3.3	3.7	4.3	4.5	5.2	5.7	9.6
Italy	5.0	4.2	4.2	3.5	4.0	4.4	4.6	4.3	4.0	5.4
Portugal	5.0	4.1	4.1	3.4	3.9	4.4	4.5	4.2	5.4	10.2
Spain	4.9	4.1	4.1	3.3	3.7	4.3	4.3	3.9	4.2	5.4

Source: Eurostat

3. The crisis

3.1 The European Central Bank System and common monetary policy

After the foundation of the EEC and the establishment of the Customs Union, the member countries, in the meeting in The Hague in 1969, agreed that a plan should be drawn up for a gradual transition to an economic and monetary union within the EEC. Several important moves followed this: in 1973, the European Monetary Cooperation Fund was set up, and in 1979 the process of monetary integration was launched, with the creation of the EMS and the European Currency Unit (ECU). The success of the EMS in promoting its objectives of internal and external monetary stability contributed to the creation of a Single Market within the EC by 1992. To achieve this, SEA was signed in 1986, thereby removing the physical, technical, and financial obstacles between members. Moreover, the idea that a single market cannot be generated without a monetary union accelerated the efforts of the member countries to create an EMU, with the aim of forming a single market. Therefore, in 1988 in Hanover, the European Council decided to found a committee under the presidency of Jacques Delors. The then president of the European Commission prepared a report in April 1989 and proposed a series of important stages to lay the groundwork for the formation of the EMU (Savas, 1999; Tur, 2000). For the establishment of an EMU, the free movement of factors of production (persons, goods, services, capital) was essential, along with the assurance of total and irreversible convertibility of national currencies, the complete liberalisation of capital movements, full integration of banking and other financial markets, the elimination of margins of fluctuation, the irrevocable locking of exchange rate parities, the creation of a common and single currency, and the transfer of decision-making power to the community organs, particularly in monetary and macroeconomic issues.

The Delors Report also indicated that the EMU could be achieved in three stages (Savas, 1999). In the first stage, measures must be taken to remove technical, physical, and fiscal restrictions, decrease regional economic disparities in the Community, coordinate fiscal policies between member states, ensure free use of the European Currency Unit (ECU), and maintain the currencies of the member states within the band ±2.25%, as proposed by the ERM.

The second stage involves making necessary changes in order to transfer decision-making power from member states to the Community, establishing a European System of Central Banks (ESCB), and narrowing the national currency band, as required by the ERM and the EMS.

The third stage requires the ESCB to take control of shaping monetary policy and to collect reserves, the coordination of fiscal policies between the member states, the delegation of power to the Community to intervene in economic policies implemented by the member states, and the use of a single currency.

During the Madrid Summit in June 1989, the Delors Report was approved, and the first stage was to be launched starting in July 1990. However, the question of when to start the second and third stages became a problematic issue, since some changes were required in the Union pacts. The Guigou Report was prepared in late 1989, in order to specify legal regulations for the EMU. Finally, on 9-10 December 1991, during the summit held in Maastricht, the EU government leaders agreed on the "Treaty on European Union," signed on 7 February 1992. The Treaty created the pillar structure of the EU: the EC pillar, the Common Foreign and Security Policy (CFSP) pillar, and the Justice and Home Affairs (JHA) pillar. The Treaty also led to the creation of the euro and the EMU. For this purpose, the Maastricht Treaty specified dates related to the establishment of the EMU, necessary economic criteria to be accomplished by the member states of the EMU, and rules regarding the fiscal policies to be applied by the member states. Finally, the Maastricht Treaty also defined the institutional structure and functioning of the ECB, whose main objective is to maintain price stability in the framework of an open market economy with free competition.

The process started by the Maastricht Treaty in 1992 was completed with the creation of the EMU, and the euro became the official currency of the Eurozone on the 1st January 2002. Adopting a common currency marks a great historical event. However, using a single currency and implementing a common monetary policy in a Union composed of countries with different economic structures has not led to the expected results. While most countries met the convergence criteria under the Maastricht Treaty, the main dynamics at force in the different economies of the EU are quite different. Eventually, the countries diverge in terms of inflation, growth, and fiscal performance. Some might argue that discrepancies in what would be considered optimal monetary policy would also exist amongst each of the participants.

Moreover, as argued by many economists, the Eurozone does not constitute an optimal currency area, because it does not meet most of the conditions prescribed in economic theory. The theory prescribes that members of an optimal currency area must have labour mobility, capital mobility, a risk sharing system, and similar business cycles across member countries. The Eurozone does not meet most of these criteria. First, labour mobility is somewhat restricted because of the different languages and cultures of the member states. Secondly, the Eurozone does not have the risk sharing system of fiscal transfers, because the SGP that was signed in 1998 in Dublin provides for a no bail-out clause, effectively preventing any fiscal transfers between member states. Accordingly, the structural circumstances of the Eurozone might have made it an unsuitable candidate for a currency union. If the theory is right, then the crisis might have been inevitable from the start.

Furthermore, the rules that were set to hold the EMU together were simply not robust. As a result, the rules were largely ineffective, and this might have also been a contributory structural factor in bringing about the debt crisis. Even if there were some penalties and clauses preventing irresponsible behaviour by any member, these were largely unenforceable. For instance, when an official transgression had been committed, it was rarely enforced, which might have further encouraged irresponsible behaviour on the part of its members (Kar, 2003). In fact, transgressions against the SGP have almost never been fully pursued.

Besides, by joining the EMU, some of the Eurozone countries, like Greece, fulfilled the expectations of investors as they could borrow at very low rates without correcting their domestic and external imbalances (Table 9-4). This situation has not encouraged these countries to implement the necessary reform packages, as they have generally opted for short-term solutions by borrowing external loans at very low rates. Finally, the implementation of different and various fiscal policies by member states with the common monetary policy caused differences in inflation levels across member states that led to a deterioration in the SGP.

3.2 Fiscal policies

The global crisis of 2008-2009 resulted in deep economic stagnation in many economies around the world. Many of the EU countries implemented expansionist monetary policies and extensive economic support packages in order to ease the effects of the crisis. By 2009, the size of these packages over GDP reached 2.3% in Spain, 1.8% in Austria, 1.7% in Finland, 1.4% in Germany, and an average of 1.1% in the Eurozone (Table 9-6). However, these expansionary policies led to increases in public deficits. Public deficits also increased in almost all European countries, as tax revenues decreased due to economic recession, and as interest rates and debt stock rose due to the financial crisis. During the period 2009-2011, it is estimated that the average budget deficits over GDP were 6% across the whole of the EU.

Most governments in the EU put in place some support systems for direct income and introduced measures to increase household purchasing power by decreasing VAT, social security contributions, and indirect taxes. Half of the total support given was through these kinds of income support mechanisms. Besides, more than half of the Eurozone countries supported the economy through public investments like infrastructure. Again, almost half of the Eurozone countries supported the private sector by decreasing social security premiums and taxes, early VAT reimbursements, and export promotions. Wage supports and active labour policies were practiced by many of the countries. Furthermore, many countries stimulated demand in other ways such as capital promotions in the non-financial sector, loans, and guarantees, thus increasing public investments. Note that these support mechanisms defined and addressed the target market and were put into action at the right time (ECB Occasional Paper, 2010). On the other hand, although the aforementioned support packages were thought to be temporary at the beginning of the crisis, due to expectations about the dimensions of the crisis and the duration of their effects the packages remained in place for longer than expected.

Despite these support packages, the EU economies could not escape a severe economic contraction in 2008 and 2009. The decrease in tax revenues due to the economic recession resulted in great public deficits which surpassed expectations. In parallel to public deficits, the EU countries saw their debt burden increase in the same period (Tables 9-1 and 9-2).

In addition to these support packages, measures implemented to save the financial institutions also led to increases in debt stock. Governments had to assume huge contingency liabilities other than deposit protection. It is estimated that the total amount of liability for the EU was around 8.6% of GDP (OECD Economic Surveys-Euro Area, 2012). Consequently, although EU member countries prevented a big collapse of the financial sector during the crisis by implementing some support packages, they in turn amassed an important amount of obligations.

The economic and financial crisis then turned into a sovereign debt crisis, as a result of a rapid increase in EU member countries' public deficits and debt stocks. Weak economic growth performance, in addition to the negative outlook in the banking sector, raised serious questions regarding the sustainability of rising public debts. Consequently, this led to an increase in the cost of loans for many countries. The doubts around the sustainability of public debt caused many EU member countries to strengthen their budget structures and balances by making serious consolidations, along with structural finance reforms, in order to regain credibility. In this sense, the EU government expenditure to GDP ratio decreased from 51.1% in 2009 to 49.1% in 2011, and general governmental incomes increased from 44.2% to 44.6% within the same period (Tables 9-5 and 9-6). As a result, the EU's budget deficit decreased to 4.5% in 2011. These figures show the effects of an increase in incomes caused by cyclical improvements and enhancement of indirect taxes, and a decrease in public investment.

In the upcoming period, the financial consolidation process is expected to continue gradually around Europe. However, the EU's underperformance in economic growth due to decreasing confidence and rising uncertainty stands in the way of rapid financial consolidation. The continuation of the consolidation process in the upcoming period is considered necessary in order to assure market sustainability of the EU's fiscal policies. Despite the relative recovery in budget balance, the EU debt burden has been steadily increasing, standing at 80%, 82.5% and 84.9% of GDP in 2010, 2011 and 2012 respectively.

In this sense, the European countries need to take stricter measures to satisfy the Maastricht criteria on structural budget balance. Furthermore, to decrease the actual public debt stock to 60% by 2030, the upper limit set by the Maastricht criteria, the EU countries have to reach a 1% primary budget balance surplus per year. However, these strict measures may decrease domestic demand, which could undermine economic growth, which is already weak, all over the Union. This is why it is important that the EU policymakers' fiscal austerity policies should not lower demand and by reassuring the financial markets.

Structural reform efforts have been carried out in order to sustain financial stability around Europe, particularly through improving collaboration between member countries in fiscal policy design within the framework of the SGP. Within this framework the European Council, European Parliament and European Commission reached a compromise on the new governance rules for fiscal policies in September 2011. To date, seven EU members have adopted new fiscal rules in their budget management strategies. Although these improvements are quite important in creating sustainable fiscal policies, increasing coordination between member countries and active participation of the EU authority in policy design would enhance the fiscal stability in the EU.

Table 9-5 Government revenues over GDP (%)

	2001	2002	2003	2004	2005	2006	2007	2008	2009	2010	2011
EU-27	44.6	44.0	44.0	43.9	44.3	44.8	44.7	44.7	44.2	44.1	44.6
Belgium	49.5	49.6	50.9	48.9	49.3	48.8	48.2	48.8	48.1	48.9	49.4
Denmark	55.4	54.8	55.0	56.4	57.8	56.6	55.6	54.8	55.2	55.1	56.0
Germany	44,5	44.1	44.3	43.3	43.6	43.7	43.7	44.0	44.9	43.6	44.7
Ireland	34.0	33.1	33.6	34.9	35.4	37.2	36.7	35.5	34.8	35.6	35.7
Greece	40.9	40.3	39.0	38.1	39.0	39.2	40.8	40.7	38.2	39.7	40.9
Spain	38.1	38.7	38.0	38.8	39.7	40.7	41.1	37.0	35.1	36.3	35.1
France	50.0	49.6	49.3	49.6	50.6	50.6	49.9	49.9	49.2	49.5	50.7
Italy	44.5	44.0	44.4	44.0	43.4	45.0	46.0	45.9	46.5	46.0	46.1
Hungary	43.7	42.5	42.4	42.6	42.2	42.7	45.6	45.5	46.9	45.2	52.9
Holland	45.1	44.1	43.9	44.3	44.5	46.1	45.4	46.7	46.0	46.2	45.5
Austria	51.1	49.8	49.7	49.2	48.2	47.5	47.6	48.3	48.7	48.1	47.9
Poland	38.5	39.3	38.5	37.2	39.4	40.2	40.3	39.5	37.2	37.5	38.5
Portugal	38.3	39.6	40.9	41.4	40.1	40.6	41.1	41.1	39.6	41.4	44.7
Finland	53.1	53.1	52.8	52.5	53.0	53.3	52.7	53.6	53.4	52.7	53.2
Sweden	56.1	54.1	54.4	54.6	55.8	54.9	54.5	53.9	54.0	52.4	51.4
UK	40.7	39.0	38.7	39.5	40.7	41.5	41.1	42.9	40.1	40.2	40.8

Source: Eurostat

Table 9-6 Government expenditure over GDP (%)

	2001	2002	2003	2004	2005	2006	2007	2008	2009	2010	2011
EU-27	46.1	46.6	47.2	46.8	46.8	46.3	45.6	47.1	51.1	50.6	49.1
Belgium	49.1	49.8	51.0	49.2	51.9	48.5	48.3	49.8	53.8	52.8	53.3
Denmark	54.2	54.6	55.1	54.6	52.8	51.6	50.6	51.5	58.2	57.8	57.9
Germany	47.5	47.9	48.3	47.3	46.6	45.7	43.7	44.0	48.1	47.9	45.7
Ireland	33.0	33.4	33.1	33.5	33.8	34.2	36.7	42.8	48.8	66.6	48.7
Greece	45.3	45.1	44.7	45.5	44.6	45.2	47.8	50.7	53.8	50.2	50.1
Spain	38.7	38.9	38.4	38.9	38.4	38.4	39.2	41.5	46.3	45.6	43.6
France	51.7	52.6	53.4	53.3	53.6	53.0	52.6	53.3	56.8	56.5	55.7
Italy	47.7	47.1	48.1	48.5	47.9	48.5	47.6	48.6	51.9	50.5	49.9
Hungary	47.7	51.5	49.7	49.1	50.2	52.2	50.6	49.2	51.4	49.5	48.9
Holland	45.4	46.1	47.1	46.3	44.8	45.5	45.4	46.2	51.5	51.2	50.1
Austria	51.1	50.8	51.3	53.8	50.2	49.1	48.6	49.3	52.7	52.6	50.5
Poland	43.8	44.3	44.5	42.6	43.4	43.9	42.3	43.2	44.5	45.5	43.5
Portugal	43.3	43.1	44.7	45.4	46.6	45.2	44.4	44.8	49.8	51.4	48.7
Finland	48.1	49.1	50.3	50.2	50.4	49.3	47.4	49.3	56.1	55.5	54.0
Sweden	54.5	55.6	57.7	54.2	53.9	52.7	51.0	51.9	54.9	52.4	51.4
UK	40.2	41.0	42.1	43.0	44.1	44.2	43.9	47.8	51.5	50.3	49.0

Source: Eurostat

4. Measures against the crisis

4.1 Emergency measures

The financial crisis which broke out in the second half of 2007 in the US real estate market became global in September 2008, with the bankruptcy of Lehman Brothers. This global crisis led to a serious economic contraction across countries around the world in 2009. The crisis still continues to affect the world economy negatively, despite all the measures taken by governments. As a result, crisis management frameworks and strategies of the EU and the US should be questioned.

These measures aimed to re-establish confidence in the financial markets and mitigate the negative impact of the crisis on the real sector. In this framework the measures may be categorised in four groups: monetary policy, fiscal policy, policies for the financial markets, and structural reform packages. In order to prevent the stress caused by the banking sector reluctant to open new credits to financial and non-financial sector during the crisis in August 2007, a great amount of liquidity (around 400 billion US$) was injected by the central banks to the financial markets. In parallel to the injection of liquidity, interest rates were reduced to ease credit allocation, i.e. FED reduced the interest rates from 5.25% in August 2007 to 2% in March 2008. Note that the ECB, which was hesitant about reducing interest rates due to inflationary expectations, ultimately ended up reducing interest rates following the collapse of the Lehman Brothers in late 2008 (Artus, 2009).After the Lehman collapse, both the FED and the ECB pursued a more aggressive liquidity and interest rate policy. The monetary base in the US increased by 594 billion US$ from August 2008 to November 2008 (Blanchard, 2009). The ECB reduced the interest rates in October 2008 from 3.75% to 1% as of March 2009. Financial markets, which became non-functional due to the effects of the crisis, have now returned to normal as a result of the adopted expansionary monetary policy.

Even though this expansionary policy stopped the transmission of the crisis, raising the capital ratios of troubled financial institutions was much more important. In this sense, a financial aid package of 3.5 trillion euros was provided to the financial institutions by the EU up to October 2008. The content of this aid package can be divided into four groups: quantitative and credit easing for the banks, debt guarantees, purchase of impaired assets by the treasury, and recapitalisation (Ait Sahalia et al., 2010; EU Commission, 2009). Moreover, the ECB acted as the lender of last resort for some commercial and investment banks.

Furthermore, expansionary fiscal policies (fiscal stimulus packages) were implemented in order to increase demand, production, and employment, from the last quarter of 2008. Although interest rates, which were around 1%, played a role in increasing consumption, the stimulus had an accelerator effect on economic recovery.

The measures taken to support financial markets, in addition to monetary and fiscal policies adopted to stem the crisis, brought along very serious social problems. In particular, the nationalisation of the debts of some banks created an insurmountable amount of public debt and this generated grave concerns about repayment. As a result, countries like Greece, Ireland, Portugal, and Spain experienced serious debt problems. In addition, the downgrading of these countries' credit score by rating agencies, together with the reluctance of German and French governments to save these countries, due to rising concerns about public opinion, impeded the resolution of the situation. Therefore, structural and institutional measures have become important, and will be further discussed in subsequent sections.

4.2 Structural measures

The Eurozone debt crisis indicated that fiscal discipline was not sufficiently effective, and hence that structural reforms were necessary to strengthen the EU. Consequently, the economic governance of the EU has been under revision, with the aim of generating permanent change along with temporary measures, such as crisis packages.

Within this reform framework, the Europe 2020 Strategy was accepted in 2010 and "Six pack" entered into force on 13 December 2011, after the SGP, enacted in 1997, was reviewed in late 2010. In addition, the "Two pack", which includes some adjustments relating to the Eurozone countries, received the support of the European Parliament on 13 June 2012. Furthermore, the Fiscal Compact, which prescribes an effective surveillance and sanction mechanism with more rigid rules for strengthening financial discipline in member states, was signed in on 2 March 2012 by 25 members, not including the UK or the Czech Republic. Note that the aforementioned agreement is not part of the Union Law, since it was concluded outside of the Union itself. Lastly, the European Stability Mechanism (ESM) was established on 27 September 2012.

European Semester

The Commission proposal, related to the commencement of the European Semester as an ex ante control of national economic and fiscal policies, was approved in the ECOFIN meeting of 7 September 2012 (European Union, 2011a). The proposal would consolidate fiscal discipline and assure coordination between economies of member states. Monitoring progress and ensuring the active involvement of the EU in countries' economic policies are key elements of the strategy.

The European Semester's six-month cycle would start with the presentation of the Annual Growth Survey, prepared by the Commission in January. This survey sets out the EU's priorities for the coming year, of boosting growth and job creation. EU Heads of State and Government would determine the economic problems of the EU and would clarify the economic priorities with respect to the Annual Growth Survey. In April, member states submit their plans to the European Commission for sound public finances (Stability or Convergence Programmes), and reforms for progress towards smart, sustainable, and inclusive growth (National Reform Programmes) within the guidelines of the Europe 2020 Strategy. In May and June, the Commission assesses these programmes and provides country-specific recommendations, as appropriate. In July, the Council of the EU formally adopts the country-specific recommendations and finally, in Autumn, the Governments present the budget draft to their Parliaments.

The Commission released the 2012 Annual Growth Report, which marked the 2012 European Semester, on 23 November 2011. The Report highlighted the need to pursue differentiated growth-friendly fiscal consolidation, to restore lending conditions, to promote growth and competitiveness, to tackle unemployment and the social consequences of the crisis, and to modernise public administration as the main policy priorities (European Commission, 2011a).

Europe 2020 Strategy

On 3 March 2010, the European Commission launched the Europe 2020 Strategy, to prepare the EU economy for the next decade. By following the Lisbon Strategy (2000-2010), which focuses on employment and growth, the Europe 2020 Strategy strives towards smart, sustainable, and inclusive growth, with greater coordination of policy at the national and supranational level.

The Strategy identifies five main targets to be realised by 2020: to raise the employment rate from the current 69% to 75%; to invest 3% of the EU

GDP in R&D; to cut down greenhouse gas emissions by at least 20%; to decrease the share of early school leavers to 10% from the current 15%; lastly, to reduce the number of Europeans living below national poverty lines by 25%, lifting 20 million people out of poverty. These targets will be met through a Single Market, an EU budget (regional development, social and consistency funds), and foreign policy tools (EU 2011b).

According to the survey carried out by the Eurobarometer and released in March 2012, the majority of European citizens find the aims of Europe 2020 realistic and attainable, and support the priorities defined within the Strategy (Standard Eurobarometer 76, Europe 2020). However, according to the progress report released on 23 December 2011, the progress made by member states towards the aims of Europe 2020 fell short of expectations. The national targets of member states were in fact not sufficient, and did not satisfy the benchmarks underlined by the Strategy (EU Commission, 2011b).

Six pack

On 13 December 2011, a new set of rules, composed of five regulations and one directive entered into force, with the objective of reforming the SGP by strengthening the surveillance of financial and macroeconomic conditions on a supranational level.

"Six pack" set an expenditure benchmark, requiring member states not to exceed the reference growth rate. If the 60% reference debt to GDP ratio is not respected, it should at least decline on a yearly basis. If member states fail to meet the benchmark, they must abide by an excessive deficit procedure (even if the deficit is below 3%). The member state must comply with a schedule that outlines an adjustment trajectory, in order to reach medium-term budgetary objectives.

In the case where a member state does not respect its obligations, a financial sanction may be imposed by the Council on the basis of a Commission recommendation, unless a qualified majority of member states vote against it. This is the so-called "reverse qualified majority" voting procedure, which makes the enforcement of the rules stricter and more automatic, therefore more dissuasive and credible (EU, 2011d).

Two pack

A new package of two proposals named "Two pack," officially supported by the European Parliament on 13 June 2012, proposed further coordination and surveillance of budgetary processes for all Eurozone members. In this sense, two draft regulations are implemented: regulation on common provisions for monitoring and assessing draft budgetary plans and ensuring the correction of excessive deficit of the member states in the Eurozone; regulation on the strengthening of economic and budgetary surveillance of member states experiencing or threatened with serious difficulties with respect to their financial stability in the Eurozone.

For this purpose, Eurozone member states are required to submit their draft annual budgetary plans to the Commission and the Euro group by 15 October. The Commission assesses the budgetary drafts, paying particular attention to the SGP and other recommendations made within the European Semester. If there is a risk of non-compliance, the Commission will ask for further revision. Member states experiencing severe difficulties with regards to their financial stability, or those receiving financial assistance, are subject to even tighter monitoring.

Like the European Semester, the "Two pack" has come under fire because the Eurozone states are required to send their budgetary drafts to the Commission, and the Commission may ask for amendments. The Commission's right to ask for a change in a budgetary draft has caused concern, on the grounds that it may impose restrictions on a national parliament with regard to their national budget.

European Fiscal Compact

The European Fiscal Compact, (formally, the Treaty on Stability, Coordination and Governance in the Economic and Monetary Union), is an intergovernmental treaty, introduced as a new stricter version of the previous SGP, signed on 2 March 2012 by all member states of the EU, except the Czech Republic and the UK.

The Fiscal Compact Treaty, which is not a part of the EU legal framework, requires ratifying states to incorporate the balanced budget rule into their national legal systems within one year. States that do not correct the rule within the timeline may face the Court of Justice. If the Court's binding decision is not applied, a sanction of up to 0.1% of the member state's GDP may be imposed. If the state is in the Eurozone, the fine is transferred to the ESM and, if not, to the EU budget. With this Treaty, the excessive deficit procedure will also become more automatic.

The "Six pack", which is part of the EU legal framework and the Fiscal Compact Treaty, which is not in the EU framework, constitute parallel regulations that would help ensure fiscal discipline in the member states. However, these regulations, which are based on fiscal consolidation, are criticized on the grounds that fiscal deficits and public debt are the results of the crisis and not its causes, on the one hand, and that the expenditure approach to public finance omits or neglects income issues, on the other. An interesting discussion was initiated about which of these two regulations (Six Pack or Fiscal Compact) would be more effective in ensuring fiscal discipline (Dullien, 2012). For now, expectations are centred more around the Six pack than the Fiscal Compact, since the former has been already approved by the member states.

European Stability Mechanism

The ESM is an international organisation located in Luxembourg, which was established on 27 September 2012 after several discussions which had been on-going since December 2010. The ESM acts as a permanent firewall for the Eurozone member countries, with a maximum lending capacity of 500 billion euros. It aims to safeguard and provide instant access to financial assistance programmes for all members of the Eurozone that experience financial difficulty. All new bail-out applications and deals for any Eurozone member state with a financial stability issue will, from now on, be covered by the ESM.

ESM member states can apply for an ESM bail-out if they are in financial difficulty. It should nevertheless be noted that ESM bail-outs are conditional upon member states first signing a Memorandum of Understanding, which outlines a programme for the needed reforms or fiscal consolidation to be implemented in order to restore financial stability. Another precondition for receiving an ESM bail-out will be that the member state must have fully ratified the Fiscal Compact. When applying for ESM support, the country will be analysed and evaluated with regard to matters of financial stability by the so-called Troika (European Commission, ECB and IMF).

Note that these stability mechanisms or sets of rules for financial and fiscal stability, designed at the supranational level, deliver much needed supranational regulation to ensure fiscal discipline and the coordination of national economic policies amongst member states. Here, the important issue concerns the effective use of all these tools and rules. Therefore, the Union's success in managing the present crisis and in preventing future crises depends more on the application of the aforementioned policies and rules than on the procurement of new measures and regulations.

5. Impacts of the debt crisis on Turkey

Economic integration between the EU and Turkey has deepened significantly over the years. Foreign trade volume between both markets reached up to 110 billion euros in 2011. The EU is Turkey's number one trading partner and leading export market. During the period 2008-2011, 3/4 of foreign direct investments (FDI) were of EU origin. Turkey takes part in the production and logistics chain of EU companies with its increasing investment opportunities. Turkey is also a candidate country undergoing accession negotiations with the EU. Moreover, Turkey's low domestic savings rate, and thus its dependency on external finance, increases the country's vulnerability against external shocks. With such deep economic ties, in terms of trade, capital flows, and investment, it is impossible for Turkey to isolate itself from the on-going crisis in the EU.

5.1 Foreign trade channel

The EU, with a share of 41.6% in the overall foreign trade volume is Turkey's number one trading partner. Almost half of Turkey's exports go to the EU. Four of the strongest EU economies (Germany, the UK, France, and Italy) are Turkey's leading export markets. Therefore, Turkey's export performance is directly linked to EU members' demand conditions. The recent economic recession in the EU has had a negative impact on the volume of Turkish exports. Even though Turkey has recently been expending effort in diversifying its export portfolio, compensation of the loss of trade volume from the EU seems impossible in the medium-term, since the lack of political and economic stability in North Africa and the Middle East limits the country's export potential. Besides, the goods demanded by these countries (construction products and basic foods) are different from those demanded by EU consumers (automotive and petrochemical industry, machinery and household electrical appliances). Furthermore, Turkey's lack of competitiveness in other probable markets such as China, India, the East Asia, and the US prevents possible increases in export volumes in those countries. As a result, the EU crisis has affected Turkey's export performance quite negatively.

On the other hand, Turkey's efforts to balance external and internal demand conditions and to reduce its foreign trade deficit is slowly starting to bear fruit in 2012. However, the on-going crisis in Europe prevents the Turkish economy from reducing its current account deficits more rapidly.

Figure 9-1 Turkish exports (2008-2011 average)

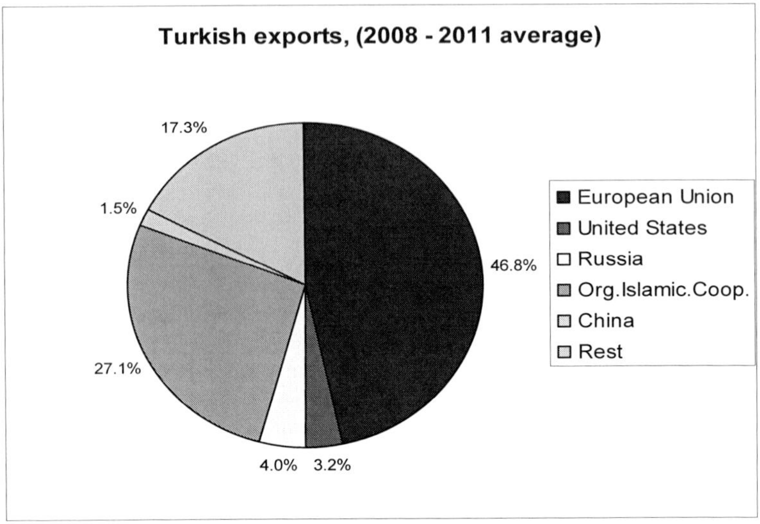

Source: Turkish Statistical Institute

Table 9-7 Turkey's leading export markets, (Share in total, %)

Share in Total Exports	2008	2009	2010	2011	Average
EU	48.0	46.0	46.3	46.2	46.8
USA	3.3	3.2	3.3	3.4	3.2
Russia	4.9	3.1	4.1	4.4	4.0
OIC	24.7	28.0	28.5	27.7	27.1
China	1.1	1.6	2.0	1.8	1.5
Other	18.0	18.1	15.9	16.4	17.3

Source: TurkStat

5.2 Credit channel

Domestic savings in Turkey are at a low level and follow a decreasing trend. Low domestic savings increase the country's dependency on external finance, and exacerbate the current account deficit. Dependency on external finance prevents sustainable and high economic growth. Moreover, when the country faces difficulties with access to external capital, economic activity records important contractions.

Following the global crisis, the Turkish economy recorded an economic recession of 4.8% of GDP in 2009, due to sudden outflows of foreign capital. This ratio is worse than that of many EU member states during the same period. In the following period, the abundance of global cash (due to huge liquidity injections of the central banks of the advanced countries) accelerated the short-run capital inflow to Turkey's banking sector, which led to a rapid credit expansion, supporting domestic demand and investment. As a result, the country recorded high ratios of growth (9.2% and 8.5% in 2010 and 2011 respectively).

On the other hand, 3/4 of foreign capital supplied by the Turkish banks are of EU origin. This means that Turkey is directly affected by any shock to the EU credit sector. Following the debt crisis in the EU, financial and non-financial institutions experienced problems, especially in terms of access to long-term foreign credits. The EU banks' efforts to strengthen their financial situation may have affected the credit levels allocated to Turkey and, consequently, the lending capacity of Turkish banks. The SMEs are particularly affected by the restrictions of loan opportunities: loans to SMEs dropped from 26.7% in 2007 to 21.4% in 2009, and were still below the pre-crisis level in 2011 with 24%.

One of Turkey's advantages in the crisis period is that the level of foreign-owned banks is still relatively low (21.9% in September 2011). This actually limited the negative effects of the EU crisis on the Turkish financial sector. The crisis also brought some handovers in the sector, as banks of US (GE, Citibank) and EU origin (Dexia, BCP Millennium, EFG) left their places to new initiatives.

5.3. Investment channel

FDIs are generally considered to be more stable source of financing and have more to contribute to the economy in the long-run, in comparison to short-term capital inflows. Since Turkey is dependent on foreign capital, and 75% of FDIs to the Turkish economy are of EU origin, the influence of the EU crisis is channelled via the flows of investment.

The economic crisis in the EU restricted the external investment opportunities of member states. In this context, net direct investments to Turkey decreased by 69% in the first quarter of 2012, as compared to the same period in 2011. Similarly, the long-term credit provided to the Turkish financial and non-financial institutions decreased in the same period. Consequently, one may observe that the crisis in the Eurozone negatively affected the Turkish economy through investment channel.

Figure 9-2 Foreign direct investments in Turkey (2008-2011 average)

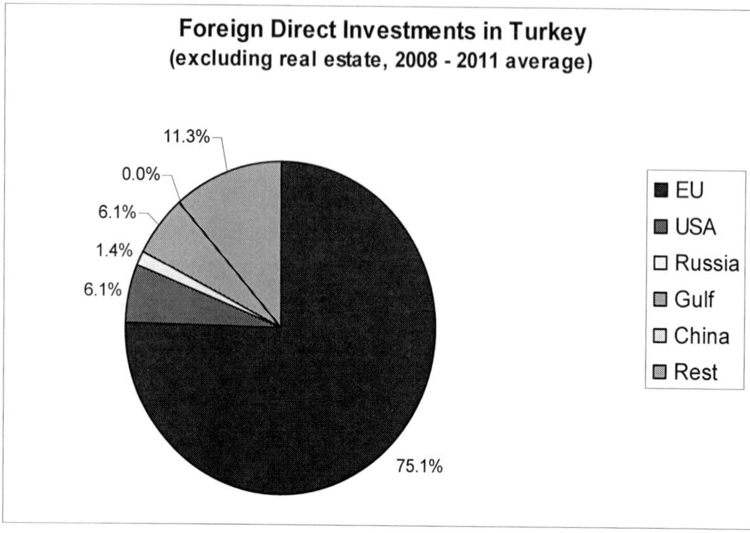

Source: Central Bank of Turkey

6. Some suggestions for the exit of the on-going crisis

The global financial crisis that started in 2008 resulted in a deep recession across many of the world's economies. The emergency measures implemented in order to reassure confidence in the financial markets and to lessen the negative impact of the crisis on the real sector did not bring the expected positive consequences. In fact, these stimulus packages resulted in a severe debt crisis in some fragile Eurozone countries. In this sense, in this framework, many structural reforms and institutional measures have been implemented in order to find a solution to the crisis. However, all these measures have had a relatively small degree of success, and the on-going crisis situation threatens the future of the Eurozone and the EU. Therefore, finding a sustainable solution to the crisis has become an issue of utmost concern for the EU member countries.

There are four different strategies put forward to exit the European debt crisis. The first option is monetary expansion. A concerted programme of monetary expansion by the ECB, with support from the ESM, would contain the crisis by supporting nominal growth. This option instigates extensive inflationary concerns in some countries, particularly in Germany. The second option, preferred by the German government, is to reduce budget deficits and public debt, and to ensure economic growth in the periphery states by implementing austerity policies, realising structural reforms, decreasing the unit cost of labour to increase productivity and hence restore competitiveness. In the first years of the programme, this option will lead to more economic contraction in the crisis country, which, on the one hand, will further deteriorate the fiscal balance, and, on the other hand, will increase the socio-economic costs of the crisis.

The third option is to allow member states which have increasing debt ratios and worsening macroeconomic balances, and hence cannot meet EU criteria, to leave the Eurozone. By leaving the EMU, the country suffers a sharp deterioration in its economy, a rapid depreciation of its new currency and an inflation spike. The country will probably announce debt default. Real depreciation will then give the country the competitive power to drive economic growth. However, allowing the exit of a member state may affect the sustainability of the Union, ultimately leading to its collapse.

The fourth option is to provide support via fiscal transfers to Southern member states which have saving deficits and therefore current account deficits (like PIIGS countries) from Northern states like Germany, which have surpluses. This solution would avoid the destructive effects of leaving the euro, but is difficult to implement without public consensus. The fourth option nevertheless opens the way to an more integrated Union.

Whichever option is adopted, we need to make a quick decision. The solution is closely related to the following questions: which option will be the least costly, who will shoulder the burden of the crisis, and what future do the Europeans imagine for the EU?

References

Aït-Sahalia, Y., J. Andritzky, A. Jobst, S. Nowak and N. Tamirisa 2010, "Market Response to Policy Initiatives During the Global Financial Crisis", *NBER Working Paper,* 15809.

Artus, P., J.P. Betbeze, C. de Boissieu and G. Capelle-Blancard 2009, "La Crise des Subprimes", *CAE Report,* 78, Paris: La Documentation Française.

Bénassy-Quéré, A., B. Coeuré, P. Jacquet and J. Pisani-Ferry 2009, "The Crisis: Policy Lessons and Policy Challenges", *CEPII Working Paper,* 2009-28.

Blanchard, O. 2009, "The Crisis: Basic Mechanisms, and Appropriate Policies", *IMF Working Paper,* 09-80.

Dullien, S. 2012, "Reinventing Europe: Explaining the Fiscal Compact", *European Council on Foreign Relations,* http://ecfr.eu. June 12, 2012.

European Central Bank 2011a, *The European Stability Mechanism*, Monthly Bulletin.

—. 2011b, *Annual Report 2011.*

—. 2010,"Euro Area Fiscal Policies and the Crisis", *ECB Occasional Paper,* 109.

European Commission 2012, *"Six-pack? Two-pack? Fiscal Compact? A Short Guide to the New E.U. Fiscal Governance"*, http://ec.europa.eu.

—. 2011a, *The 2012 Annual Growth Survey: Frequently Asked Questions,* Brussels.

—. 2011b, *Progress Report on the Europe 2020 Strategy to the Communication from the Commission to the European Parliament, the Council, the European Economic and Social Committee and the Committee of Regions, Annual Growth Survey 2012*, Brussels.

—. 2011c, *European Economic Forecast 2011*, Autumn.

—. 2009, "Economic Crisis in Europe: Causes, Consequences and Responses", *The European Economy Series,* 7.

European Union 2012, *First Alert Mechanism Report on Macroeconomic Imbalances in Member States*, Brussels MEMO/12/104.

—. 2011a, *European Semester: A New Architecture for the New E.U. Economic Governance,* Brussels, http://europa.eu July.

—. 2011b, *Existing Tools for Boosting Growth and Jobs*, http:// ec.europa.eu July 14, 2011.

—. 2011c, *The European Semester: Who Does What and When?,* August.

—. 2011d, *E.U. Economic Governance "Six-Pack" Enters into Force*, Brussels MEMO/11/898.

—. 2010, *E.U. Economic Governance: The Commission Proposes a Reinforced Macroeconomic, Budgetary and Structural Surveillance*, Brussels IP/10/859.

Eurostat 2012, *Government Finance Statistics*.

IMF 2010, *Fiscal Monitor, Balancing Fiscal Policy Risks*, April.

Karluk, R. 1998, *Avrupa Birliği ve Türkiye*, Istanbul: Beta.

Kar, M. 2003, "Avrupa Para Birliği ve Ortak Para Politikası", in Kar, M. and H. Arıkan (eds), *Avrupa Birliği Ortak Politikalar ve Türkiye*, Istanbul: Beta.

OECD 2012, *Economic Surveys–Euro Area*, March.

Savas, V.F. 1999, *Çağımızın Deneyi Euro,* Ankara: Siyasal Kitabevi.

Tur, O. 2000, *Avrupa Para Birliği ve Sermaye Hareketlerinin Serbestleşmesi*, Istanbul: Beta.

Standard E.U.robarometer *76 Europe 2020*, Autumn 2011.

CHAPTER TEN

COUNTRY RISK AND FINANCIAL CRISIS

EL THALASSINOS
UNIVERSITY OF PIRAEUS, DEPARTMENT OF MARITIME STUDIES

1. Introduction

Rating companies, as well as specific departments of multinational corporations, are analysing, more or less subjectively, the evolution of a country's risk. Rating grades appear to be important support-tools in decision-making; the provided ratings are used by decision makers as such, without any critical attitude.

The phenomenon of globalisation has multiplied the understanding of country risk, and crises occurring often, and without being predicted, have stressed the fact that the assessment processes, regardless of who makes them, have significant shortcomings. Countries like the so-called PIIGS in Europe, which currently faces economic and social problems, are for the reasons presented in a delicate situation.

In this context, the paper aims at finding answers to the following questions: What are the relevant variables in the analysis of a country's risk assessment during a debt crisis? What are the problematic areas and how can they be treated? What are the necessary measures required to deal effectively with the crisis? What is the burden for society, for the state, and for the political system?

The paper is organised into three sections. The second section presents a literature review for the concept of country risk, from the point of view of globalisation. In the third section, an analysis is made of the determinants of country risk and how the concept of country risk is used as a tool in decision making. In the last section, some considerations are made concerning a country's risk perspective.

2. Concept of country risk

The concept of country risk is closely related to economic globalisation as a process, creating advantages and disadvantages and later leading to country risk. According to the IMF (2005) and Bouchet (2003), this is due to at least the following three reasons:

- Difficulty in assessing the situation.
- Fragmented/incomplete information.
- The “knowledge problem”.

The semantic fields of country risk include nationalisation, expropriation, a problem of property rights and contracts, armed conflicts, inconvertibility, debt defaults, etc. However, one of the factors affecting country risk is the exposure to default on international loans, due to specific internal events in the debtor country, conducted wholly or partly under governmental control. As a result of the economic and/or political failure of a foreign country in which an enterprise carries out certain activities, country risk is also affected. Finally, a set of parameters of macroeconomic, financial, political and social nature may contribute to the formation of risk in relation to emerging countries.

Most countries are affected by systemic crises, with events characterised by a great diversity in terms of initial macroeconomic conditions, causes and triggers, the level of development of affected countries, the degree of openness towards the rest of the world, and by existing institutional frameworks and external conditions.

A number of understandings of the term “country risk” are highlighted in the literature. It is considered to be the result of sovereign actions, of political decisions, but also of economic or financial risk (Thalassinos 2007, 2008). In the first category, political risk is highlighted, broadly covering those actions taken by national governments which are harmful to foreign private companies, or the uncertainty often driven by the vacuum of power and law, due to changes in the political regime.

According to Calverley (1990), country risk represents the potential financial losses due to problems arising from macroeconomic and/or political events in a country. Sovereign risk is defined as the risk that a government will, at some stage, either be unable or unwilling to meet its obligations. This refers to the estimation of the probability of default on sovereign external debt, while transfer risk has to do with the possibility that even if a project is generating sufficient cash flow in local currency to meet its obligations, the government does not have enough foreign currency available to make the foreign exchange remittance to service the debt.

Certainly, a country risk analysis that focuses only on political risk would be shallow. The vision would then be too narrow and simplistic, in a context where the risk has a much larger sphere. In recent years, financial deregulation (or, according to some, regulation in itself) and connections between states and economies have added political risk to economic, financial and even systemic risk, as is the case of the Eurozone during the recent period.

Although there is limited literature on country risk theories, there is sufficient evidence for the consequences of the risk. There are many situations where country risk cannot be treated using traditional theories (Beetsma, 1996; Caprio, 2003; Roubini, 2004; Cerra, 2005). Therefore, it is necessary to try to explain the meaning of some particularities, such as the following:

- Variability of indicators in comparison with a period's average: How the risk is developing through time.
- Possibility that an unfavourable event takes place, with a certain probability for additional losses: An effective prediction about an unfavourable event and the estimated losses.
- Possibility/threat of a loss which can be caused by internal or external vulnerabilities or unforeseen causes.
- Probability that the profitability of an investment will be less than expected, or a set of stress tests or sensitivity analysis.
- Negative effect of a political and/or economic change in other countries.
- Impossibility for borrowers to repay the loan and interest due to imbalances in their current accounts and/or internal or external deficits.
- Losses due to appreciation or depreciation of currencies in a certain period.
- Uncertainty regarding a loss, or possibility that losses are greater than expected, so immediate measures must be taken in an attempt to stop the losses.

Moreover, recent papers have multiplied the approaches to the country risk concept, and the number of entities that deal with its analysis have become significantly larger. Other studies in past last decade (Arteta, 2008; Reinhart, 2009; Giordano, 2009) have developed new perspectives according to which risk can be contemplated as the perspective of the economic actors reached by risk creditors, banks, investors (financial or industrial risk), and exporters (commercial risk).The type and the nature of risk specifies the entity generating the risk, and the responsibility it takes. Authors such as Calverley (1990) have developed the notion of sovereign and transfer risk, and also the type of crisis that leads to the manifestation of risk. Sovereign and political risk are evoked (and clearly differentiated), as well as economic and financial risk (Sargent, 1977).

Moreover, a country risk approach depends on the type of state considered, or on the nature of the considered agent (Kolb, 2011). A difference should be distinguished, for example, between sovereign and country risk. In general, the note given by analysts to sovereign risk coincides with the maximum state score, the so-called sovereign ceiling (ECB, 2010). No local agent receives a rating higher than that of their sovereign ceiling. This approach is not always the correct one. For example, during the Russian crisis in 1998, Gazprom continued to honour its own debt while the Russian Federation has suspended payments.

3. Determinants of country risk

Three concepts are used by most rating agencies, which set their own thresholds for alert: solvency, the debt versus the states' wealth; sustainability, the evolution of the states' wealth versus debt evolution as a long-term orientation; liquidity, the ability for debt payment on maturity as a short-term orientation. The conclusions of such an analysis are usually addressed, without claiming completeness, to banks, credit institutions, investors or exporters.

Investors are interested in industrial risk sizing. This includes the inadequate management of manufacturing or sales processes, and may even extend to expropriation or financial risk sizing, in terms of changes to the remuneration of securities, while lenders are concerned with non-payment or late payment risk. Among the determinants of country risk, the external debt relative to gross domestic product is an important factor. It should be noted that the currency in which this debt is expressed is crucial—a major part of the debt expressed in foreign currency provides an additional risk, if the national currency is experiencing depreciation. The external debt relative to export volume, or the external debt relative to the ability to attract foreign currency, is also important. In some cases, this can be considered as an alert signal corresponding to over-indebtedness. From this perspective, the emphasis needs to be placed on a favourable development of exports, which improves the prospects for external debt repayment.

The external debt service, relative to GDP and to volume of exports, are indicators frequently used by the World Bank to rank countries, in accordance with the level of debt affecting country risk. Foreign exchange reserves greater than the equivalent of three months of imports are normally acceptable, but are not if the total external debt level exceeds 50% of GDP. The inflation rate and real interest rate may also reach dangerous levels when they exceed the threshold of 10.5%. The existence of agreements with the IMF, an essentially positive aspect generating trust, may also hide a potential crisis. Lastly, political risk and psychological factors may have a negative effect on country risk.

The economic structure of income plays a part in the balance of payments flexibility. In this context, a balance of payments analysis is of particular importance in tracking the various disturbances, the level of supply versus demand, savings versus investment, and private versus public savings. Also, the current account deficit which determines the status of the international creditor or debtor of the state under analysis may affect country risk.

In many cases, country risk issues begin with the deterioration of the fundamental economic and political structure of a state. Warning signals, such as excessive debt or declining reserves, should be regarded as symptoms of increasing risk. Activities such as identifying vulnerabilities, finding the origins of problems, and assessing difficulties—either short-term or long-term—are considered part of the fundamentals of analysis.

Institutions that carry out country risk assessment and issue reports are either the rating companies, the most notable being Moody's, S&P and Fitch. Insurance companies such as Compagnie Française d'Assurance pour le Commerce Extérieur (COFACE), consulting firms such as North South Export in France, Business Environment Risk Intelligence in London, and financial publications such as Institutional Investor, Euro Money Publications, Banks' Reports are also involved in ratings assessment.

The factors used by agencies in conducting evaluations include the balance of payments and the current account, the level of debt, the public deficit level, the structure and the economic growth of the country, the exchange rate and the convertibility of the local currency, the GDP and the GDP per capita, the labour cost factor and productivity, the level of reserves, the interest rates, the inflation rate, the liquidity of the banking sector, the political environment, and other international agreements.

The ratio of the above criteria and the evaluation methodology are unknown to the public. The criteria and factors are divided into two categories: firstly, the quantitative factors, which are considered as objective criteria; secondly, the qualitative factors, which are considered as subjective criteria. However, the proportionality of objective to selective criteria in the final rating model has remained unknown.

Country risk, when used as a tool in decision making, is a policy for determining where to invest, what to invest in, and how to invest. What is the likelihood of default or debt service difficulties? Which foreign stock markets are reliable? What international fixed-income investments are profitable? Where can one find trustworthy trading partners? What is the proper way to minimise transfer risk? A strategic investment decision should always be linked to the international situation, taking into account the following factors: risk aversion, the perception of uncertainty, the host state's characteristics regarding social and economic structure and momentum, the labour costs and level of qualification, the attractiveness of the local market and the local institutional framework with respect to investment policy, the taxation system, income policy, and other macroeconomic figures and limitations.

4. Conclusion

Despite readability and rapidity, a recognised degree of simplicity and other advantages, the rating is not free of subjective elements. Models are not explained very well, and scoring systems do not necessarily converge.

With regards to the activity of rating agencies, some critical remarks can be made, taking into consideration their announcements for the PIIGS countries in recent times. It seems that the agencies did not fully take into consideration the fundamentals of the economies, the measures taken by the EU, or the consistency of the rescue packages. They are too critical of countries, and this attitude can often influence markets negatively, while they are less critical of certain dangerous financial products.

There is also minimal concurrence in their market. Only three agencies represent more than 97% of the business. The capacity of the rating process and the level of objectivity are sometimes questionable. The ratings can have a pro-cyclical effect, and the reactions from agencies can be too late and too strong, which can encourage speculation. The pro-cyclical effect derives from chains of events of this type. The continuous downgrade rating followed by speculative pressure may worsen the outstanding loan conditions, which leads to higher interest rates and in turn attracts less investment.

The inflation rate does not necessarily entail an escalation of country risk. Trade openness of emerging markets enhances the inflation rate, and its decrease is not synonymous with development. The problem of external debt, obtained by totalling public debt and private operators' debt, is not always a negative sign. Two elements of significant interest here are not necessarily negative signs: first, a tendency towards long-term debt; second, a counterparty to borrowing, seen as a development engine and not an obstacle.

Finally, private debt levels should also be supervised. The levels in some cases are particularly high, and are influenced by an underestimation of risk as in the case of the US and Japan, a point which should provoke serious consideration.

References

Arteta, C. and G. Hale 2008, "Sovereign Debt Crises and Credit to the Private Sector", *Journal of International Economics* 74-1, p. 53-69.

Beetsma, R.M.W.J. 1996, "Serving Public Debt: The Role of Expectations. A Comment", *The American Economic Review* 86-3, p. 196-200.

Bouchet, M.H., C. Ephraim and B. Grosslambert 2003, *Country Risk Assessment,* London: Wiley & Sons.

Calverley, J. 1990, *Country Risk Analysis,* London: Butterworths.

Caprio, G. and D. Klihgebiel 2003, "Episodes of Systemic and Borderline Banking Crises", in Klingebiel, D. and L. Laeven (eds), *Managing the Real and Fiscal Effects of Banking Crises,* World Bank Discussion Paper, 428, p. 31–49, Washington, D.C.: World Bank.

Cerra, V. and S.C. Saxena 2005, "Growth Dynamics: The Myth of Economic Recovery", *IMF Working Paper,* 147.

European Central Bank 2010, *Financial Stability Review,* Frankfurt.

Giordano, R. and P. Tommasino 2009, "What Determines Debt Intolerance? The Role of Political and Monetary Institutions", *Bank of Italy Economic Research Department Working Paper,* 700.

Heffernan, S.A. 1986, *Sovereign Risk Analysis,* London, Boston: Allen and Unwin.

IMF 2005, *Yearly Reports.*

Kolb, W.R. 2011, *Sovereign Debt: From Safety to Default,* New York: Wiley & Sons.

Reinhart, C.M. and K. Rogoff 2009, *This Time is Different: Eight Centuries of Financial Folly,* Princeton, NJ: Princeton University Press.

Roubini, N. 2004, "Private Sector Involvement in Crisis Resolution and Mechanisms for Dealing with Sovereign Debt Problems", in Haldane, A. (ed) *Fixing Financial Crises in the Twenty-First Century,* London: Routledge, p. 101-142.

Sargent, N. 1977, "Country Risk", *Federal Reserve Bank of San Francisco*.
Thalassinos, E. 2007, "Trade Regionalization, Exchange Rate Policies and EU-US Economic Cooperation", *European Research Studies Journal* X-1/2, p. 111-118.
—. 2008, "Trends and Developments in the European Financial Sector", *European Financial and Accounting Journal* 3-3, p. 51-68.

CHAPTER ELEVEN

"DE-COUPLING" IN GLOBAL ECONOMIC ACTIVITY: TRENDS AND SOME PREDICTIONS FOR THE FUTURE

SUMRU ALTUG
KOÇ UNIVERSITY, CEPR AND KU-TUSIAD ERF

1. Introduction

The recent global financial crisis is being viewed as the most synchronised recession since the Great Depression in the 1930s (see Imbs, 2010). While developed countries have entered a period of low growth and recession, the effects on emerging and developing economies have been much more uneven. In this paper, we will discuss the phenomenon of "de-coupling" in the recent global financial crisis and its aftermath. We will also briefly touch upon what such "de-coupling" portends for global economic activity in the future.

Studies that seek to establish commonalities and similarities in the business cycle responses of individual countries have uncovered evidence of significant heterogeneity across countries sharing similar geographical or political groupings.[1] Other studies have documented the existence of "de-coupling" of business cycle activity across developed and emerging economies, in an era of increased trade and financial integration since 1985. Kose et al. (2012) find that global factors have diminished in importance for the behaviour of key macroeconomic aggregates, whereas

---

[1] For studies that include emerging or developing economies, see Rand and Tarp (2002), Girardin (2005), Benczur and Ratfai (2010), Male (2011), or Altug and Bildirici (2012). Aolfi et al. (2010) provide evidence on historical business cycles for the Latin American countries. Canova and Schlaepfer (2011) and Altug and Canova (2012) examine the business cycles in the Mediterranean countries.

group-specific factors have become more important. They also find that country-specific factors have become more important in accounting for the co-movement of output, consumption, and investment for emerging economies, but less so for developed ones. This suggests an enhanced role for policies in the former group, which rely on domestic saving rather than foreign capital to boost investment. Other studies have also considered price level and labour market behaviour. Mumtaz et al. (2011) find that there has been "de-coupling" in global business cycles as regards the behaviour of output and that there is some evidence for increasing similarities in inflation rates, although the bulk of inflation is still accounted for by regional factors. Altug et al. (2012) examine the cyclical behaviour of industrial production (IP) and employment growth for 20 developing and emerging economies. They find evidence that cyclical phenomena are "de-coupled" for the developed countries and a set of emerging economies, based on the behaviour of both IP and employment growth. Interestingly, they also find that industrial production and employment growth are "de-coupled" from each other for many emerging countries.

The remainder of the paper is organised as follows. Section 2 presents the "de-coupling" phenomenon during the global financial crisis. Section 3 brings some clarification as regards how the cyclical responses of countries can be explained. Section 4 focuses on the factors that affect business cycles in Mediterranean countries. Finally, Section 5 concludes with some predictions for the future.

2. "De-coupling" during the global financial crisis

Before we relate some of these findings to the account for behaviour of global economic activity in the present and the future, we will discuss the performance of different groups of countries, depending on how they fared in the aftermath of the 2008 global crisis. We can categorise the behaviour of the individual countries as (i) countries that continued to grow during the crisis; (ii) countries that have surpassed their pre-crisis GDP levels; (iii) countries that have attained their pre-crisis GDP levels; and (iv) countries whose GDP remains below pre-crisis level. The following graphs show the performance of the different countries in each group.

From these figures, we observe that a variety of countries did not experience a recession during the recent global crisis, including dynamic economies in East Asia such as Australia or Indonesia, as well as countries such as India and Poland. Likewise, a group of prominent emerging economies, including Turkey, Brazil, Mexico, South Korea and Russia, experienced relatively short, V-shaped recessions, only to attain strong rates of growth in the aftermath of the crisis, which allowed them to surpass their pre-crisis levels of real GDP.

Figure 11-1 The performance of the different countries in terms of real GDP (2005Q1=100)

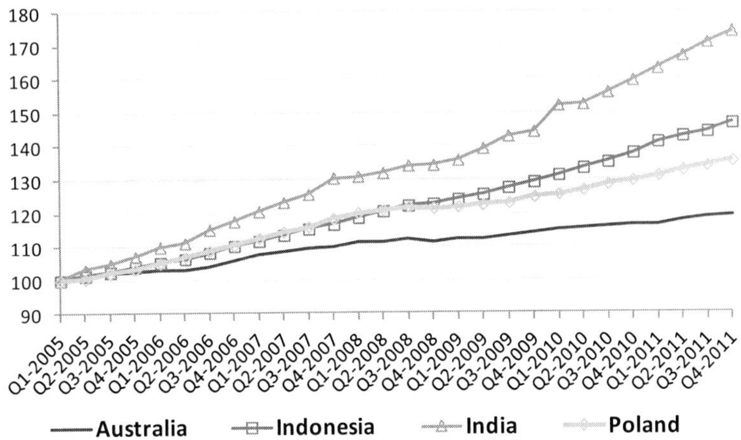

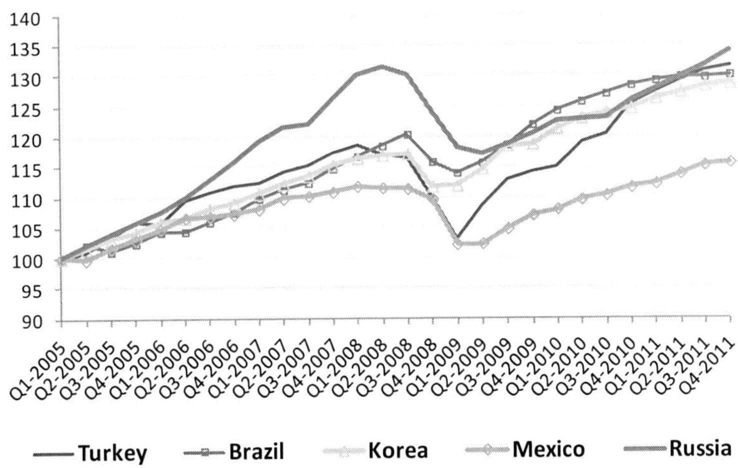

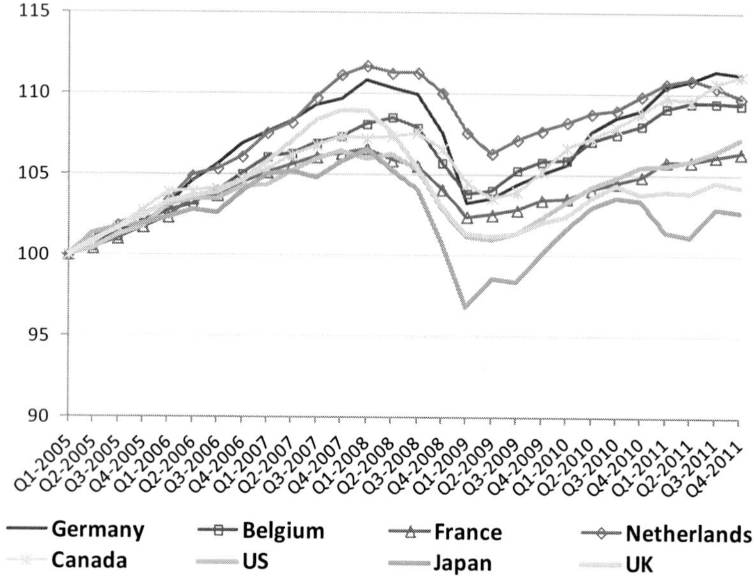

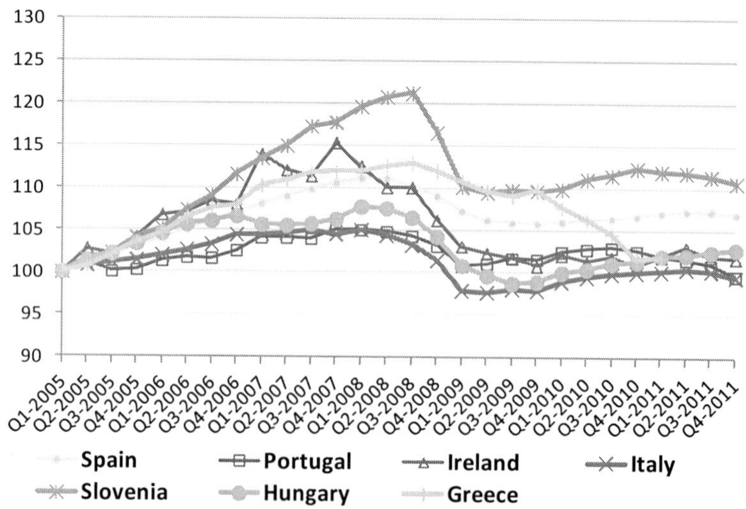

By contrast, the G-7 economies (with the exception of Italy) together with other European economies such as Belgium and the Netherlands have endured what might be termed as U-shaped recessions: countries such as Canada, Germany, Belgium, and the Netherlands have experienced faster and stronger recoveries from the global crisis, while Japan, France, the UK, and the US have tended to show larger declines in output and a slower rebound. The final group of countries comprises those that suffered asset price bubbles and large private or public indebtedness in the run-up to the crisis, and that are now grappling with large fiscal deficits and unsustainable levels of debt. These results themselves suggest a form of "de-coupling" in global economic activity, and also point to a variety of factors in determining the response of each country.

3. What explains the cyclical responses of countries?

A few recent studies have sought to identify the institutional determinants of differences in the performance of countries in the recent global recession. Giannone et al. (2010b) argue for the role of an institutional feature, such as excessive credit market liberalisation, in accounting for such differences. De Carvalho Filho (2011) argues that a monetary policy regime such as inflation targeting was important in determining the extent and severity of the 2007-2008 global financial crisis across countries. Essers (2012) seeks to account for the observed heterogeneity in developing country growth experiences in the recent global financial crisis by examining the role of variations in political arrangements across countries.

Taken together, these findings suggest that cyclical fluctuations are driven by a more complex set of factors than previously considered. While the nature of trade and financial links and the role of alternative policy regimes have often been considered, country-specific and idiosyncratic differences also imply a role for institutions, especially informal institutions such as norms, codes of conduct or other behavioural factors in the transmission of global or common shocks. Despite such mounting evidence, however, much of the literature on understanding business cycles around the globe has been "institution-free."

There are recent studies showing that membership in a common currency area—a much touted institutional arrangement to further European trade and financial integration—has done little to dispel such differences. (See, for example, Giannone et al. 2010a or Canova et al. 2012). In a recent contribution, emphasizing the *durable* nature of institutional arrangements, Altug et al. (2012) associate average business cycle characteristics and business cycle synchronisation with a set of institutional factors in a set of developed, emerging and transition countries from all continents. They find that the relationship between the two is strong, even after accounting for the impact of macroeconomic and structural factors. Specifically, they find that stronger governance in a society tends to be associated with more vigorous expansions, while both capital market development and civil liberties dampen business cycles. They also find that similarities in the institutional environment measured by composite indicators of governance and of labour and capital development are strongly related to business cycle synchronisation, after controlling for a key set of macroeconomic and structural factors.

4. What factors matter for Mediterranean business cycles?

The Mediterranean region is an interesting laboratory for examining the factors determining the behaviour of business cycles across countries and how synchronised or how "de-coupled" they are. Canova and Ciccarelli (2012) and Canova and Schlaepfer (2011) examine the cyclical behaviour of countries in the Mediterranean region. Surprisingly, they find that neither standard measures of development, wealth or monetary indicators, nor different degrees of trade or financial openness, can explain the differences among countries in this region. In a related paper, Altug and Canova (2012) describe the business cycle characteristics of up to 45 European, Middle Eastern and North African countries, with special emphasis on the Mediterranean countries. The interest in their paper lies in considering countries in the southern European periphery such as Greece, Italy, Portugal, and Spain, which have been the subjects of the recent Euro area debt crisis, together with countries that have been subjects of the "Arab Spring", such as Tunisia and other North African and Middle Eastern countries.

They juxtapose the cyclical behaviour of the Mediterranean and non-EU countries, on the one hand, and non-Mediterranean countries and EU countries, on the other. Their findings suggest considerable heterogeneities across the different groups. Consistent with other studies, they find that the EU-15 countries—typically "core" EU countries—tend to suffer milder contractions in terms of their amplitude. Surprisingly, however, there is little difference in the duration of contractions. They also examine the *cumulated* output loss/gain during contractions and expansions, respectively, and find that the non-EU Mediterranean and North African countries suffer most during contractions, while the Middle East and North African countries tend to experience the smallest output gain during expansions.

They also examine business cycle synchronisation across the different groups, and find that this is low within the Mediterranean region, and even lower within the non-EU Mediterranean group. However, the synchronisation between Mediterranean and non-Mediterranean countries and between non-EU Mediterranean and non-Mediterranean countries is higher and significant. Thus, there are important business cycle heterogeneities within the Mediterranean (and the non-EU group), and countries in these groups have cycles which are more synchronised with countries outside the group. Also interesting is the fact that while Mediterranean EU countries have cycles that are well synchronised with the cycles of other EU countries, non-EU Mediterranean countries have low synchronisation with EU Mediterranean countries.

Thirdly, they examine the fraction of countries sharing the same phase of the business cycle, i.e., a recession or expansion, at any given time. They find evidence for a number of recessions, including the recessions associated with the oil shocks of the 1970s and 1980s, as well as the ERM crisis of 1992, for their sample as a whole. The recession of 2007-2008 emerges as the most global of all recessions, with more than 80% of the countries in their sample being in that phase over this period. However, they find evidence of much greater heterogeneity for the behaviour of the Mediterranean and non-EU Mediterranean countries, many of which tend to display recessionary activity at idiosyncratic times throughout the sample period, and some which have not been affected by the recent global financial crisis.

Motivated by the findings of Canova and Ciccarelli (2012) and Canova and Schlaepfer (2011) regarding the failure of standard explanations in accounting for business cycle facts in the Mediterranean, Altug and Canova (2012) instead relate such facts to a set of institutional and cultural indicators. As in Altug et al. (2012), they consider a variety of institutional indicators to measure the quality of governance in a society, the extent of its civil liberties, and the nature of its monetary, labour, and capital market institutions.[2] Following some of the recent literature, they also consider a set of cultural indicators that measure cultural attributes deemed to be important by members of a given society. These include attitudes towards acceptance of inequality and power distance, individualism, the importance of trust and respect, as well as indicators that measure the importance of family ties. As in Altug et al. (2012), they find a role for

[2] Specifically, they consider (i) an aggregate index of the Worldwide Governance indicators provided by the World Bank, which measure different dimensions of governance grouped as: voice and accountability; political stability and absence of violence/terrorism; government effectiveness; regulatory quality; rule of law, and control of corruption; (ii) the Civil Liberties Index prepared by Freedom House; (iii) an index of central bank independence, due to Cukierman et al. (1992) and others, and an index of employment protection laws due to Botero et al. (2004).

indicators of overall governance and monetary institutions, such as central bank independence, in affecting the nature of business cycles for their sample of countries. However, in a novel finding, they also uncover evidence for the importance of family ties in affecting business cycle features and business cycle synchronisation in the Mediterranean!

Taken together, the findings described in Sections 3 and 4 show that cyclical phenomena are driven by a variety of complex factors that have only recently begun to be analysed by economists. Such factors include the institutional environment in a society such as regulatory quality, the rule of law, political stability, the presence of civil liberties, as well as the quality of its monetary, labour and capital market institutions. Surprisingly, more intangible aspects of individual interactions, including those involving mutual trust, perceptions of inequality, individualism, or even family ties, are also emerging as important determinants of real activity.

5. Some predictions for the future

In our view, this line of research and the developments that have led to the global economic crisis suggest that the future course of the global economy will depend on the institutional responses that countries take. Indeed, as Diamond and Rajan (2009) argue, the ability of many emerging economies to avoid the worst effects of the 2007-2008 crisis were due to the institutional and policy reforms that such countries enacted in response to previous crises. Yet, the institutional and political changes that are required to overcome the current crisis seem daunting.

As Douglass North (1990) has argued, institutions are "*the humanly devised constraints that shape human interaction*." The notion that institutions provide the framework for a regularised form of interaction among different agents seems especially pertinent today, as we witness tremendous changes in the global economy. Doubtless, one of these changes is the emergence of new countries and regions that are expected to play an increasingly important role in global economic life in future years. India and China, the poor, large countries of yesteryear, are today being transformed into global economic powers. The global financial crisis of 2007-2008 that erupted as a result of the subprime crisis in the US is also leading to a new perspective. As the developed countries have entered a period of low growth and weak performance, many emerging economies have continued to experience significant dynamism, suggesting that their role in international governance, global institutional structures and decision-making needs to be re-thought and re-configured.

The severe strains in the Eurozone, long considered by many to be a successful implementation of a free trade area and currency union, also constitutes another factor in this global shift. Many prominent economists and economic historians have argued for policy prescriptions that make use of the lessons of the Great Depression or the implications of standard economic frameworks, such as the structure of an optimal currency area. However, while fiscal adjustment is being prescribed as the cure for the Euro area problems, one of the most important lessons from previous eras of fixed exchange rate regime is being ignored: by design, the burden of adjustment is biased towards deficit countries, with surplus countries not having to adjust in order to correct imbalances. How the Eurozone will evolve in the future is adding to the uncertainty in the international policy environment.

Clearly, for many countries, the transition to a new policy regime is turning out to be more difficult than expected. Will the EU undertake steps for further economic (i.e., fiscal, and political) integration? How will the countries of East Asia evolve? Will regional trade and investment increase in importance? Will a country such as China be able to sustain its model of development based upon massive domestic investment and saving, at the expense of domestic consumption? Will global economic activity become two-speed or multi-speed? What will Turkey's place be in this new order? These are some of the pressing issues that urgently await answers.

As the economic recession continues in the West, and the EU grapples with the sovereign debt crisis, emerging economies in Asia and elsewhere have continued to display strong economic growth. This has created a further debate concerning the "de-coupling" of emerging and developed economies and whether emerging market growth can be sustained in the face of weak performance by the developed economies. With increased globalisation, the future of both emerging and developed economies will depend on their mutual reactions and the institutional changes that these beget to the current crisis and beyond. Our analysis suggests that much recent policy advice, which focuses primarily on macroeconomic indicators and conditions and ignores the institutional and cultural environment in a given society, is not likely to succeed.

References

Aguiar, M. and G. Gopinath 2007, "Emerging Market Business Cycles: The Trend is the Cycle", *Journal of Political Economy* 115, p. 69-102.

Altug, S. and M. Bildirici 2012, “Business Cycles in Developed and Emerging Economies: Evidence from a Univariate Regime Switching Approach,” *Emerging Markets Finance and Trade* 48-6, p. 4-38.
Altug, S. and F. Canova 2012, “Institutions and Culture Matter for Business Cycles?”, *KU-TUSIAF ERF Working Paper,* 1217.
Altug, S., B. Neyapti and M. Emin 2012, “Institutions and Business Cycles,” *International Finance* 15-3, p. 347-366.
Altug, S., B. Tan and G. Gencer 2012, “Cyclical Dynamics of Industrial Production and Employment: Markov Chain-based Estimates and Tests”, *Journal of Economic Dynamics and Control* 36, p. 1534-1550.
Aolfi, M., L. Catao and A. Timmerman 2010, “Common Factors in Latin America's Business Cycles”, *CEPR Discussion Paper*, 7671.
Benzcur, P. and A. Ratfai 2010, “Business Cycles around the Globe”, *Manuscript,* Central European University.
Botero, J., S, Djankov, R. La Porta, F. Lopez-de-Silanes and A. Schleifer 2004, “The Regulation of Labour”, *Quarterly Journal of Economics* 119, p. 1339-1382.
Canova, F. and M. Ciccarelli 2012, “ClubMed? Business Cycles in the Mediterranean Basin”, *Journal of International Economics* 88-1, p. 162-175.
Canova, F., M. Ciccarelli, and E. Ortega 2012, “Do Institutional Changes Affect the Business Cycle? Evidence from Europe”, *Journal of Economic Dynamics and Control* 36-10, p. 1520-1533.
Canova, F. and A. Schlaepfer 2011, “Mediterranean Business Cycles: Structure and Characteristics”, *Manuscript.*
Diamond, D. and R. Rajan 2009, “The Credit Crisis: Conjectures about Causes and Remedies”, *The American Economic Review* 99-2, p. 606-610.
Essers, D. 2012, “Democracy and External Shock Resilience in Developing Countries: Evidence from the Great Recession”, *University of Antwerp, Institute of Development Policy and Management Working Paper,* 2012-02.
Filho, I.C. 2011, “28 Months Later: How Inflation Targeters Outperformed Their Peers in the Great Recession"', *The B.E. Journal of Macroeconomics* 11-1, p. 1-46.
Cukierman, A., S. Webb, and B. Neyapti 1992, “Measuring the Independence of Central Banks and its Effect on Policy Outcomes”, *The World Bank Economic Review* 6, p. 353-398.
Giannone, D., M. Lenza, and L. Reichlin 2010a, “Business Cycles in the Euro Area”, in Alesina, A. and F. Giavazzi (eds), *Europe and the Euro,* Chicago: University of Chicago Press, p. 141-167.

Giannone, G., M. Lenza and L. Reichlin 2010b, "Market Freedom and the Global Recession", *CEPR Discussion Paper,* 7884.
Girardin, E. 2005, "Growth-cycle Features of the East Asian Countries: Are They Similar?", *International Journal of Finance and Economics* 10-2, p. 143-156.
Imbs, J. 2010, "The First Global Recession in Decades", *IMF Economic Review* 58, p. 327-354.
Kose, A., C. Otrok and E. Prasad 2012, "Global Business Cycles: Convergence or Decoupling?" *International Economic Review* 53-2, p. 511-538.
Male, R. 2011, "Developing Country Business Cycles: Characterizing the Cycle", *Emerging Markets Finance and Trade* 47-S2, p. 20-39.
Mumtaz, H., S. Simonelli and P. Surico 2011, "International Comovements, Business Cycle and Inflation: A Historical Perspective", *Review of Economic Dynamics* 14-1, p. 176-198.
North, D. 1990, *Institutions, Institutional Change and Economic Performance,* Cambridge: Cambridge University Press.
Rand, J. and F. Tarp 2002, "Business Cycles in Developing Countries: Are They Different?", *World Development* 30, p. 2071-2088.

NOTES ON THE CONTRIBUTORS

Jean-Pierre Allegret

Jean-Pierre Allegret is Professor of Economics at the University of Paris Ouest Nanterre La Défense, and is affiliated to Economix research centre. He holds a PhD in International Economics from the University Pierre Mendes in Grenoble (France) in 1991. He is the author of books and studies on international monetary issues, such as the implementation of the euro, the financial liberalisation in emerging economies and the new architecture of the international financial system. In 2009, he published a book on "Exchange Rate Regimes in Emerging and Transition Economies" co-authored with K. Josifidis and E. Beker-Pucar, Press of the University of Novi Sad-Faculty of Economics Subotica. In collaboration with P. Le Merrer, he wrote a study on the global economy entitled "Economie de la Mondialisation, Opportunités et Fractures", de Boeck, Brussels. He has published in academic journals such as Economic Modelling, Louvain Economic Review, Open Economies Review, Panoeconomicus, Post-Communist Economies, The Review of International Organizations, The Review of International and Political Economy, The Journal of Economic Integration, The European Journal of Development Research, Revue Economique, Revue Française d'Economie. Jean-Pierre Allegret is a member of the Editorial Board or Associate Editor of several international journals (Panoeconomicus, Economic Research Guardian, Journal of Business and Finance, and Practical Ideas in Economics and Finance).

Sumru Altuğ

Sumru Altuğ is a professor of economics at Koç University, Istanbul, Turkey. She received B.A. and M.A. degrees in Economics from the University of Pittsburgh (1978, 1980) and a Ph.D degree in Economics from Carnegie-Mellon University (1985).

Prof. Altuğ held an Assistant Professor position in Economics at the University of Minnesota (1984-1994) and visiting positions at the University of Wisconsin (1988-1989), Duke University (1990-1991) and Virginia Polytechnic Institute and State University (1994-1995). She was a Visiting Fellow at the National Bureau of Economic Research in 1986, and has been a Research Fellow at the Centre for Economic Policy Research, London, UK since 1997. She also held chaired professor positions at the

University of Durham and the University of York in the UK during 1999-2002. She has served as an Associate Editor for the Economic Journal (2000-2003) and as a member of the Economic and Social Research Council Politics, Economics, and Geography (PEG) Research College, UK (2001-2003).

Prof. Altuğ is the author or co-editor of several well-known texts in macroeconomics, including "Dynamic Macroeconomic Analysis: Theory and Policy in General Equilibrium" and "Asset Pricing for Dynamic Economies", issued from Cambridge University Press in 2003 and 2008, respectively. She has also published papers on business cycles, intertemporal models of consumption and labour supply, investment, productivity and growth, among others. Her most recent work is a monograph entitled Business Cycles: Fact, Fantasy, and Fallacy, published by World Scientific in 2009.

Ali Arı

Born in Izmir in 1980, Ali Arı received his BA in Politics (2002) from Marmara University (Turkey), both his MA and PhD in Economics (2003, 2009), from Toulon University (France). Dr. Arı has been an Assistant Professor at the Department of Economics in Kirklareli University (Turkey) since 2010. Currently, Dr. Arı is the Director of the Centre for European Studies and the Head of Department of Economics at Kirklareli University.

His main research interests are in international finance, macroeconomics, political economy and Turkish economy, topics on which he published in several international journals. Dr. Arı is a member of editorial and advisory boards of international journals, and is a member of several economic associations. Dr. Arı is also the founding Editor of the Journal of European Theoretical and Applied Studies.

Adem Baltacı

Adem Baltacı is an Assistant Professor in the Faculty of Economics and Business Administration at Kirklareli University, where he is also the vice-chair of Department of Business Administration. He received his BA in Public Administration from Istanbul University in 2002, his MA in Management and Organisation from Marmara University in 2003, and his Ph.D. in Management and Organisation from Sakarya University in 2009. His fields of interest include human resources management, performance appraisal, industrial competitiveness, and intercultural organisational behaviours. He has published papers in various journals related to these topics.

Yüksel Bayraktar

Born in Ankara in 1979, Yüksel Bayraktar received both his MA and PhD in Economics (2003, 2010), from Kocaeli University (Turkey). Dr. Bayraktar has been lecturing at the Department of Economics at Istanbul University since 2010. His main research interests are in international finance, macroeconomics, political economy, and Turkish economy, topics on which he has published in several journals.

Hüseyin Burgazoğlu

Hüseyin Burgazoğlu has been a research assistant in the Faculty of Economics and Business Administration at Kirklareli University since 2009. He completed his undergraduate studies at Bogazici University (Turkey) in 2007. Currently, he is a PhD candidate at Istanbul University, in the Department of Quantitative Methods. His research interests include multivariate statistical methods, mathematical modelling, and performance appraisal.

Raif Cergibozan

Raif Cergibozan is a research assistant at Kirklareli University and is affiliated to the Centre for European Studies. He received his BA from Marmara University, Department of Economics (2009) and his MA from Istanbul Technical University, Department of Economics (2011). He is now a PhD candidate in economics at Galatasaray University. His areas of special interest are financial crises, labour markets, international trade, time series analysis and macroeconometric models.

Abdullatif Çeviker

Abdüllatif Çeviker is an Assistant Professor of economics at the Faculty of Political Sciences in Istanbul Medeniyet University. He earned his PhD in Economic History from Marmara University. His main research interests are international trade history, technology history and diffusion of innovations. He is currently working on Turkey's trade with Balkan countries in the inter-war period. His works have been published in various journals and proceeding books.

Cemil Erarslan

Born in Istanbul in 1980, Cemil Erarslan received his BA, MA and PhD in Economics from Kocaeli University (Turkey) in 2001, 2003, 2009 respectively. Dr. Erarslan has been lecturing in the Department of Economics at Kirklareli University since 2010.

His main research interests are in macroeconomics, global financial crisis, new economy and political economy, topics on which he published in several journals and books. Dr. Erarslan is also Editor of the Kirklareli University Journal of Faculty of Economics and Administrative Sciences and was assistant editor of the Kocaeli University Journal of Faculty of Economics and Administrative Sciences.

Ayfer Gedikli

Assistant Professor Ayfer Gedikli studied financial economy in her doctorate programme. After the PhD, she worked as vice general manager in different state-owned enterprises. In 2009, she returned to academic life and started working as assistant professor and deputy dean in the Faculty of Economics and Administrative Sciences in Kirklareli University. Currently, she is a member of Istanbul Medeniyet University, Department of Economics. Her main research interests are globalisation, financial crises, their effects on the growth and development of emerging countries, regional development and poverty.

Cécile Bastidon Gilles

Cécile Bastidon Gilles has been an Assistant Professor at Toulon University since 2003 and is a research fellow at the LEAD (EA 3163). She completed her PhD at the University Aix Marseille, where she was lecturer between 1998 and 2003. Her research interests focus on financial intermediation, interbank markets, and monetary policy. In prior works she has focused on international lending and debt problems, with a special interest in the question of the optimality of international last-resort-lending. She currently works on several research projects in theoretical macroeconomic modelling.

Philippe Gilles

Philippe Gilles is a Professor of Economics at Toulon University, honorary Dean of the Faculty of Economics, Director of the research Master programme "Financial Macroeconomics & Development" and research fellow at the LEAD (EA 3163). He has co-founded and co-directed the LEAD (2006-2011). Prof. Gilles served as vice-president of University Sud, Toulon-Var between 2007 and 2011. He completed his PhD at the University Aix Marseille, where he was an Assistant Professor till 2001. His research interests lie in the area of international macroeconomics, with a focus on the history of financial crises. In prior work, he focused on the history of economic thoughts and development economics. In addition to four academic books and numerous published articles, he is the co-author of several study reports for the European Commission.

Mehmet Hondur

Mehmet Hondur got his B.S. in Economics from METU in 2000, MBA & MS in Finance from University of Maryland, College Park in 2007. He has been working as an economist in the Economic Modelling Department of Ministry of Development of Turkey. His main topics of interest are macroeconomic policy analysis, design and fiscal policy. He is pursuing his Ph.D. at the Public Finance Department in Hacettepe University.

Muhsin Kar

Muhsin Kar received his BA from Ankara University, Department of Economics, his MA in Economic Development in Leicester University and his Ph.D. in Economics in Loughborough University. His main research area is the role of the financial sector in economic development and European economic integration, and he has several publications in referred academic journals. He is currently the Head of the Department of Economics in Necmettin Erbakan University, Konya, Turkey.

Fatih Özatay

Fatih Özatay received his Ph.D. in Economics from the Ankara University in 1986. He joined the Research Department of the Central Bank of Turkey in 1987 and worked as an economist and acting director general until 1995. In the same year, he started to work at the Faculty of Political Sciences of the Ankara University as a Lecturer, and at the Turkish Treasury as an Advisor. In May 2001, he was appointed as vice Governor at the Central Bank of Turkey and also served as the member of the Monetary Policy Committee. He has been working as a Professor at the Department of Economics at the TOBB University of Economics and Technology (TOBB-ETU) and the Director of the Finance Institute at the Economic Policy Research Foundation of Turkey (TEPAV) since April 2006. His main areas of interest are financial crises, monetary policy, and the Turkish economy. His two recent books are "Financial Crises and Turkey" (2009) and "Monetary Economics: Theory and Policy" (2011).

Kıvılcım Metin Özcan

Kıvılcım Metin Özcan is a Professor of Economics at Necmettin Erbakan University, Konya. She received her PhD from the University of Oxford. Her research interests are macroeconomic modelling and time series analysis of aggregated macroeconomic and financial data. Her work has appeared in Oxford Bulletin of Economics and Statistics, European Journal of Operational Research, Journal of Business and Economic Statistics, Empirical Economics, Applied Financial Economics, Russian and East European Finance and Trade, Canadian Journal of Development Studies, Substance Use and Misuse, Emerging Markets Finance and Trade, Applied Economics, Physica A, Journal of Business Economics and Management, Journal of Economic Cooperation and Development, Multinational, Finance Journal. She is a fellow of the Economic Research Forum at Cairo, Egypt and a Board member of the Institute for Strategic Thinking in Ankara, Turkey.

Ata Özkaya

Dr. Ata Özkaya is a researcher and lecturer in Galatasaray University in the Department of Economics, Centre for Economic Studies. He holds a B.S. in Electronics and Communication Engineering and M.S. in Electronics and Communication Engineering from Istanbul Technical University. He worked for Alcatel as senior telecommunication engineer. He holds an MA degree in "Microeconomics, Econometrics and Industrial Economics" from University of Paris 1 Panthéon-Sorbonne, and MA degree in "Economic Theory" from Galatasaray University. His PhD studies are on "Logical structures for decision-making under risk and uncertainty" in 2007-2009 at University of Paris 1 Panthéon-Sorbonne and "Public debt stock sustainability in Turkey and liquidity crises" in 2009-2011 at University of Nice-Antipolis. Dr. Özkaya has been qualified by National Council of Universities (CNU) of France.

The research areas on which Dr. Özkaya has publications and review works are Decision making under risk and uncertainty; Game Theory; Time series modelling of stochastic process; Endogenous growth and R&D competition; Public debt stock sustainability; Chaos Theory; Financial crises and multiple equilibria; Turkish public debt crises; Epilepsy crisis modelling and human brain mapping.

Eleftherios Thalassinos

Professor El Thalassinos has been lecturing at the University of Piraeus since 1984. He is also visiting professor at the Hellenic Open University. He held a European Chair Jean Monnet and a Jean Monnet Module and he is visiting research fellow in two European and one US universities since 1995. He has graduated from the University of Athens (BA in Economics, 1976), De-Paul University of Chicago (MBA in International Business, 1979) and the University of Illinois at Chicago (Ph.D in International Economics and Quantitative Methods, 1983). He has taught at the

University of Illinois, State University of Chicago, Roosevelt University of Chicago and the University of Antwerp, Belgium.

His research interests are in the areas of European integration, business economics, time series analysis and international finance. His work has appeared in various journals, the European Research Studies Journal, the Journal of Energy, the European Finance and Accounting Journal, the International Journal of Services, the International Journal of Migration, the International Research Journal of Financial Economics, in various National and International Conference Proceedings and in European projects.

Professor Thalassinos is the founder and General Editor (since 1998) of the European Research Studies Journal, and a member of the editorial board of several international journals. He also served as a Chairman of the Department of Maritime Studies of the University of Piraeus (1998-2006) and now he has been Director of Graduate Studies (2004-today). He was appointed conference Chairman for the International Conference on Applied Business and Economics (ICABE) between 2007 and 2012 and for the International Conference in Applied Economics between 1993 and 1996. He was also the Editor for the Greek edition of the Foreign Policy magazine for the period 2000-2003.

Güray Vural

Güray Vural holds a BA degree in Management from Middle East Technical University (Turkey) in 1994, and a MA degree in European Studies from Hochschule Bremen University of Applied Sciences. Güray Vural worked in the Turkish banking sector during 1994-2004 in different capacities, first as an internal auditor and then as the head of the Treasury Operations department in a private bank. He has been working at the Delegation of the European Union to Turkey since May 2004, as the sector manager in charge of macroeconomics, economic and monetary policy, financial services, SME finance, and statistics. Moreover, Mr. Vural was a part-time lecturer at the Middle East Technical University, the Department of Business Administration, for the course "European Economic Integration" between 2005 and 2010.

Dilek Yiğit

Dilek Yiğit holds a B.A. in International Relations from Ankara University. She received her M.A. in International Relations from Ankara University and an M.A. in European Politics from University of Essex. She obtained a Ph.D from Ankara University. She is a chief of division at Undersecretariat of Treasury, Directorate General of Foreign Economic Relations.

INDEX